AF560362

MODERN TEACHING OF RURAL SOCIOLOGY

MODERN TEACHING OF RURAL SOCIOLOGY

[Strictly According to the UGC Syllabus for B.Ed. Course]

By

BHARAT SINGH

ANMOL PUBLICATIONS PVT. LTD.

NEW DELHI - 110 002 (INDIA)

ANMOL PUBLICATIONS PVT. LTD.
4374/4B, Ansari Road, Daryaganj
New Delhi - 110 002
Ph.: 23261597, 23278000
Visit us at: www.anmolpublications.com

Modern Teaching of Rural Sociology

First Published, 2004

ISBN 81-261-1864-4

PRINTED IN INDIA

Published by J.L. Kumar for Anmol Publications Pvt. Ltd., New Delhi - 110 002 and Printed at Mehra Offset Press, Delhi.

Contents

Preface

Education is a vast discipline and Teachers' Training is a vital part of it. The responsibilities of the educationists and educators are focused on the task of providing better training to the future teachers for their better learning and proper development. Needless to say that this responsibility can only be exercised, if the trainers are equipped with the required knowledge of the subject concerned. That's why it becomes essential for making adequate provisions for each course to the student-teachers or teacher trainees. The present series is designed for providing a solid workable base for all course-papers. It has been prepared strictly according to the syllabus of the B.Ed class, prescribed by the UGC for different universities.

No doubt, there are so many other books on the subject, available in the market, written by worthy authors. However, every writer has his or her own style and way of presentation. The present work also has its own features and characteristics.

In preparation of this series of texts, the editor had to refer to the works of other authors and information sources. The editor feels a deep sense of gratitude for incorporating their ideas in the text. Hopefully, this series would serve as a 'ready to refer' tool for all teachers, teacher-students and others.

— Editor

One

Historical Background

Rural Sociology or the science of the laws of development of rural society in general has come into being only in recent times.

The Origin

Reflections on rural society, indeed, are as old as the rural society itself. In the past, social thinkers had made attempts to comprehend the life processes of the rural world and to advance solutions of the problems arising therefrom. A comprehensive survey of the views of eminent thinkers belonging to various countries in the past epochs regarding rural life and its problems as they emerged in the changing rural society in various stages of development has been made in the "Systematic Source Book in Rural Sociology" Vol. I, edited by Sorokin, Zimmerman and Galpin. It reveals how some of the basic features of rural society and urgent problems of changing rural life had commanded the interest and attention of earnest social thinkers of ancient, medieval and early modern periods and impelled them to make sociological reflections, though they would betray to the well-equipped modern rural sociologists a lack of scientific methodology.

An Organised Study

It was since about the middle of the nineteenth century that more systematic observations on the history of the origin and transformation of rural society have been advanced. The impact of the capitalist industrial civilization upon the rural economy and social structure, in various parts of the world, forced the attention of scholars to the study of the trends of rural social development. Research in the subject of the origin and the nature of village communities which were undergoing transformation was launched.

Olufsen, Maurer, Maine, Hexthausen, Gierke, Elton, Stemann, Innes, Coulanges, Nasse, Laveleye, Baden Powell, Ashley, Pollock, Maitland, Lewinski, Seebohm, Gomme, Guiraud, Jubainville, Slater, Vinogradoff, Meitzon and others are some of the outstanding scholars who have thrown light on rural society from various angles.

Subsequently eminent scholars, professors and others interested in the phenomena of the rural life have published in various countries enormous material dealing with its various aspects.

Systematic Order

However, rural sociology as an organized discipline consciously developed, is of very recent origin. Due to historical reasons it has originated in the U.S.A. and slowly tends to draw attention elsewhere as its importance is being realized. During what is called "Exploiter Period" of American society (1890-1920), a period when the American rural society witnessed allround decay, a considerable literature, describing and analysing the problems arising out of its growing crisis, came into existence. This literature, however, did not explore, locate, and formulate the fundamental laws governing the development of rural society. It created the prerequisites for the birth of the science of rural society but did not still create that science. However, the beginnings of rural sociology may be traced to those " streams " of publications.

The first valuable work on the subject was the Report on the Country-life Commission appointed by President Theodore Roosevelt in 1907. A number of Doctorate theses based on the study of the rural community comprised further significant literature dealing with problems of rural life and providing, revealing information thereon. Finally a group of rural church and school studies made by individuals interested in an investigation of maladjustments in rural life constituted the third "stream" of publications. This literature served as the basis for creating the science of rural sociology in the U.S.A.

The Countrylife Commission, under the chairmanship of Dean Bailey, the eminent scholar of rural problems, circulated

5,00,000 questionnaires to farmers and leaders of rural life and received nearly 1,00,000 replies. The Commission, on the basis of this investigation, published a report in which they attempt to analyse and diagnose the defects and deformities of rural society. "This report actually provided what might be called a charter for Rural Sociology."

"An American Town," "Quaker Hill" and "A Hoosier Village," of which James Michel Williams, Warren H. Wilson and Newell L. Sims were respectively authors, represented further studies of the American rural community. These studies were based on statistical and historical data and field-interview techniques and were submitted as research documents at the Columbia University between 1906 and 1912. Dr. Warren Wilson, along with others interested in the processes of rural life, carried on a number of rural church studies. These studies, together with some rural school studies and "The Social Anatomy of an Agricultural Community" by Dr. C. J. Galpin based on an investigation into rural life made by him at the Agricultural Experiment Station of the University of Wisconsin in 1915, comprised additional literature germane to rural sociology until 1916.

"Rural Sociology" by Prof. John M. Gillettee published in 1916 served as the first college text book on the subject. Subsequently, a number of writers devoted themselves to the study of rural life and published valuable works which also enriched the literature on the subject. The publication of "A Systematic Source Book in Rural Sociology" in 1930 recognised as an "Epoch-making" work contributed decisively to accelerate the advance of rural sociology.

Later on, other intellectuals also focussed their attention on the subject and helped its further development.

Sorokin, Zimmerman, Galpin, Taylor, Kolb, Brunner, Sims, Dwight Sanderson, Landis, Redfield and Smith are some of the outstanding social thinkers in the U.S.A. whose intellectual labour resulted in a phenomenal advance of the new science of rural sociology.

The founding of the journal "Rural Sociology" in 1935 (at present a monthly) and the establishment of "Rural Sociological Society of America" in 1937 were further landmarks in the history of its growth.

In the U.S.A., rural sociology, though a new science and still in a state of immaturity, is commanding wider and wider interest among social thinkers today. More than eight hundred professors and research workers are engaged in developing that science in that country.

Current Scene

In other countries also, increasing attention is being paid to study and systematise this branch of study.

The various studies organized by the League of Nations and embodied in a number of monographs, together with the recent studies made by such organizations as UNO, UNESCO, FAO and others, have also contributed to the rapid advance of rural sociology.

Such is the history of the genesis and growth of rural sociology, the youngest amongst all sciences. It has started taking roots and is slowly but securely spreading itself in various parts of the world including India which needs it the most in view of its very large rural population with innumerable complex problems.

Area and Scope

As in the case of every young science, especially of a young social science, a great controversy has taken place over the question of the definition and scope of rural sociology among scholars engaged in the endeavour to develop it.

Disputed Matters

Is rural sociology a distinct science or is it merely an application of the general principles of sociology (or the science of society as a whole) to the sphere of rural social phenomena? Should rural sociology restrict its scope merely to the life processes of rural society or should it also include as an integral part, a study of rural and urban social life, comparative as well as in their mutual inter-connection and interaction and, further, have as its central concept what Zimmerman describes as "The mechanism and effects of urbanization and ruralization upon a population"

Further, should rural sociology only provide scientific knowledge about rural society and laws governing its development or should it also serve as a guide and suggest practical programmes of reform or reconstruction of that society in the economic, social or cultural fields? In short, should rural sociology merely give an objective authentic composite picture of the changing rural life in all its multifold and multiform aspects or also function as an ideological instrument to remould it according to a social purpose and a practical plan?

These are some of the principal problems over which extensive controversy is at present raging among sociologists. Such a disagreement among social scientists is not a characteristic peculiar to the field of rural sociology. Even regarding sociology in general, neither a clear, universally accepted definition nor a unanimous view of the scope of its study have as yet emerged among sociologists. The sub-domains of the single concretely whole domain of social life are so intermingled, interacting and even overlapping, that it is difficult to isolate one of them, study it and evolve a distinct science disclosing the laws of its structure and its evolution. Hence it is that disputes take place among social thinkers regarding the method and approach to be adopted to evolve a social science.

Fundamental Issues

In spite of a wide divergence of views among rural sociologists regarding the definition, scope, and objective of rural sociology and also about the emphasis to be laid on this or that factor of the rural society as the point of departure of its study, there also exists a number of basic agreements among them.

All rural sociologists recognize that the social life of the community is divided into two distinct segments, rural and urban. Though these segments interact among themselves, each is sufficiently distinct from the other.

All of them hold the view that social life in rural setting exhibits characteristics and tendencies which are peculiar to it, which constitute its specificness and which, therefore, sharply distinguish it from social life in urban setting.

All of them unanimously declare that the prime objective of rural sociology should be to make a scientific, systematic and comprehensive study of the rural social organization, of its structure, functions and objective tendencies of development, and on the basis of such a study, to discover the law of its development.

Since every science, social or natural, has for its aim the discovery of the hitherto hidden law of development of a domain of nature or society, the basic task of rural sociology, they unanimously declare, is to discover the law of development of rural society.

An Active Section

A Systematic study of the rural social organization, its structure, function and evolution has not only become necessary but also urgent after the advent of Independence. The very process of achieving national freedom and transfer of power from the British to the Indians as also the colossal and very significant consequences which have followed this achievement, have revealed the signal importance of a careful, all-comprehensive, and methodical study of the rural society in our country.

The extensive participation of the rural masses in the long drawn out national liberation struggle; the devastating communal frenzy which swept over the rural social world and resulted in the uprooting of a great section of the village population in a number of provinces; the deep ferment which is, at present, seething in the agrarian area and which frequently bursts out in varied forms of struggles between different strata of the people; the numerous prejudices which are corroding the life of the rural people and which manifest themselves in various caste, linguistic, provincial and other forms of tension, antagonism and conflict; and similar other phenomena reveal that rural India is not so inert and quiescent as it was once assumed to be.

Welfare Governance

The grave problems pertaining to rural society outlined above have been brought to the forefront in the post-independence period. The Constitution of the independent India has already fixed the goal towards which Indian society is to develop. A secular state, based on universal franchise and with the welfare of its citizens as its prime objective as provided for in the directive principles of the Constitution, is the national ideal which has emerged after the transfer of power. The realization of such an ideal, however, is a most complex and stupendous task which a people can set to itself.

To evolve a truly secular state in a country which is a citadel of the most stubborn religious prejudices rampant among its people; to create a social and cultural atmosphere for the intelligent exercise of universal adult franchise by the citizens who are living within the traditional, authoritarian, joint family, caste and semi-feudal social framework and the overwhelming majority of whom are illiterate; to develop a welfare economy in a country where the entire productive system is increasingly deteriorating; to implement such directive principles of the Constitution which accept the need to provide such rights as the right to work, the right to social security, and the right to education to citizens when even the task of providing primary necessities to them is increasingly becoming more and more difficult; — to fulfil such a programme it is vitally necessary to have a precise and thorough understanding of the Indian social structure and its developmental tendencies.

Racing Behind

Those who desire to strive for such a creative social transformation have to bear in mind that India is overwhelmingly an agrarian country; that not less than three-fourths of her population is engaged in agriculture; and that the agricultural economy, which forms the material basis of the life of this vast mass of the population, determines their social organization (the institutional matrix within which their life processes flow) as well as moulds their psychological and ideological life. Further, since the rural society forms the major sector of the Indian society, the specific programme of the re-casting of the former must inevitably play a decisive role in any scheme of transformation of the latter on a higher economic and cultural basis.

Sophisticated Academics

Statisticians, economists, sociologists, social workers and government agencies have, hitherto, overwhelmingly focussed their attention on the study of the phenomena of the problem of the urban society, though by far the greater portion of the Indian humanity lives in the rural area amidst conditions of immense material and cultural poverty. Even the literature dealing with the factual data about the life of the rural people is very meager. It is true that there has grown a literature, though insufficient, devoted to the study of different kinds of soil, manure, seeds, techniques of agriculture, land holdings, land tenures, processes of marketing of crops and other matters pertaining to agrarian economy. There are even some fragmentary studies delineating the life history of some castes and tribes and indicative studies of some villages. However, uptil now, neither the problems of the rural society have been formulated in all their bewildering complexity and variety, nor have scientific diagnosis and solutions to these problems been offered.

The study of the Indian rural society, which varies from state to state, from even district to district, due to their extreme geographical, economic, historical, ethnic and other peculiarities, hitherto made has been spasmodic, insufficient and often superficial. Such a study cannot give an authentic, composite picture of the variegated landscape of the rural life, nor can it serve as a guide for evolving a scientific programme of reconstruction of the rural society, so essential for the renovation of the entire Indian society.

In fact, a concrete and comprehensive study of the rural society in all its aspects, ecological, morphological, institutional and cultural, has hardly begun.

Village Society on Way to Progress

It is, however, urgently necessary to make a scientific and systematic study of the rural society, of its economic foundation and social and cultural superstructure, of its institutions and their functions, of the problems arising from the rapid process of disintegration which is undergoing and which even threatens its breakdown.

(1) India is a classic land of agriculture. Its long past history, its complex social organization and religious life, its varied cultural pattern, can hence be understood only if a proper study is made of the rise, growth crystallisation and subsequent fossilisation and break up of the self-sufficient village community, the principal pivot of the Indian society only till recently.

(2) Due to historical reasons, the existing Indian rural society has become a veritable mosaic of various types of rural societies and hence reveals a diversified cultural pattern. The culture of the hunting and food gathering tribes; the culture of the primitive hoe-agriculturists; further, all the varied cultures of peoples

engaged in agrarian production with the plough and the bullock, as also the modern culture of a rural people influenced by new technical and economic forces — all these cultures are juxtaposed in the contemporary rural India. Further, the Indian rural humanity is also being influenced by the ideological currents of the modern era. Consequently we find in the Indian rural world today, the persistence of primitive cults of magic and animism, polytheism, pantheism of the ancient world, monotheism and other idealistic philosophic world outlooks inherited from the ancient medieval periods as also a minor current of modern rationalist world view. This has transformed it into a veritable museum of different and even conflicting cults and ideologies.

(3) The unique agrarian socio-economic structure of India experienced a decisive transformation as a result of the impact of the British conquest and rule. On the eve of the British conquest of India the Indian rural society was composed of a multitude of villages. Each village lived almost an independent, atomistic, self-sufficient social and economic existence. The village represented a closed society based on economic autarchy and social life governed by caste and community rules.

In the economic sphere, the village experienced a steady transformation during the British period. Its economic self-sufficiency was dissolved. It slowly began to produce for the Indian and the foreign market and, not as before, for meeting the needs of the village population. The village economy became increasingly an integral part of the national and even world economy. The influx of cheap foreign and, subsequently, of indigenous industrial goods into the village, progressively undermined the village artisan industries. The old self-sufficient economy based on an equilibrium between the village agriculture and the village artisan industry was thus disrupted.

In the social field, the rule of custom enforced by the joint family, the caste and the village panchayat, was gradually replaced by the reign of laws made by the centralized British state in India and administered by its own revenue, executive and judicial officials posted in the village. This considerably undermined the powers of the joint family, the caste and the village panchayat.

The introduction of the modern means of transport and communication accelerated the processes mentioned above.

Every aspect of the village life, social, economic, political and cultural, experienced a steady transformation. The old pattern of village life, the old structure of village society, became appreciably changed.

Since the transformation was mainly brought about by a foreign power to serve its own political and economic interests, it resulted in the destruction of the old type of the rural society without its being replaced by a socially healthy, economically progressive and culturally more advanced new type. The transformation culminated in the emergence of the present impoverished and culturally backward village which, moreover, lacked stability and a definite structural design.

The Indian agrarian economy is at present in a state of acute crisis. This has resulted in the unbearable economic misery of the rural people. The agrarian situation has consequently become almost explosive.

It is, therefore, vitally necessary to focus attention on the crisis of the rural economy. The solution of the crisis is the essential pre-condition not only for eliminating poverty of the rural population but also for building a prosperous national economy which can guarantee a higher material standard of life to all citizens.

It should be noted that the role of social institutions in accelerating or retarding the fulfilment of an advanced programme of agrarian re-construction is greater in India than in any other country. Programmes and policies of rural renovation based on pure economic factors have not, therefore, met with appreciable success. The role of such institutions as the caste and the joint family organization in thwarting such programmes and policies has not been hitherto properly grasped. The necessity of Rural Sociology becomes all the more important in India.

The Justification of Study

To reconstruct such a rural society on a higher basis, it is urgently necessary to study not only the economic forces, but also the social, the ideological and other forces operating in that society. It is a complex and colossal task.

As referred to above, only stray, spasmodic efforts have been hitherto made to study the life processes of the Indian rural society. No systematic study has still been launched to study that society in all its aspects, to study its life processes in their movement and, further, in their interconnections.

In fact, Indian Rural Sociology or the science of the laws governing the specific Indian rural social organism has still to be created. Such a science is, however, the basic premise for the renovation of the Indian rural society, so indispensable for the renovation of the Indian society as a whole.

Two

The Rural Folk

The first task confronting the rural sociologist is to define the rural people and distinguish them from the urban population. Various approaches have been suggested for that purpose by eminent thinkers. Classification adopted by Government Census Departments in various countries is, however, generally accepted as the most convenient, though it may vary from one country to another.

Rural-Urban Population Compared

The next task before the student of the rural people is to determine the ratio of rural and urban populations. In many countries, this ratio in a great measure indicates the level of living of the people as a whole since it shows the relative proportion of industry, and agriculture and hence the total wealth of the people. The ratio, further, considerably influences the apportionment of social amenities within the country. It thereby serves as a guide for evolving a correct programme for social advance. One of the great mistakes committed by a number of reformers and social engineers is to transplant mechanically the techniques adopted for reform in a country inhabited by a small agrarian population and with a vast area of land to a country inhabited by an overwhelmingly agrarian population and with scarce land resources. The recent effort to introduce measures adopted to improve the agrarian sector of the U.S.A. which is overwhelmingly industrial to predominantly agrarian backward countries of Asia is an instance of such an error. Even within the same country a detailed study of the ratios of rural-urban population in different regions is essential because these differences considerably alter the nature of problems relating to those regions. For instance, the problems of Gujarat and those of Bihar are different as there is a difference in the proportion of rural-urban population of these states.

Population Density

The next important problem is that of the density of the people living on land. Sociologists, after adequate investigation, have reached the conclusion that the average density beyond a particular limit indicates an undesirable over-concentration of the people in that area. This is because the density of the population affects production and distribution and also generates various social reactions which greatly influence the total life of a society. The density of the population further affects the level of the standard of living of the people.

A systematic study of the density of the population in different regions and districts in India and also of the proportion of various groups belonging to diverse castes, religions, and vocations which comprises the population, will unfold the variegated picture of the complex social life of the Indian people with all its multiple tensions, antagonisms as well as mutual adjustments among these groups.

Longevity of Life

The study of birth rates, death rates, rates of suicides, specific bodily diseases and such other matters regarding the rural population is another important aspect of a demographic study of the rural society as it reveals the quantitative and qualitative growth or decline of the rural people. Further, when this study is correlated to that of the social, economic and religious life processes of various social groups, it provides intelligent and correct criteria of evaluating the norms of those groups.

Villagers' General Health

Apart from a study of the death and survival rates prevailing among the rural people, there are also other means to determine their vitality such as a study of their general health and longevity. Further, estimates of mortality prevailing among separate groups such as infants, females and old people; upper, lower and middle social strata; and land labourers, farmers, artisans, and other social categories, will give a detailed picture of the vitality of various sections of the rural people.

Categorisation on Age and Sex Basis

Another aspect of the life of a population which requires a close study is their distribution in age and sex groups. The analysis of age groups gives us a correct understanding of the proportion of the people who are of productive age and those who are to be sustained by the society. The preponderance of children and the aged over the working section of the people would considerably influence their economic and social life.

Similarly the analysis of the sex composition is also essential, since it is generally recognized by sociologists that "sex mores, social codes, social rituals, and social institutions are all likely to be affected where extremely unbalanced sex ratios are found."

Various Groups

Caste, race, nationality and religious composition of the people has a great social significance. It gives rise to a rich, complex, diversified social life and varied patterns of culture. More often it breeds animosities, antagonisms and conflicts. We know how in India in recent years the multi-religious composition of the Indian people engendered ghastly communal Hindu-Muslim riots. We know how nationality conflicts are steadily corroding the body politic of India.

A very peculiar type of social grouping which is found in India is the caste grouping. A student of the Indian society who fails to study closely and carefully this variety of social grouping will miss the very essence of that society. Looking to its important role in India a separate chapter has been devoted to the sociological significance of caste elsewhere.

A systematic, co-ordinated and inter-related study of the rural people from various angles is an urgent need.

Domestic Life

Among the institutions that compose rural society, the family is the most important. It has been its very foundation. It plays a decisive role in the material and cultural life of the rural aggregate and in moulding the psychological characteristics of the rural individual as well as the rural collectivity. In fact, according to some thinkers, family and familism impress their stamp on the entire rural structure. Familism permeates it from top to bottom.

A systematic study of rural family, of its structure, functions, evolution, and interrelations with other institutions of the rural society is vitally necessary for the rural sociologist.

The Indian rural society provides a classic field for the study of the institution of rural family. Within it are found many types and patterns of family organization which humanity has hitherto evolved.

Family Organisation and Setup

Prof. Rivers has distinguished four types of institutions which have been designated by the term family, viz., the clan, the matrilocal joint family, the patrilocal joint family and the individual family composed of only parents and minor children.

According to one group of sociologists, these four types reveal four main stages of the evolution of the family form corresponding to four stages in the evolution of society. The first type corresponds to the hunting and food gathering stage of social evolution; the second to the phase of hoe agriculture and the beginnings of domestication of animals; the third — a classic type — to the phase of agricultural economy based on the plough and domestication of animals, and, finally, the fourth type to the modern industrial capitalist phase of human existence. As a result of the growth of market economy in the agrarian area and of the impact of urban socio-economic forces on the rural society, the last type is increasingly becoming predominant today.

The Indian rural society provides a great laboratory to test this view, since it includes within its fold the relics of the clan as well as matrilocal and patrilocal family types and the recent individual family group also. A methodical study of the structure and functions of these various family types and their correlation with the stages of civilization to which they correspond will throw a floodlight on the history of Indian humanity and will enable Indian historians to evolve a correct sequence of the developmental phases of the Indian society.

Joint Family under a Father Figure

In almost all fully developed agrarian societies depending on plough agriculture, patriarchial joint family has been found to be the predominant family form in rural areas. Outstanding rural sociologists have made a close study of the characteristics of this type of family. They have observed the basic structural, psycho-social, and functional features of this type of the rural family which distinguish it sharply from the urban family. They are as under:

Greater Homogeneity: The rural family is far more homogeneous, stable, integrated and organically functioning than the urban family. The ties binding the members of the former, for instance the husband and the wife, parents and children, are stronger and last longer than those in the case of the urban family. A glance at the Indian countryside will corroborate this view. The Indian village still remains a cluster of joint families though, due to a number of historico-economic causes, the joint family has been exhibiting a tendency of slow but steady disintegration. The rural family is composed not only of the members of the family but also frequently includes distant relations which hardly happens in the dovecotes of the urban society.

Based on Peasant Household: Another essential characteristic of the rural family is that it is generally based on the peasant household. All its members are engaged in the agricultural occupation. Work is distributed among them mainly on lines of age and sex distinctions. "The Community house, common land and common economic functions along with the common kinship bond create the peasant household." Since the members of the rural family form a single economic unit and constantly co-operate with one another in agricultural operations, since they hold property in common usually managed by the eldest member of the family, since also they spend most of their time together, the psychological traits they develop are very similar.

Greater Discipline and Interdependence: The rural family is characterised by greater discipline among its members than the urban family. Further, since there is considerably less state or public provision for meeting the educational, cultural, or social needs of the people in the rural area than in the urban, the rural family attempts also to satisfy these needs of its members. It thus serves as a school, a recreation centre, as well as a maternity or a non-maternity hospital.

Dominance of Family Ego: The interdependence of the members of the rural family and the dependence of its individual member on it are, therefore, far greater than in the case of the urban family. This welds its members into a homogeneous, compact, egoistic unit, strengthens emotions of solidarity and co-operation among them and fills them with family pride. They develop more collectivist family consciousness and less individualistic emotion. In a rural society, a family is discredited if any of its individual members perpetrates an infamous act. Similarly the glory of his or her achievement also accrues to the family from which he or she springs. The urban family in contrast to the rural family, is less authoritarian of the family even at the cost of their lives.

Authority of the Father: Since the rural family is a more integrated and disciplined unit than the urban family, the head of the rural family exercises almost absolute power over its members. It is he who distributes the work of the peasant household among the family members on lines of sex and age differences; arranges marriages of sons, daughters, nephews and nieces; administers the joint family property according to his wisdom; and trains the youngsters for future agricultural work and social life. All initiative and final authority are vested in him. In fact "the head of the family has had the rights and authority to be the ruler, the priest, the teacher, the educator and the manager of the family." Thus, the family, through its head, subordinates its individual members to itself. The latter are completely submerged in the family; hence they hardly develop any individuality or personality. Such a family type can only be a nursery for the growth of family collectivism but not of individuality. The urban family in contrast to the rural family, is less authoritarian but also less co-operative. This is due to a variety of reasons. First, it is not a single productive unit administered by the family head since its adult members are mostly engaged in occupations unconnected with, and outside the home. Further, educational, recreational and a number of other needs of its members are satisfied by extra-family institutions like school, club, and others. Property of its earning members, too, tends to be individual, ,since it is derived out of extra-family occupations. In the sphere of marriage also, its members are increasingly exhibiting independence and marry persons of their own choice.

Closer Participation in Various Activities: One striking feature of the rural family lies in the fact that its members, being engaged in work connected with the peasant household, spend practically the whole day together. In contrast to this, the members of the urban family engaged in different occupations or being educated outside home, spend only a small portion of the day together. Even their recreational centres such as clubs and others lie outside the home. Hence the home becomes only a temporary nightshed for the members of the urban family.

The Urban Culture

Rural society has been increasingly urbanised in modern times. In proportion to its urbanization it exhibits the characteristics of urban society. The rural family more and more develops centrifugal tendencies. Its economic homogeneity based upon a single cumulative economic activity of its members declines. Joint family property tends to be disrupted since its individual adult members begin to demand its partitioning. Being increasingly engaged in different occupations, they earn independent separate incomes which they retain as their own. They live less and less together and spend only a fraction of the day in association. They begin to seek extra-familial centres like clubs, hotels, unions, associations, cafeteria, which are also slowly growing in and around rural areas. All this results in the growth of individualistic psychology among them which weakens family emotion and egoism so vital for the vigorous functioning of a homogeneous family.

The individual hitherto submerged in, and subordinated to, the family tends to become atomistic. He more and more breaks away from the family restrictions. He develops his own initiative and independence. This inevitably results in the weakening of the family authority, family ties, and the family itself.

According to the views of such eminent sociologists as Sorokin, Zimmerman and others, the social and political organization of all agrarian societies during their subsistence stages bears the fundamental traits of rural family, the basic unit of rural society. These traits they characterise as familism.

"Since the family has been the basic social institution of the rural social world, it is natural to expect that the whole social organization of agricultural aggregates has been stamped by the characteristics of the rural family. In other words, all the other social institutions and fundamental social relationships have been permeated by, and modelled according to, the patterns of rural family relationships. Familism is the term used to designate this type of social organization ..... Familism is the outstanding and fundamental trait in the gestalt of such a society."

These sociologists enumerate a number of important characteristics of such societies bearing the stamp of familism. They are as under :

***Marriage Earlier and its Higher Rate*:** The members of these rural societies marry at an earlier age than those of urban societies. Further, the rate of marriage in the former is higher than that in the latter.

***Family, Unit of Social Responsibility*:** Since family is the unit of rural society, it is the family collective that pays the taxes and discharges social responsibilities. The individual is also appraised according to the status of the family to which he or she belongs.

Family, Basis of Norms of Society: Further, ethical codes, religious doctrines, social conceptions and legal norms governing rural societies have always condemned anything which would weaken the stability of the family. They have preached implicit obedience to parents on the part of sons and daughters and to husband on the part of wife.

Family, its Impress in Political Form: The political organizations of those rural societies have been also based on the conception on which rural family rests. Their political ideology has conceived the relation between the ruler and the ruled as that between the head of the family and its members, i.e., paternalistic. "King, monarch, ruler, lord have been viewed as an enlarged type of family patriarch the predominant type of political organization in the rural community is represented by the institution of the village elder, the head, elected by the peasants as the family elder is either openly or tacitly elected by the family members. The whole character of the village chief's authority and administration is a mere replica of the paterfamilia's authority and administration."

Co-operative rather than Contractual Relations: The relations between the members of the rural society are basically co-operative in contrast to those between the members of the urban society which are preponderatingly contractual. This difference, according to the view of the outstanding sociologists, is the result of the difference between the rural and urban families. "In a rural family the solidarity of its members is organic and spontaneous. It springs up of itself-Naturally as a result of close co-living, co-working, co-acting, co-feeling and co-believing. Any contractual relationship between its members would be out of place and contradictory to the whole tone of family ..... it is no surprising, then, that purely contractual relationships have been but little developed in familistic societies." The members of the urban family on the other hand have separate interests as well as individualistic 'psychologies. They have more or less lost collective family feeling. The urban society bears this characteristic of the urban family. Spontaneous cooperation and solidarity-feeling are found to be appreciably less among the urban people than among the rural people.

Family, Unit of Production, Consumption and Exchange: The economic structure of the rural society also bears the traits of the rural family. It is based on family ownership. The production and consumption are familistic. The market is less developed. Exchange has more the characteristics of simple barter than of full-fledged monetary transactions. The entire code of laws regulating the economic relationships within such a society bears the stamp of familism. In contrast to this, the urban economy is predominantly a commodity economy and therefore the economic and hence the general social relations between the members of the urban society are competitive and contractual.

Dominance of Family Cult and Ancestor Worship: The ideology and the culture of rural society also exhibit traits of familism. The cult of family dominates. Religious and other ceremonies have for their object the security and property of the family. Ancestor worship is almost universally prevalent. Even the relationships between its gods and goddesses are familistic, they being related to one another as father, mother, brother, sister, etc.

Dominance of Tradition: As a result of all these factors rural society is marked with much less mobility than urban society. Tradition severely governs its life processes. It undergoes change with extreme slowness.

Social Trends

To sum up, until the impact of the Industrial Revolution and the competitive market economy, familism was the heart of village communities. Subsistence agrarian economies and rural societies based on them were familistic through and through. However, the rise and development of modern industries steadily undermined subsistence agrarian economy and brought the rural economy within the orbit of capitalist market economy. This transformation together with the growing pressure of various urban forces brought about the increasing disintegration of the old rural family. The rural society, too, more and more lost its familistic traits.

In India, due to lack of sufficient industrial development, the forces of urban society have not penetrated rural society to the same extent as in the U.S.A., Great Britain and other industrially advanced countries. The rural family consequently retains its specific traits to a far greater extent in India. Urban industrial development affects the rural family in many ways. It creates new occupations such as those of factory and workshop workers, of clerks, typists, and others. The members of the rural family develop a desire to take to those occupations, demand their share in the joint family property and migrate to towns and cities. This process undermines the joint family based on a common occupation of its members and joint family property, income and expenditure.

Modern industries produce a number of articles cheaply and on a mass scale. They reach out to the village population who purchase them. Thus the peasant family which was formerly producing cloth and other necessities with primitive techniques more and more ceases to produce them now. Thus it loses a number of its economic functions with the result that the scope of the collective labour of its members narrows down.

Capitalist economic development transforms the social and political environments of a people also. In India, British capitalism transformed the socio-economic structure of the Indian society and, further, established a centralized State. This resulted in a number of consequences. Private and State agencies increasingly established schools, dispensaries and administrative and judicial machinery in the village. The rural family which served as the school for its members no longer functioned as such, since its members now began to receive education outside the family. Also not the grandfather or the grandmother, the embodiment of traditional medical knowledge, but the doctor appointed by an agency unconnected with family, now increasingly treated the members of the family. Caste and panchayat councils were deprived of their functions as guardians of law and dispensers of justice. The customary law was replaced by the new law of the centralized state which operated through its administrative and judicial organs. The process progressed in proportion as the urbanization of the country advanced.

The historical tendency of the rural family is towards its increasing disintegration and loss of functions. The more this tendency grows, the more the family ego and solidarity feeling cradled in and nourished by the collective labour and life of its members weaken and atomistic individualistic psychological traits develop among them.

During the last hundred and fifty years, the traditional joint family and the familistic rural framework have been undergoing a qualitative transformation. The basis of rural family relationships is shifting from that of status to that of contract. The rule of custom is being replaced by the rule of law. The family is being transformed from a unit of production to a unit of consumption. The cementing bond of the family is being changed from consanguinity to conjugality. Further, the family is ceasing to become an omnibus social agency, it being shorn of most of its economic, political, educational, medical, religious and other social and cultural functions. Instead, it is becoming a specialized and affectional small association. From a massive joint family composed of members belonging to a number of generations, the family is increasingly shaping as a tiny unit composed of husband, wife and unmarried children. Familism, too, is gradually dropping off. The rural society is acquiring quite a new gestalt.

A systematic study of the rural family from many angles has never been so necessary as at present in India. Its methodical, intensive and extensive study will provide proper direction for evolving a programme of appropriate measures to realise grand objectives that are embodied in the Constitution of the Indian Union. Rural sociologists in India require to launch a very comprehensive campaign of study to locate the laws of the transformation of one of the most classic familistic civilizations that has emerged in the history of humanity.

Three

Village Life, through the Ages

After having surveyed the chief characteristic differences between the rural and urban segments of social life, we will now proceed to analyse the structural pattern of the rural society since it provides the matrix within which the whole drama of rural life is unfolded.

The village is the unit of the rural society. It is the theatre wherein the quantum of rural life unfolds itself and functions.

Like every social phenomenon the village is an historical category. The emergence of the village at a certain stage in the evolution of the life of man, its further growth and development in subsequent periods of human history, the varied structural changes it experienced during thousands of years of its existence, the rapid and basic transformation it has undergone during the last hundred and fifty years since the Industrial Revolution—all these constitute a very fascinating and challenging study.

Old is Gold

The rise of the village is bound up with the rise of agricultural economy in history. The emergence of the village signified that man passed from the nomadic mode of collective life to the settled one. This was basically due to the improvement of tools of production which made agriculture and hence settled life on a fixed territorial zone possible and necessary.

How humanity, in different parts of the world, passed from the nomadic hunting and food gathering stage to that based on *roving hoe* agriculture and thereafter, on settled plough agriculture carried on by means of draft animals, has been one of the most difficult and complex problems in the field of social research.

With the invention of the plough, man could develop stable agriculture, the basic source of assured food supply. Man's nomadic mode of life ceased. No longer men roamed in herds from place to place in search of means of subsistence. They settled on a definite territory and organized villages based on agricultural economy. Agrarian communities with villages as their fixed habitation and agriculture as their main occupation came into existence. This event marked a landmark in the history of mankind, inaugurating a higher phase of social existence. Agriculture assured the community, for the first time, a relatively stable food supply in contrast to previous stages of social life. While food supply derived from, such sources as hunting, fishing, fruit gathering and migratory hoe agriculture had always been insufficient and precarious, grain and other types of food products derived from plough agriculture could be counted upon and also be stored for use in periods of emergencies, thereby assuring relative food security for the future.

In the agricultural phase the struggle for existence became relatively less acute for man. Further, at a certain stage of the development of agricultural economy, due to the greater productivity of agriculture, a section of the community could be liberated from the necessity of participating in food production and could therefore concentrate on secondary industrial or ideological activity. This gave momentum to the growth of technology, arts, sciences and philosophy. It also brought about, though slowly, the significant transition in the social organization of humanity, from an organization founded on kinship and clan to that based on territorial ties. With the development of agriculture at a certain level, mankind took a leap from totemistic collectivist clan society to territorial civil society with its distinct multi-class social structure and the resultant institution of the state.

Civilization thus began with the development of agriculture. The village — the first settled form of collective human habitation and the product of the growth of agricultural economy—thus historically gave birth to rural society, and from the surplus of its food resources, nourished the town which subsequently came into existence.

Aggregates of Different Kind

In the history of different peoples living in different parts of the world, different types of villages emerged with the rise and spread of agriculture. This was mainly due to differences in geographical environments in which those peoples lived. Further, the early village of a people also underwent changes in time due to its subsequent technical, economic, and social evolution as well as due to the impact of other societies on it.

The history of the village, in time and space, reveals such diverse village types as the Saxon village, the German Mark, the Russian Mir, the self-sufficient Indian Gram, the village of the feudal Europe which was an integral part of the manor; and finally the modern village, which is an integral part of national and world economic systems, with its variants such as the U.S.A. village, the typical West European village, the village of the backward modern countries of Asia, the village of the Soviet Union based on collectivized agricultural economy and others.

Hence the student of rural society should study the village, the basic unit of rural society as it originated and underwent a constant state of development and change due to the action of its own developing internal forces as also due to its interaction with other societies.

Village Aggregates Classified

Eminent sociologists have advanced a number of criteria to classify village communities.

(1) According to one criterion the village aggregates have been classified according to the types which evolved during the period of the transition from man's nomadic existence to settled village life. Thus villages have been divided into three groups: (i) the Migratory agricultural villages where the people live in fixed abodes only for a few months; (ii) the Semi-permanent agricultural villages where the population resides for a few years and then migrates due to the exhaustion of the soil; and (iii) the Permanent agricultural villages where the settled human aggregates live for generations and even centuries.

(2) According to the second criterion villages have been classified into grouped (or nucleated) villages and dispersed villages. In grouped villages the farmers dwell in the village proper in a cluster. They work on the fields which lie outside the village site. Since they dwell together in a single habitat, they develop a compact life. In the case of the non-nucleated dispersed village type, the farmers live separately on their respective farms. Their habitats being thus dispersed, their social life assumes a different form.

(3) Village aggregates have been also classified according to a third criterion, that of social differentiation, stratification, mobility and land ownership.

According to this criterion, village aggregates have been grouped into six broad types viz. (1) that composed of peasant joint owners; (2) that composed of peasant joint tenants; (3) that composed of farmers who are mostly individual owners, but also include some tenants and labourers; (4) that composed of individual farmer tenants; (5) that composed of employees of a great private landowner; and finally (6) that composed of labourers and employees of the state, the church, the city or the public landowner.

Case for Systematic Classification

A systematic classification of Indian village aggregates on the basis of the above criteria and a study of their history will provide valuable information about village communities in India, about varied types of social institutions which have come into being in rural India, and also on the complex cultural patterns which have influenced and been influencing life processes of the Indian rural people.

An exhaustive survey of Indian villages co-relating the village types classified according to three principles will help to disclose the laws of the rise and development of Indian village communities. It will also help historians and sociologists to locate the laws of the peculiar development of Indian society and, further, will assist rural workers to evolve scientific programmes of rural reconstruction.

Difference between Urban and Rural

Social life in the countryside moves and develops in a rural setting just as social life in the urban area moves and develops in an urban setting. Their respective settings considerably determine rural and urban social life.

A correct comprehension of the specific characteristics of the rural framework is, therefore, indispensable for a proper grasp of the distinct features of rural social life. Such a study constitutes the first task of the rural sociologist and can be accomplished by studying in contrast the distinctive features of rural and urban settings. A brief outline of the principal points of contrast between the rural and urban settings will show how the different structures and life-processes of rural and urban societies are to a great extent the consequence of the difference between those different settings.

The Distinction

Outstanding sociologists have laid down a number of significant criteria for distinguishing the rural social world from the urban social world, such as the social composition of population, "the cultural heritage," the magnitude of material wealth, social stratification of the population, the degree of the complexity of social structure and social life, the intensity and variety of social contact and others. They have finally attempted to trace the sharp differences and contrasts between the two types of social phenomena, rural and urban, largely to the basic differences between the rural and urban settings.

The following are the most important criteria for distinguishing the rural social world from the urban social world

(1) Occupational differences.
(2) Environmental differences.
(3) Differences in the sizes of the communities.
(4) Differences in the density of the population.
(5) Differences in the homogeneity and heterogeneity of the population.
(6) Differences in the social mobility.
(7) Differences in the direction of migration.
(8) Differences in the social differentiation and stratification.
(9) Differences in the system of social interaction.

The following table reproduced from "Principles of Rural-Urban Sociology" reveals the decisive differences between the rural and the urban worlds.

	Rural World	Urban World
Occupation	Totality of cultivators and their families. In the community are usually a few representatives of several non- agricultural pursuits.	Totality of people engaged principally in manufacturing, mechanical pursuits, trade, commerce, professions, governing, and other non-agricultural occupations.
Environment	Prèdominance of nature over anthropo-logical environment. Direct relationship to nature.	Greater isolation from nature. Predominance of man-made environment over nature, stone and iron.
Size of community	Open farms or small communities, " agriculturalism" and size of community are negatively correlated.	As a rule in the same country and at the same period, the size of urban community is much larger than the rural community. In other words, urbanity and size of community are positively correlated.
Density of population	In the same country and at the same period the density is lower than in urban community. Generally density and rurality are negatively correlated.	Greater than in rural communities. Urbanity and density are positively correlated.
Heterogeneity and homogeneity of the population	Compared with urban populations, rural communities are more homogeneous in racial and psychological traits (Negative correlation with heterogeneity).	More heterogeneous than rural communities (in the same country and at the same time). Urbanity and heterogeneity are positively correlated.
Social differentiation and stratification	Rural differentiation and stratification less than urban	Differentiation and stratification show positive correlation with urbanity.
Mobility	Territorial, occupational and other forms of social mobi-	More intensive. Urbanity and mobility are positively

	lity of the population are comparatively less intensive. Normally the migration current carries more individuals from the country to the city.	correlated. Only in the periods of social catastrophy is the migration from the city to the country greater than from the country to the city.
System of interaction	Less numerous contacts per man. Narrower area of the interaction system of its members and the whole aggregate. More prominent part is occupied by primary contacts. Predominance of personal and relatively durable relations. Comparative simplicity and sincerity of relations. "Man is interacted as a human person."	More numerous contacts. Wider area of interaction system per man and per aggregate. Predominance of secondary contacts. Predominance of impersonal casual and short-lived relations. Greater complexity, manifoldedness, superficiality and standardized formality of relations. Man is interacted as a "number" and "address."

A Different Approach

One of the important aspects from which rural social life is increasingly being analysed is the aspect of its spatial organization.

What factors determine the growth of varied types of villages, what factors operate to combine a cluster of villages into an agrarian region, what factors tend to transform an agrarian region into a cultural, linguistic or political region, and how do regions evolve into a province-these problems are of considerable significance in the study of rural society.

Regional Factors

Sociologists have attempted to locate the factors explaining this process. According to them, some of the important factors, which have determined the structural pattern of the village, the formation of regional and other bigger units and the interrelations of the village with those units, are as follows:

(1) Natural conditions like relief, configurations, soil, water resources and others; (2) the stage of agrarian economy, whether it is the nomadic stage, the stage of fixed subsistence agriculture or that commercial agriculture; and (3) the nature of social conditions such as needs of defence, forms of property and others.

Habitats in Two Categories

The first great division which has been made of village communities from the ecological angle is that of nucleated or grouped villages and dispersed habitats. This distinction is vital from the point of view of the study of the entire social life of the rural community. The members of a rural community who dwell in villages have generally stronger social urges, exhibit a stronger feeling of social cohesion, and possess greater ability for co-operation than those who are dispersed and live on their respective farms. Each type of habitat furnishes a different framework for social life. The nucleated village is marked by "proximity, contact, community of ideas and sentiments" while in dispersed habitats "everything bespeaks separation, everything marks the fact of dwelling apart."

Larger Rural Regions

The study of the emergence of a larger rural area is one of the most baffling problems confronting the student of rural society. The factors which have combined to evolve homogeneous rural regions demand a very careful examination. Again we find that the larger rural regions change their characteristics with the change in the techno-economic, socio-economic and socio-political forces. The epoch of self-sufficiency evolved one category of regions. Under the impact of Industrial Revolution and production for market, a totally new type of rural areas came into being. The change from market economy to planned economy, where the agrarian sector is consciously developed as a part of the total life of the community, is creating in some countries and will create in other countries a new type of regional units. And, above all, the gigantic development of productive forces which is evolving an international economic and cultural community in the modern epoch is forcing the students of human society and especially of rural society to discover the appropriate variety of rural regions which will be in consonance with this development.

Efforts are being made to define economic, linguistic, administrative, religious and cultural regions in various countries. Efforts are also being made to find out where these regions coincide and also to study the laws which bring about this concurrence.

The works of Sanderson, Kolb, Taylor and others which embody an intensive study of rural economic and cultural zones in the U.S.A. have thrown considerable light on the phenomenon of the development of such zones. Various studies of primitive tribes— their geographical milieu, technical equipment, economic organization, social institutional structure, religion, arts and culture and, further, their transformation under the impact of communities belonging to various stages of civilized life—also furnish rich material for discovering the laws of rural development. Works dealing with the role of geographical factors—such as mountain, river, desert, sea, rainfall, various species of trees and animals—in indirectly or directly influencing the nature of economic organization, social institutions, styles of architecture, and beliefs and other ideological elements of man's life, also provide valuable clues for a correct understanding of the emergence of varied rural cultures.

The environmental and regional approach will help to distinguish chief village types and village social structures. It will also assist in scientifically classifying principal regional, district and provincial units. It will also aid in locating the underlying factors which have operated to create distinct culture-areas. And finally it will help to evolve a systematic account of the evolution of Indian society as a whole.

Need for an Ecological Map

A detailed map of India indicating various natural and economic regions; indicating the areas inhabited by populations living in various stages of economic development; showing linguistic regions including regions based on different dialects as well as different variations of the main language; and showing, further, religious regions based on different, religious beliefs prevailing among the people; will throw great light on some of the most burning problems of Indian society and will also assist those engaged in the difficult task of reforming rural society to locate some of the fundamental causes of the present crisis of that society.

Prevalent Conditions

The Great majority of the country folk live in small or large nucleated settlements, and areas of dispersed habitations are few :the Himalayan zone is perhaps the only extensive area of true dispersal, of the type found in European highlands, elsewhere, even in the hills, the normal unit is the small hamlet rather than the homestead. This is enforced partly by the paucity of water-points, partly by the needs of defence—still visibly attested by the watch-towers of Pathan villages. In the Assam-Burma Ranges defence is also an important factor: villages are on hilltops or spurs, often stockeded; it must be remembered that in these jungly hills the valleys are extremely malarial, and that communication is easiest along relatively open ridgeways. Bengal — especially the En delta — is *sui generis*: there is indeed much settlement that is not nucleated, but "dispersal" appears an exceedingly inappropriate term for the dense stipple of separate homesteads, hardly isolated except in the most literal sense of the word when, during the rains, each is an island on its little earthen plinth. Other more or less dispersed zones are found in the Assam jungles, or in the great floodplains by farmers using the rick khadar for high-value crops after the rains. But in both groups the very small hamlet — say 6 to 12 huts — is the rule, rather than true dispersal: and in the latter case the huts are often only temporary, inhabited during the dry weather by people normally resident in big villages on the bluffs above.

These are anomalies: in the great homogeneous plains nucleation is almost invariable. In the past defence played its part, and in areas open to constant disturbance (e.g. the Sutlej/Jumna and Jumna/Ganges Doabs, Rohilkhand, the fringes in Central India, Khandesh, the Raichur Doab) villages are often grouped around a petty fort; and even today the close-packed houses, with blank outer walls and low doorways, massed into a ring with few entrances, present a defensive aspect. Often there is not much in the way of site selection; one place is as good as another, and the village rises are as often as not their own creation, the rubbish of generations. But any discontinuity, any break in the almost imperceptible slope produces linear settlement patterns: especially notable are the bluffs above flood-plains and the margins of abandoned river courses. The bluff villages tend to be larger than those on the drier interfluves; they have the advantage of two types of terrain, the upland doab and the valley-bottom with its tamarisk brakes and the excellent soil of its chars or diaras — the floodplain islands — submerged in the rains and liable to disappear completely in floods, but cropping up again sooner or later. These alluviated areas are often given over to cash crops of high value; near large towns they are often used for market gardens, easily irrigated by wells taking advantage of the high water-table.

Settlement lines tend to occur also at the marked break of slope where steep residual hills grade into a fan, which has usually a fairly high water-table. Lateritic shelves along deltaic margins are also important building sites, poor in themselves but offering rough grazing, scrubby woodland (the source of a great range of minor necessities from tiber to illicit alcohol), and providing space for dry crops, the flats below being entirely given over to paddy. They form as it were neutral ground between the jungly hills and the waterlogged paddy-plain. Here not only the general arrangement of settlements but also the village itself is often linear; islands of lateritic and older alluvium in the deltas are often completely ringed with houses. Linear settlement is also, of course, prominent in the deltas and wider floodplains themselves, strung out along levees or artificial embankments, and in places (e.g., Kerala and the Contai area of SW Bengal) along old beach ridges. Very often such sites are the only dry points in the rains and the only water-points in the hot weather.

There is in general very little that looks like a "Plan," other than that dictated by such site factors as alignment along bluffs or levees, grouping round a fort or a tank; but within the seemingly chaotic agglomeration there is, as a rule, a strong internal differentiation, that of the separate quarters for various castes.

These points are best brought out by a close view of a specific village, not indeed 'typical' (no single village could be that) but certainly the most random of samples. Our example is in the Deccan, more precisely in the Bombay-Karnatak.

Aminbhavi lies seven miles away from Dharwar; an old settlement, going back at least thirteen centuries, originally walled and moated. Essentially its site is governed by the junction of the Dharwar rocks, forming poor red soils around the mosque-crowned hill to the W, with the crystallines which have weathered into deep black cotton soils in the E. It is a typical black soil agricultural village, with a rainfall of about 24 ins. devoted mainly to dry crops (cotton, jowar, wheat, pulses, safflower, in that order), tending to become a satellite of Dharwar, the market of its dairy and agricultural produce. On the poorer land to the W is rough grazing, supporting a few shepherds, and immediately W of the village the common or gauthana, an essential part of its economy, the centre of all harvesting.

Caste and community largely govern the layout. Of its 4,106 inhabitants, Lingayats, the sturdy agricultural caste of the Karnatak, number some 2,650. Next come 550 Muslims, an unusually high proportion, but the place was of some importance in the days of the Bijapur Kingdom, and the first element in its name is indeed that of some forgotten Muslim (Aminbhavi roughly — Amin's Well). But the culturally dominant groups are the Jains (250) and the Brahmins (75); this is an Inam(landlord) village, most of it belonging to the Desai (Jain) and Deshpande (Brahmin) families, whose wadas (more or less equivalent to manor houses) stand on the best sites, within large compounds. The Desai provide the village patel or headman. For the rest, each caste tends to occupy a solid block of contiguous houses in a lane named from the caste; where, as with the leading family residing in it. Besides those mentioned, there are 300 Talwars (domestic servants and agricultural labourers), 200 Harijans ("untouchables"), and smaller groups of other low castes — Wadars (quarrymen), and so on. These groups live on the circumference of the village, or even beyond the old moat.

Occupations likewise are still mainly on a caste basis: the Lingayats provide the bulk of the tenant-farmers, Talwars and Harijans, landless agricultural labour; carpenters, smiths, cobblers, washermen, barbers are all separate castes. Apart from these crafts and agriculture, there is some handloom cotton weaving, a subsidiary occupation of the Lingayats.

Houses are generally built on to each other, or at least the mud walls of the compounds are continuous. The house layout is as standard as in any English working class street. In front is a porch (katte), used for drying agricultural produce, as a formal reception room, as "a place of female gossip when the master of the house is out," and above all as a sleeping-room in the stifling summer nights. Behind this is the main room, some 25 ft. square, part of which is a cattle pen, at threshold level; the remainder, raised some 2 or 3 ft. is the general living-room, for sleeping, eating, more intimate entertainment of guests, and perhaps handicrafts. The most prominent object is the pile of grain stored in gunny bags and sadly depleted towards the end of the agricultural year. Behind is a separate kitchen (with a corner for the bath) and the backyard with manure-pit and haystacks. This is the standard pattern; construction is similar in all groups (except the lowest), differences in economic status being reflected merely in size, except that the well-to-do have more separate single-purpose rooms. Jains and Brahmins do not live so tightly packed as the rest, either in the spacing of the houses or within them.

The poorest castes live in wretched one-room wattle huts with thatched roofs. Apart from these all houses have walls 1 or 2 ft. thick of mudbrick, with few (and high) or more likely no windows: Indians in general have a doubtless well-founded burglar-phobia. The flat roof is supported by wooden posts and made of mud on a framework of crude beams and babul (acacia) branches; they have rounded mud parapets and clay rain water pipes.

As for services, these are mostly grouped around the main village lane: market-place for the weekly bazar, eight shops (four grocery, two cloth, one tailor, one miscellaneous) and a number of booths selling tea and bidis, the cheap crude cigarettes of the Indian masses. Near the market-place is the room of the village panchayat or caste council, an ancient institution generally fallen into dustbin but now being fostered as the first step in local government. Associated with this tiny 'urban core' are the government establishments — Police Station, Post Office, grain warehouse. There are three mosques, one giving its name to the Idgah hill in the W, and eight temples, including that of the Deshpandes, as well as the Lingayat math, a centre of religious and charitable fellowship. The professions are represented by an Ayurvedic (indigenous) dispensary, a Urdu school for the Muslims, and separate schools for boys and girls. The boys' school is the most modern building in Aminbhavi, its stone walls and red-tiled roof standing in sharp contrast to the monotony of mud walls.

Finally we may note the large masonry-lined public well, sunk in what was once the moat; it is no mean excavation, an apt reminder of the all importance of water-supply in Indian life.

Once more, no one village can be typical of the whole sub-continent; but many of the features detailed above can be parallelled over and over again in most parts of India. Our random sample is at least very representative.

Shades of Life

The aspect of the village varies not only with the general regional setting, with building materials and house-types, but with social factors. The generally greater emphasis on caste in the S takes social fragmentation allied with spatial separation to the extreme, segregating the untouchables in outlying cherish or sub-villages, sometimes located several hundred yards from the main villages of which they are service-components. This is indeed the climax of geographical differentiation; apartheid. A typical cheri may consist of two rows of huts with a narrow central "street" in the middle this widens to make room for a tiny temple. The huts have thick mud walls, roofed with palmyra thatch, and low mud porches scrupulously swept. To enter one must bend double; the only light comes from the door and from under the leaves and the furniture consists of a few pots and pans, a couple of wooden chests, and the essential paddybin, 4 to 6 ft. high and 3 to 4 in diameter, raised from the ground to escape the rats, and built up of hoops of mud. Poor as they are, these dwellings are yet homes, and obviously loved as such: their cleanliness, the surrounding mangoes, coconut and palmyra palms, redeem them from utter squalor. The nadir is reached in the bustees of Calcutta and the revolting camps of casual tribal labour found on the outskirts of the larger towns: shelters (they cannot be called even huts) of matting, of rags, of petrol tins beaten flat, on waste spaces open to the sun and reeking with filth.

A geographical study of Indian house-types would be a work vast in scope and rich in instruction; a few of the more striking instances are mentioned in the regional chapters. Social factors are no less important than environmental, at least once we go beyond the fundamental antithesis of the NW (or SW Asia) type and the thatched gable of the more humid areas. Not only the site and layout of the village, but the "geography of the house" often reflects age-old religious and magical traditions; the round huts of some lower castes in Telengana, with bold vertical stripes of white and rusty red, are clearly culturally rather than geographically influenced. At the other extreme from the rude massive huts of Bundelkhand we have the elaborate courtyard house of the richer U. P. farmer, with some pretensions to elegance — the survival of decayed traditions — in doorways and arcading. Some Indian domestic building indeed reaches a high standard of artistry: the carved timber of Kumaon or of the small towns of the Konkan, the restrained but excellent brick details and the very pleasant white bungalow-style houses, with low gables of semi-cylindrical tiles, found in small Maharashtra towns. Environmental influence is well seen in the flat-roofed blank-walled box standard in the Punjab and Wn U. P. — so strongly reminiscent of arid SW Asia, and fitting so well into the four-square planned villages of the Canal Colonies. Against these may be set the Bengal house, matting-walled, with thatched gables pitched high to shed the rain and ingeniously designed to take the strain of cyclonic gales. In Madras " We see flat-roofed stone houses in the Ceded District (Deccan), so constructed as to protect the dwellers from the severe heat of the sun, the rocks and slabs locally available being used. In contrast we find in Malabar timber entering into the construction. Here the buildings are on high ground and have sloping roofs, both necessitated by the high rainfall..... In the Tamilnadu we have brick houses with open courtyards, reflecting an equable climate and moderate rainfall."

As for what life in the Indian village is really like, who knows save the Indian villager? A few officials like M. L. Darling, whose Punjab rural rides compare with Cobbett's, a few devoted social workers, Indian and European, Christian and otherwise. But even then there is the difference between living in the village from cradle to grave (or burning-ghat), and living in the village with a territorial-and social and psychological — base outside. The alien may perhaps glean something from that rich harvest of salty rural proverbs (a comparative anthology of them would be fascinating) which are as vital a part of India's cultural heritage as the lyrical and metaphysical visions of her sages. Not that this latter strain of culture is absent from the village; the great epics Ramayana and Mahabharata pass from lip to lip in folk-versions, to some extent at least every man is his own poet, and not a few of the noblest figures in India's predominantly devotional literature sprang from the village rather than the schools: Kabir the weaver and Tukaram. The things that strike the outsider, then, are not perhaps ultimately the most important: the flies and the sores, the shrill clamour of gaunt pi-dogs, the primitive implements, the utter lack of sanitation.

At its worst the Indian village is infinitely depressing: in the plains where so much ground is cultivated that the scanty village site cannot grow with its growing population, or where a few miserable huts cling to shadeless stony rises in the drier parts of central India or the Archaean Deccan. Yet cheerfulness keeps breaking in, in the most unfavourable circumstances; fatalist as he is and must be, the peasant often displays an astonishing resilience and refuses to be broken by his often bitterly hard geographical and social environment. And over much of the land the villages have their amenities, even their beauties: in the plains and deltas they rise out of the sea of cultivation, emerald or gold or drab grey in the stubble season, like dark green islands, shaded in mango or orange trees, tamarinds, bamboos, palms. The tank or the well, the shade of the great banyan or the porch of the headman's hut, are essentially free clubs for the women and the men-folk respectively. Though the substratum of life — the gruelling round of the seasons — remains and will ever remain the same, though a miserable livelihood exacts an exorbitant price in endless toil, there have been great changes, material and psychological, since Edwin Montagu, Secretary of State for India, spoke in 1918 of the "pathetic contentment" of the Indian village. Pathetic it still too often is; contented, less and less; which is as it should be. "These idyllic village communities confined the human mind within the narrowest possible compass." This is overstated; there were the epics and the proverbs; but the horizons were far too narrow for a full life. Now new motifs are changing the tempo of life in the large villages: perhaps a radio, perhaps a mobile film unit, more and more frequently a school. The mass movements launched by Congress have not always been amenable to a thus-far-and-no-farther policy: the peasant has other enemies than British imperialism, and Congress taught him organisation. All are helping to break down the isolation and lack of information which rendered the villager so helpless a prey to the money-lender, the retailer, and the grain broker — often all three being one and the same person. Perhaps the most powerful agent of change is the battered, ramshackle motorbus, packed to the running-board and coughing its way through clouds of dust along the unmetalled roads to the nearest town. There may be loss as well as gain in all this; but it is idle to bewail the break-up of integrated codes of life — too often integrated by religious, social, and economic sanctions which were a complete denial of human dignity. In any case the disintegration set in long ago with the impact of world market; and it is high time that new horizons should be opened, that the villager should see whence the forces that have subverted his old life have their origins and what of good they may bring.

Infrastructure

A structure is something concrete and visual as also something abstract and conceptual. It is objective and subjective and the grades of objectivity and subjectivity differ from people to people depending on their social conditioning. A structure has a form or gestalt which may be sharply defined and simple or indistinct and vague. For a casual observer the habitation area called a village has a gross form in most cases. This form gets disturbed and becomes indistinct in certain ways and still something called "a village" remains with its objective boundaries and its subjective feelings for those who live in a village as also for those who are its neighbours. In some recent field work in certain areas of Maharashtra (the region where Marathi is spoken) I felt forcibly the gestalt aspect of the entity we call a village. The question presented itself to me in a negative way. As I viewed certain villages and walked through them I found myself asking why the area was called a village at all.

Various Types

It would be very difficult to experiment about the gestalt of a village but one can define certain types of villages. For a casual observer the habitation area called a village has a gross discernible form in some cases. This form tends to be obliterated in certain ways and yet a village remains a felt entity for one who lives in it. In Maharashtra there appear to be three types of villages which are differently constituted as regards their gestalt.

One type is the tightly nucleated village with the habitation clearly defined from the surrounding cultivated fields. These villages are situated on high plateau of the Deccan.

In such villages, while the habitation area is well marked, the boundaries of the village together with its fields are never perceived. The fields owned by one village merge into those owned by another except where a hillock or a stream or a highway forms the boundary.

The second type of village is found on the west-coast (the Konkan) near the coast. The villages are generally strung along length-wise on the two sides of a road. The houses stand in their own compounds with their fruit and cocoanut gardens and are fenced on all sides. One walks or drives through fences on both sides of the road all the time. There are numerous tiny streams joining the Arabian sea and there are also spurs of the western mountains (the Sahyadri) coming right into the ocean where the streams join the sea they widen considerably, are forbidable at low tide and have on both sides strips of the salt marshes called Khajana. These natural obstacles divide one village from the other. Where these are absent one village merges into the other and a casual traveller does not become aware of having crossed from one habitatic area into another. The gestalt has changed not merely as regards form but also as regards the inter-relation of the background and the gestalt.

In such villages the exploitation of land is of two types—horticulture and agriculture. The gardens of cocoanut and arecanut palms and plantain, jack fruits and cashewnuts are planted near the house and fenced in, while the rice fields may lie a little away from the houses though in some areas they come right to the steps of the houses. There is no sharp distinction between the habitation area and the cultivated area.

The third type of the village was found in the Satpura mountains on the north-western boundary of the Marathi-speaking region. The Satpura mountains are made up of seven main east-west folds with undulating high valleys in between.

The houses are situated in their own fields in clusters of two or three huts, all belonging to a single close kinship group. They are either the huts of a father and grown-up sons or brothers and their wives. Sometimes a woman and her husband may have a hut in the same cluster as that of the father and brothers of the woman.

The next cluster of huts may be as far as a furlong or two away depending on how big the holding of each cluster is. The village boundaries are many times not defined by streams or hillocks because the houses belonging to one village are situated on separate hillocks or divided by streamlets. Added to this scattering is the habit of the Bhils to change the location of habitation on the smallest pretext ranging from a mishap to just wish to be near a friend or even just wanting a change.

In this area the village loses its gestalt completely, on all four sides. The habitation area is not distinguished from the cultivated area and the widely scattered houses of such villages are many times nearer to the houses in the next village than to the houses of its own village.

The clusters of habitation illustrated above may belong to two or three villages and but for the stone heaps erected by the revenue department to mark the boundaries it would be difficult to separate one village from the other.

Roads in Use

The function of the roads is different in these three types. In the first type (the tightly nucleated villages) there are two types of roads.

(a) The roads connecting different villages meant for inter village communications ;

(b) Internal streets or narrow alleys connecting housing areas ; sometimes a main arterial road may pass through or near a village and owing to modern ribbon development may become the main street of the village but such cases are very few. One can generally distinguish between roads connecting, villages and streets connecting internal habitation areas.

In the case of the villages of the second type, the main road in the village is generally also the main arterial road joining the villages of the coast for miles and miles in one linear direction. Such roads are seen in most villages of the west-coast from Bombay to Cape Comorin. The road from Cape Comorin to Trivandrum in the extreme south-west of India is a typical example of such a road.

In the third type of village there are no village streets because no houses are aligned along streets. There are only footpaths leading from one house cluster to another and the continuation of these leads to houses in the next village.

As a consequence of these different ways of grouping houses in habitatic areas, the individual dwelling or a cluster of dwellings gain individuality—are seen as a gestalt—to the same degree that the village or the whole habitation area loses its individuality or distinctness. In the tightly packed Deccan villages one loses sight of the individual houses which are but vaguely felt as parts of a big conglomerate. In the linear coastal village a house being situated in its own compound and separated from the next house, has a greater individuality is however blurred to a certain extent as a single house in the Deccan villages. This individuality is however blurred to a certain extent as a single house is but one in a long row of similar houses. It is the row which impresses itself on the observer rather than the individual house. In the Bhil area the individual house or houses cluster is a gestalt whose individuality is not disturbed by the proximity of the other houses. On the other hand, the widely spaced houses or cluster are not experienced as a unity making one village separating itself from a similar unity called another village.

The first type of village is the one found all over the Maharashtra plateau as also in other parts of India like Uttar Pradesh, Gujarat, Andhra, Mysore and Orissa.

The second type of village is found as already stated all along the west coast. Whether the same type is found also on the eastern coast I do not know.

The third type of village is found in parts of the Satpura region as also along the coast slightly in the interior. There are villages of scattered homesteads in the coastal area where sometimes the only way of internal communication is walking over the narrow bunds of the tiny rice fields, a very tricky business for strangers especially when all the fields are full of water. Though this type is found in some hilly regions as also in some parts of the coast it cannot be called a jungle type or a primitive type either, as there are a number of jungle people who live in villages where the houses are clustered together in a nucleus but are not as tightly packed as in some of the Deccan villages. The Gonds and the Kolams in Maharashtra and Andhra and the Katkaris in Maharashtra, the Bette Kuruba, the Jenu Kuruba, the Erawa and the Sholega of Mysore also live in villages made up of many huts.

The Warli of the west coast and the Chenchus living in the Nallamalai hills live sometimes either in an individual family house apart from others or in a cluster of a few houses which cannot rightly be called a village.

Communication, a Boon

The nucleated Deccan villages show a clear distinction between communications within one village and communications with other villages. In modern Marathi there are words which are used exclusively for roads within a habitation area. There are also words as in Sanskrit which are used for both internal and external communication arteries but there is a whole series of words which denote various types of roads inside a habitation area. Ali, Galli, Bol are some of these words. Ali is a row of houses of one caste, or one profession; Brahmin Ali means a road both sides of which there are Brahmin houses, Tambat Ali means a road both sides of which have the workshops of the makers of brass and copper pots. Galli is a narrow street. " Galli Kuchchi " is an expression used for narrow roads full of mean houses. "Kuchchi " might have relation with word `Kancho' used for a certain type of communication in Gujarat.

We find that an explanation of the various words used for an internal system of communication involves reference to social structures like the family and the caste. It would appear that these words have primarily reference to a type of habitation area with the larger habitation area called a village and secondarily mean communication arteries with a village. They reflect a differentiated society, leading to a separate area for houses leading to sub-areas and hence to internal communication channels. The differentiation with an inhabited village may be based on lineage or caste and we will describe it presently.

Whatever the place name suffixes, the most common word for an habitation area in Marathi is 'Gaon' and in Telugu it is "Oor."

Mutual Relationship

In Maharashtra each 'Gaon' has habitation clusters a little away from the main habitation area. These clusters are called

'Wadi' and are said to belong to a 'Gaon.' In the same way in the Andhra Pradesh there are clusters of huts a little away from the main village which are called 'Palli' or 'Guda' which are said to belong to an 'Oor.' The interrelation of the Wadi and Gaon is manifold. The Wadi people sometimes call the Gaon to which they belong 'Kasaba' or 'Pethi' words which mean an area where various types of craftsmen (Kasabi) live or where there is shopping and market centre. The hereditary village servants and village craftsmen live in the Gaon. The village headman, the Patil, also must live in the Gaon, the revenue records and office are situated in a Gaon. A Wadi is generally a cluster of agnatically connected households. It may sometimes have just one big family with its farm servants and livestock. Sometimes people live in temporary huts in Wadis and have more permanent houses in the Gaon. Sometimes a Wadi is a settlement of a particular caste which by the nature of its occupation may need a larger space than is available in a Gaon. In the eastern parts of the Satara district many villages have Banagar Wadis a few furlongs away from the main village. The Banagars are shepherds who need large compounds near their houses for their mixed heards of sheep and goats. It also seems probable that this is an immigrant element which has made a separate settlement near a village with the consent of the villagers. In the same way there are Ramoshiwadis, i.e., hamlets where only the Ramoshi live.

They were counted among criminal tribes. Wadis are called generally after clan name or after a tribe or a caste. Vagh Wadi, Shinde Wadi, Kamat Wadi are names of the first type. Banagar Wadi, Ramoshi Wadi, Brahman Wadi are of the second type.

The Wadi originally is a cluster of hutments belonging to one family or belonging to two or three families whose fields lie in the immediate neighbourhood. Sometimes these are temporarily inhabited during the sowing and the harvesting season for facility of work in the field and the necessity to guard the crop.

Sometimes when the population is growing and there is available land for new settlement and the habits of the people are semi-nomadic, an originally compact village splits into different habitation areas. Recently, I came across such a village in the jungle tract of the Shrikakulam district of the Andhra Pradesh.

The village is called Devanpuram. The original village was a settlement of two tribes, the Jatapu and the Savara. The Savara went a few furlongs away and had their own settlement. The Savara settlement split and one part has gone about a mile away over the hills and has a settlement there. Devanpuram is thus an Oor with three Pallis-(1) A Jatapu palli, (2) a small Savara palli called China Savara palli and (3) a bigger Savara palli called Pedda Savara palli. This split has occurred since the last survey. If they remain in their present situations, the three parts may be acknowledged as three separate villages with the same name but separate headmen; for example, the villages called 'Gondi.' The two villages are within a mile of each other. The one near the road is as usual Jatapu-Gondi and the one nearer the hills and a little more inaccessible is the Savara Gondi. Generally, the most important and the most independent of these Wadis or Wada is that of the fisher folk and in a recent study we found that in one village the Koli or Bhoi are successfully defying the authority of the main village.

Nucleus under Change

A village is thus an ever-changing nucleus of habitations from which tiny clusters separate and remain attached or separate completely to form a new nucleus. The quality of being a 'gestalt' objectively and subjectively is thus a dynamic quality which makes it difficult to give a definition of a village which would apply to all villages. This difficulty will be more apparent when we look closer into the internal structure of a village.

Among many semi-nomadic primitive agriculturists a village may endure for as few as three years. When the soil round about is exhausted the whole village moves off to somewhere else. Villages which were registered as existing at a particular place during the last elections are no longer there.

In the plains the villages are generally permanent and of long standing and hundreds of epigraphic records have shown that villages with the same boundaries have existed for over a thousand years.

In Maharashtra, there is a great variation as regards villages and the families they contain. For a particular caste there may be only one family (with one clan-name), for other castes there may be several families so that for one caste there is village exogamy while for the other castes there may be marriage within a village.

In the South, multi-clan village is the rule. In the North, where there are no clans, villages are supposed to be peopled by descendants of one ancestor for each caste and there is strict exogamy. This exogamy applies even when people of separate ancestries and Gotras come and live in the village.

Habitation on Caste Basis

Generally, a village in India is, however, socially a far more complicated structure and the complexity is reflected in the way houses are built and roads existed. A village generally has more than one caste. In the North and sometimes even in Maharashtra there may be only one lineage of a caste, but generally in the North and almost as a rule in the Dravidian South, each caste in a village is made up of more than one lineage and clan. A map of a village will show almost invariably that the habitation area of each caste is separated from that of the other by a greater or a lesser distance. A few castes may live in houses situated side by side but others live apart. The castes which are always separated from the others are those whose touch was supposed to pollute the rest—the so-called untouchables. Their habitation area has generally a distinct name. In Maharashtra there is a Maharwada in almost every village. Mang is another untouchable caste which has its dwelling cluster separate from the rest of the village and also from the Mahars. The same is the case in Andhra Pradesh where the Mala live apart from the rest of the village. The Madiga live near the Mala but have a separate cluster of houses. The Maharwada or the Mala and Madiga Wadi are generally at the end of a village, hence the Sanskrit name Ante-Vasi (living at the end) and the Marathi name Vesakar (living near or outside the wall of a village. The Kumbhars (potters) also live a little away from the rest of the village and their part of the village is called Kumbhar Wada. Villages which have weavers in their population also have a separate area where weavers live. If there are a number of Brahmin houses they, have an area for themselves. The shepherds live so far away that their habitation area is termed a Wadi of the village.'

This tendency to have separate sub-areas for habitation within a larger unit called a village can be explained in various ways and on different grounds like caste-hierarchy, ideas of impurity and pollution, the need for certain occupations to have room for carrying out the different processes needed for their craft. The first reason applies to the house complexes generally, the second applies to the distance found between the untouchable quarters and the rest, the third applies to castes like potters, brick-makers, weavers and dyers, shepherds, wool carders and blanket makers, etc. To me it appears that there is an inherent tendency in the Indian culture to form separate groups and remain separate. The arguments listed above all strengthen this tendency and the phenomenon called 'caste,' apart from its hierarchical structure, is the direct outcome of this tendency. The primary group is the large family, sometimes unilateral sometimes bilateral. This group extends into the caste. The family as well as the caste are based on territory. The smallest territorial unit is the area in which the house and the family land are situated, the largest territorial unit in that part of linguistic area through which a caste has spread. Rarely is any area, small or big, in sole possession and occupation of a single family or a single caste so that we find in each such area a check-pattern of sub-areas belonging to families, clans, and castes. I have not seen anywhere either castes or tribes living inter-mingled. However tightly nucleated and crowded a village, the check-pattern sub-areas were always there.

This tendency is seen even among the primitives. The Bhils are divided into endogamous sub-divisions. They have villages of mixed population where sometimes allied tribes like Dhanak and untouchables live. Each of these has a separate habitation area and within each area there are house-clusters belonging to different lineages.

This is but a preliminary study of habitation areas and their structure. The way people build their houses, the way they group them, the way arteries of internal and external communication are formed would lend itself to ecological and anthropological analysis and may help to establish environmental-geographical as well as cultural zones and by linking with social institutions like the family and the caste will help to understand the meaning of the social institutions. It will perhaps reveal the fact that the unity or uniformity of Indian culture is based on tiny check-patterns fitted one into the other rather than a unicolour homogeneity.

Four

Rural Sphere

There are numerous individuals and groups who desire and strive for improvement of the material and cultural life of the rural people.

They can be broadly divided into the following three categories (i) The Philanthropic group; (ii) The Reformist group; and (iii) The Revolutionary group.

Philanthropic Category

The Philanthropic group does not view the problem of the material and cultural poverty of the rural people in the context of the institutions and the basic structure of the rural society. It holds the conviction that it is possible to ameliorate the position of the rural people through direct humanitarian effort, without changing those institutions and structure. It evolves economic, educational and other programmes of village uplift which embody such items as creation of charity funds to help the village needy, moral appeals to landlords and such other groups to relax their pressure on peasants, establishment of hospitals and schools, and others.

The basic feature of the standpoint and the programmatic approach of this group to the problem lies in the fact that it attempts to improve the conditions of the rural population within the matrix of the existing institutions and structure of the rural society, by means of purely humanitarian endeavour.

Reformist Category

The Reformist group subscribes to the view that it is the malfunctioning of the existing rural social system and its institutions (and not the social system and its institutions in their basic essence), which is the social-genetic cause of the economic misery and social and cultural backwardness of the rural people. They therefore, work for a healthy functioning of the social system and its institutions, or, at most, for reforming them. They assert that once this institutional reform is accomplished, it will result in the all-sided betterment of the life of the rural population.

The distinguishing characteristic of the standpoint and the programmatic approach of this group to the problem lies in the fact that for elevating the conditions of the rural people at present it does not regard it necessary to replace the existing social system and its institutions by new ones but strives only to reform them.

Revolutionary Category

Finally, there is a third group whose standpoint and programmatic approach to the problem are based on a revolutionary conception. They think that the abysmal poverty, crass ignorance, and cultural backwardness of the mass of the rural people are fundamentally due to the existing social system and the institutions which are its organs to sustain that system. The social system and its institutions, they feel, cannot but breed these evils. They declare, therefore, that both the programme of individual aid and relief and that of institutional reform will be unable to achieve the desired end. They contend that no reform can appreciably liberate the rural people from want, disease, illiteracy, and lack of culture. They argue that new wine cannot be filled into the old bottles.

Thus, according to this group, the evils of the rural society are not the result of any malfunctioning of the rural social system or its institutions but are inherent in this system and institutions themselves, are the inevitable product of the natural functioning of the present social order. This group, therefore, evolves and attempts to carry out a programme of a revolutionary transformation of the rural social structure from its economic base upward.

While laying decisive emphasis on its social revolutionary objective, this group includes in its programme a number of items of the first two programmes. It however, links its struggle to implement those items with the struggle for the change of the entire social system.

These three groups with their diverse and even conflicting programmes are at present struggling for hegemony in the agrarian area.

Programmes for Rehabilitation

Various individual groups, associations and parties, each according to its own light, are thus engaged in the movement of rural uplift and reconstruction. Among them are individual philanthropists and philanthropic bodies; social, political, religious, economic and educational organizations including welfare associations; missionary groups; Governmental institutions and others.

We will make a few observations regarding the work of these groups and organizations.

Exclusive Concentration on One Aspect of the Rural Life

Some of them exclusively concentrate on one single aspect of the rural life like education, economic welfare, sanitation, crusade against reactionary social customs and practices, religious superstition, ethical uplift or fight against disease. They isolate one aspect of the rural life from its other aspects. The, organic unity of the rural life and the interrelations and interdependence of its many aspects are thus lost sight of.

This results either in the abortion or limited success of their programme even when dealing with one single aspect of the rural life.

Predominantly Emotional Approach

Most of these groups and organizations, while inspired by ethical and humanitarian motives, lack scientific training for the work they undertake. They forget that an objective study of the rural society and its conditions is vital for evolving a correct programme and methodology of work and that merely good intentions are no guarantee of successful social work. They forget that a patient gathering of factual data pertaining to the life of the rural people and a detailed concrete study of their specific prerequisites for formulating a correct programme of rural work. A study of the psychological traits, ethnic and communal composition, customs and beliefs of the rural aggregate, is also indispensable for the purpose. Further, these groups and organizations require to have a concrete knowledge of the economic structure of the rural society, the specific system of land tenure prevailing in it, the various socio-economic groups bound up with its economy and with different and even conflicting interests, the religious and other ideologies which have a hold over their mind, the particular types of family and other social institutions existing there and many other things. Such knowledge is necessary because the task before them is not the renovation of a vague and vast rural society, in general, but of a specific type of rural society; not the amelioration of the abstract rural people but of a particular rural people with local limits, defined past and crystallized present conditions. It is, therefore, essential to study the particular rural society and its people in concrete details. Then alone, it is possible to evolve an appropriate programme of rural work for the recuperation of a particular rural society and the advance of the specific rural aggregate living in that society. Then alone, also, it is possible to locate the specific social, economic, psychological, ideological and other obstacles in the way of the fulfilment of that programme. A rural aggregate in Gujarat is different from that in Saurashtra, Bihar or Maharashtra.

Many individuals and organizations oriented to the work of rural reconstruction and uplift lack this understanding. They evolve naive programmes of rural work which, not being based on concrete detailed knowledge of the specific rural society and its people, fail or meet with partial success. This breeds the sentiment of defeatism among them and results sometimes in their abandoning of the rural work altogether.

Lack of Co-ordination of work

Lack of co-ordination of activities in various spheres marks the work of some organizations and groups. Further, their activities are often based on conflicting value systems.

This, too, is detrimental to the success of the programme. It is obvious that all activities should be co-ordinated and should constitute a single organic stream of total work. Also it is evident that a single principle must determine and permeate the diverse activities in diverse fields. Otherwise there will ensue mutual negating of activities.

Insufficient Ability to Assess the Results

Some groups and organizations exhibit insufficient ability for a proper assessment of the results of their efforts in various domains of rural work. Since they have, therefore, no adequate conception of the cumulative result of their activities, they get a hazy notion regarding their advance towards their objective. Inability to properly evaluate their work in terms of productivity also denies them that power of self-criticism which is also vital for a correct planning of next stages of work.

When work is not properly planned and correctly assessed, there is also the danger of deviating from the correct road to the goal.

Sporadic and unplanned forms of rural welfare work are also sometimes launched. In a number of instances, they degenerate into mere fads. This reveals unconscious lack of earnestness or absence of scientific understanding of the problem on the part of their sponsors. We find a mushroom growth of such efforts embarked upon by individuals and even institutions in the rural area. This tends to make the picture of the rural reconstruction work chaotic to some extent, and often leads the rural people to become victims rather than beneficiaries of such endeavours since they yield unstable and distorted results.

Absence of Proper Sociological Perspective

The principal weakness characterizing these organizations however, generally lies in their lack of proper sociological understanding of the problem of rural reconstruction. To evolve a successful programme of rural reconstruction at a higher level, it is quite necessary to know the law governing the development of the rural society. The structure, the functioning and the objective tendencies of development of the existing rural society, the interconnectedness and the interdependence of various elements of that society (technical, economic, social, political, ideological), and the relative significance of those elements in determining the life of the rural society and their respective role in the total social change, require to be comprehended.

To change society consciously, we must have a science of society. Rural sociology is the science of rural society. The laws of the structure and development of rural society in general can aid us in discovering the special laws governing a particular rural society. Without the science of rural society, it is not, therefore, possible to get an authentic picture of a particular rural society. Rural sociology alone can provide a correct, organic, synthetic and multi-sided knowledge of a specific rural society and the tendency of its further evolution.

Essential Element

Rural sociology will help the rural worker to make a correct diagnosis of its ills and will, further, enable him to evolve a correct prescription or programme to overcome those ills. If the diagnosis of the ills is erroneous or imperfect, the prescription itself will be unscientific and therefore futile. The uniformed rural worker will adopt unhistorical and inappropriate means to cure the defects and deficiencies of the rural social organisms. The social ills may have a deep-seated cause in the very social system itself and may be merely symptoms proclaiming the general disease of the social organism. Not knowing this, the rural worker will engage himself in a symptomatic treatment of the social ills which, as all physicians know, gives no relief or gives only a partial and temporary relief.

There is another grave danger for a rural worker who is ignorant of rural sociology. The present social evils are the features of the present society and therefore cannot be overcome by methods adopted to cure the social evils of bygone societies. For instance, solutions of the evils of self-sufficient society would not be adequate for the solution of the maladies of the present competitive commodity society. If the rural worker is unaware of this fact, he will attempt to graft the former on the present society. He will recommend the resuscitation of the techniques, political systems or ethical concepts of the past societies to overcome the crisis of the present one. Such a view is unscientific. The evils of the present rural society arise out of its own inner structure and can be cured by means determined by its own trend of development.

The programme of rural reconstruction should be derived from a strict sociological analysis of the actual conditions and tendencies of the actually existing rural society and evaluation of the actual forces at work within it.

Here comes the decisive creative role of rural sociology which is as indispensable for the purpose of rural reconstruction as the science of medicine is to a medical practitioner.

Five

Society under Change

Like all other phenomena the rural society too has been changing since its emergence. Its technology, economy and social institutions, its ideology, art and religion, have undergone a ceaseless change. This change has sometimes been imperceptibly slow, sometimes strikingly rapid, and at some moments even qualitative in character resulting into the transformation of one type of rural society into another type.

To discern change in a system, to recognize its direction, to understand the objective and subjective forces which bring it about and, further, to consciously accelerate the process of change by helping the progressive trends within the changing system— this constitutes a scientific approach to and active creative intervention in the life of a system.

Forces at Work

We will now refer to the forces and factors, conscious or unconscious, which bring about change in rural society.

Close investigators of rural society have enumerated a number of these forces and factors, the following being the principal among them.

Common Reasons

Natural forces such as floods, earthquakes, famines and others affect the territorial zone in which the rural people live. They have a disastrous effect on the flora and the fauna of the zone which often considerably influences the economic life of the people, and, in the case of earthquakes of dangerous intensity, even sometimes results in large-scale loss of human life and material devastation. The rural collectivity lives in the midst of a specific geographical and geological milieu and manipulates them through agriculture, mining and other operations. Hence a profound change in earth structures modifies or sometimes even convulses its life processes.

These are the natural forces which bring about change in rural society.

There are human factors, too, which operate to alter that society.

Technology as a Tool

As observed earlier, man carries on his struggle against the environment by means of tools. He has, therefore, been ceaselessly engaged in improving the old tools and inventing new ones. Though the inventors create new tools consciously, they are unable to prognosticate the social consequences of their inventions which are sometimes far-reaching. The invention of new tools, new means of transport and communications, and the discovery of new materials such as iron, new chemical substances and others, result in the change in the life of the rural people, in their economy and even in the structures of their social and political relations. The far-reaching economic, social and political outcomes of outstanding inventions like the plough, the steam engine and others, were not and could not be predicted by their inventors.

As Prof. Ogburn observes, the invention of radio led to about 150 major changes in social life.

The invention of steam-driven machinery in England resulted in the evolution of modern industries, which, at a certain stage of their development, needed foreign market. This led to the political and the economic expansion of Britain and the rise and growth of the British Empire. Once the power-driven technique was invented, it was adopted by other nations also. Western nations, in steady succession, developed modern industries and, due to the need of foreign market for their industrial products, conquered other countries and built up empires. This changed the economic and political life of those nations as well as of those who were subjected to them. The societies of the countries of both the dominant as well as the subject nations were either completely transformed or appreciably modified.

What is true of the national societies is also true of the rural society since it is an integral part of the national society.

Various Conscious Methods

Next we will survey the methods and devices adopted by social groups and organizations to consciously bring about the alteration or transformation of the rural world.

Eminent sociologists like Sims and others have collected and mentioned various techniques and methods used by these groups and organizations. The following are the chief among them

***Persuasive Method*:** The protagonists of this method seek to convince the rural population of the necessity of effecting changes in the rural society in various spheres, technical, economic, social and others, through organized propaganda campaign. They endeavour to popularise among them various rural reforms or rural reconstruction programmes and exhort them to implement these programmes.

The distinguishing characteristic of this method lies in the fact that its proponents restrict their effort only to the propaganda of their programmes. They do not themselves initiate or participate in implementing the programmes. They leave this to the rural people themselves.

This is because the exponents of this method have almost limitless faith in the force of argument. They hold the view that it is possible by means of a suitable argument to convince the rural people of the need for change in the rural social structure, to kindle in them the urge for such a change, to popularise among them an appropriate programme of rural reform or reconstruction and, through this, to rouse them to practical activity for the accomplishment, of that programme.

***Demonstrative Method*:** This method is also known as the method of propaganda through example or by deed. The exponents of this method endeavour to popularise their programme of rural reconstruction or specific reform by themselves implementing it on a miniature scale. They declare that the rural population would be more easily convinced of the advantages of a programme of rural change if the advantages of such a programme are demonstrated in action. They consider this method more effective than that of mere oral and written propaganda.

For instance, they organize demonstration farms to convince the farmers of the superiority of a new technique and new and better methods of agricultural production. They start model agricultural colonies based on the co-operative principle to rouse the farmers to the recognition of the economic advantages of co-operative farming so that they themselves, on their own initiative, may combine or integrate their individual uneconomic or semi-economic holdings and embark on the road to co-operative or collective agriculture. They establish a few educational and health centres so that the rural population may recognize the benefits of education and hygiene and, thereafter, themselves start schools and health centres in the entire rural area.

"Compulsory" Method: The state itself often intervenes and, through legislation, brings about changes in the rural life or the rural social structure. It is not the will and the initiative of the rural people but of the state that determine and accomplish those changes. During the War, "To rural America, along with the rest, coercive measures were applied. Among other things, production was made compulsory, prices were fixed, the disposal of food stuffs prescribed and time of labour regulated by law."

In India, a number of states have recently enacted anti-zamindari laws to alter land relations in the rural areas.

Such "compulsory" intervention of the state in the life of the rural people has been increasing in modern times.

Method of Social Pressure: This method is adopted by a rural individual, a group or a class to achieve a desired change in the life of the rural people or in the rural social or economic structure. The means resorted to vary widely. They may include petitioning, passive resistance, individual and group satyagraha, processions and marches, strikes and demonstrations, even individual terrorism (for instance killing of moneylenders or landlords by farmers or tenants), mass revolts, revolutions and others.

These forms of pressure and struggle have been growing more and more prevalent in modern times.

The rural sociologist has to carefully analyse and study these forms of struggle since they have been playing a significant role in transforming rural societies of various countries in the contemporary epoch.

Contact Method: "It is generally recognized that one of the most effective means of social change is found in contact of cultures where peoples of different cultures come in touch with one another, cross-fertilization takes place."

In the medieval age, the town and the village lived almost independent social, economic and cultural existence. This separatism was increasingly undermined as a result of the extension and wider and wider ramification of modern means of transport and communication all over the country and resultant closer and closer contact of urban and rural populations. Further, the village economy was transformed and became an integral part of the national and even international economy. This created and multiplied the points of contact between the rural and urban societies and their populations. This increasingly led to the changes in the socio-economic structure of the rural society and the life of the rural people.

The historical tendency is towards a growing urbanization of the rural society due to the stronger impact of the urban forces on the latter.

Educational Method: The increasing spread of modern education among the rural people through the establishment of schools and other educational institutions has been one of the very effective means to bring about changes in the rural life and the rural social structure. The village people, when they are initiated in scientific knowledge of life and the world, would find it easy to break with superstition which affects their consciousness and keeps them conservative.

A group of social thinkers invest the educational method with decisive importance in bringing about the rural change.

We have referred above to some of the principal methods observed by some of the eminent rural sociologists, which have been operating to bring about the rural change.

These methods should be carefully studied by those who desire to evolve a programme of rural reform or reconstruction. They should assess the value of these methods and assign them a proportional significance while elaborating such a programme.

Trends in Social System

The main changes are noticed in the caste, the joint family system and village administration through Panchayats which together formed the base of the old social edifice. The rise of internal markets, assisted by the extension of railways and roads, and the expansion in foreign trade of agricultural commodities transformed the old self-sufficient economy of the village based on barter into a market economy, based on cash. With the gradual urbanisation of the village, the rigidity of the division of labour among the community softened. The old caste barriers to economic mobility have been slowly giving way. The expansion of towns, the diversification of employment opportunities in trade and services and the glamour and attractions of city life have created a steady drift towards the city. This has been responsible for loosening the hold of the joint family system on the members. There has also been continuous drain on the intelligentsia among the rural population. The two World Wars drew from the village population into military service hundreds of thousands who imbibed a new outlook on life. After their return from the distant theatres of war they have added a new ferment to the social urges of the rural community, already seething with discontent under the pressure of poverty. The advent of freedom with a new promise and hope, the acceleration of economic and social reform measures, resulting in the abolition of large landed estates and the protection of the rights of the tenants and labourers, the political enfranchisement of the vast population under adult suffrage, have all widened the horizon of economic standards in the village and have further complicated the problems of adjustment and of devising a new social order for the villages.

Age-old Customs

The significant among the factors of change in the social order have been the rise in the age of marriage, the improved status of women, the lesser vogue of caste despotism and of purdah, the removal of the disabilities of sections of population under caste hierarchy and in general, the realignment of family relations. But it must however be said that while glimpses of change in outlook are noticed among the educated in the village community, in respect of social disabilities, the old order is kept intact in the observances of the privileges. Untouchability, access to places of public convenience as wells, etc., and public worship were the three crucial barriers and all the three have given way under legislative compulsion and educative propaganda. The inner change of heart, which is the result of enlightened education, is yet far from achievement. In one respect no change is visible. The tanner and sweeper still live on the outermost fringe of the village, often on opposite sides, though the Brahmin is losing his halo and the untouchable, the stigma. The two tests of free association in a modern society are food and marriage. In the village, they are still as strong a barrier as they were and education has done nothing to weaken them. The cow is more the object of veneration, than a problem in economic improvement.

Living Style

In objective terms a standard of living consists of three main elements: (1) the level of consumption or the composition of goods and services of a specific quantity and quality consumed by an individual, family or group within a given period; (2) social services and free services, particularly those which relate to health, education and recreation, and (3) working conditions which affect not only the worker's health and earning capacity but also the size and regularity of his income. As a dynamic concept, it implies in the first place the eradication of poverty, among the rural community and in the second, improving the content of living of all categories of workers with regard to consumption, social and free services and conditions of work.

Examined on the basis of the above terms, it would be difficult to answer the question whether there has been an improvement in the standard of living of the rural community. While the view is often held that the rise in prices during the war period ushered in a period of prosperity, evidence is lacking as to the category of the population which was actually benefited and the extent of increase in prosperity. While a relative improvement in the standard of living of the strata of economic land-holders may be accepted, the available data indicate that there has been a deterioration in the other sections of the agricultural population who form the majority.

Sophisticated Style

Aesthetic culture is an integral part of the total culture of a society. It expresses, in art terms; the ideals, the aspirations, the dreams, the values, and the attitudes of its people, just as its intellectual culture reveals its knowledge of the natural and social worlds which surround them.

A systematic study of the aesthetic culture of the Indian rural society, in its historical movement of the dissolution of old types and the emergence of new ones, is vital for the study of the changing pattern of the cultural life of the rural people. Further, since art reflects social life and its changes, such a study will help the rural sociologist to comprehend the movement of the rural society itself as it progressed from its past shape to its present one. It will also reveal the changes in the psychological structures of the rural people and its sub-groups.

Eminent sociologists have enumerated the following principal arts comprising the aesthetic culture of rural society:

(1) Graphic Arts such as Drawing, Painting, Engraving and others which have two dimensional forms.

(2) Plastic Arts which "involve the manipulations of materials to yield three dimensional forms — that is to say — carving and modelling in high and low relief and in the round."

(3) Folklore comprised of "myths, tales, proverbs, riddles, verse together with music."

(4) Dance and drama which combine the three forms mentioned above and therefore are "synthetic" arts.

Main Characteristics

Outstanding rural sociologists like Herskovief, Sorokin, Zimmerman, Galpin, and others have also located a number of specific characteristics of the aesthetic culture of the rural people living in society based on subsistence economy. The following are the important among them:

Art was fused with life. As Sorokin remarks, "The arts were not sharply differentiated from religion, magic, intellectual pursuits, and other activities. Aesthetic elements penetrated to practically all daily occupations including agricultural work and they were an inseparable part of religious and other cultural activities."

The people as a whole took part in artistic activities. This is in contrast to the situation in the present society where the people are divided into artists who perform art and the audience which enjoys it. This antithesis was not known to earlier society.

A social group, a family, or the village people as a whole, did not break itself into actors and spectators when they engaged themselves in artistic activity. Men, women, and children of the group, all participated in it; "they were both the actors and the audience." There were very few professional artists in that society. In the social division of labour artistic work was not still separated from the total social work so as to create a special body of social workers like artists.

Art was predominantly familistic. The pre-modern society, the life of the rural aggregate had familistic character. Consequently, the rural art, which was fused with the life of the rural people, also bore the impress of familism. "The significance, the manifestations, the content and the symbolism of rural aesthetic activities were permeated with familism. Births, marriages, deaths and sickness of members of the family were the main subjects of rural art."

The technique of art was simple. This was due to comparatively low level of general technique of the period, on which the technique of art depends. The instruments of rural art were the products of the village artisan industry. Often the family itself made some of these in the home. This is in contrast to the instruments of modern art which are the products of modern industries and are therefore complex, highly specialised, varied and multifold. A simple drum (Dhol Nagara, Dholak, Duff, Khanjri, Nobati); a flute made out of simple reeds or handy wood;

a few stringed instruments not complicated in structure (Ektar, Ravanhatha); some metal instruments of simple design like gongs, bells, Mantras, some wooden instruments like Kartal; ordinary metal vessels of domestic use like Thali, Gagar, Lota or drinking pot, tongs; such natural objects as branches of trees, feathers of birds, shells, conches; these constituted the technical prerequisites of art in the pre-modern Indian rural society. Further, art performances were organized not in theatres and concert halls as in modern times but either in domestic premises or in open village spaces. The village drama was enacted not on any imposing stage equipped with colourful curtains, spotlights, and rich scenery in the background. Much of the realism was achieved not by suggestive or symbolic artifice but was created by histrionics.

Art had agrarian life processes as its main content. Since art was fused with life, it depicted the life of the rural people in its various aspects, economic, social and religious. For instance, "The most common of the work songs of non-urbanized agricultural peoples were those that accompanied collective agricultural occupations, hunting and fishing, grain grinding and milling, flax-thrashing, corn-thrashing, ploughing and seeding, fruit-picking and so forth...... Some of their religious and magical songs were concerned with love, death, mourning, health and fertility, others dealt with agricultural activities and were sung as a part of the religious and magical rites connected with spring, summer fall and winter festivities, still others honoured the grove, wood, field and corn deities ...... Both work songs and religious songs were inseparably connected with daily life and with the religion and magic that centred in agriculture." Even a cursory survey of the songs of the Indian rural people corroborates the above view. Agricultural work processes like sowing, reaping, and harvesting; or other work processes like the fetching of water from the well by women; or sentiments of gratitude to gods for successful agricultural operations or plaintive appeal to them for their fruition, form the main thematic content of those songs. Dance, another form of art, had also, for its predominant content the real agrarian life processes. Similarly, the folklore composed of legends, myths and stories, mostly dealt with the same theme either in a direct or symbolic form. Ornamental and decorative rural arts also bore the impress of the rural environmental and social milieu. The specific flora and fauna found in the rural area provided material for design. Rural artistic creations in these and other spheres "are based on rural environment and occupation; trees, flowers and plants, horses, cattle and other animals, birds and, fish and peasant houses." Further, geometrical designs characterizing those arts had a magical meaning bearing on various agrarian life processes. The rural sociologists have also observed that "Agricultural characteristics are most clearly manifest in songs, music, dances, stories, proverbs, riddles, literature, pantomimes, festivals, dramatic performances, and similar forms of the arts; they are less conspicuous in designs, ornamentations, architecture and sculpture, but even here if properly interpreted, the agricultural stamp is noticeable."

Art creations were predominantly collective creations, collective inspirit. This is one of the most striking features of the rural art. While in the urban area, songs, stories, dramas, and such other art pieces, have been the products of individual artists, practically the entire folklore of the rural people, comprising rural songs and tales as well as rural dramas, has been the collective creation of generations of rural artists. Their authorship cannot be traced to individual artists since no individual artists created them. They remain, therefore, almost always anonymous in origin. As a result of this, the rural art has been overwhelmingly collective in spirit. It has expressed the fears, joys, aspirations, and dreams of the collectivity even more than most of the social art of the urban society. Further, it has been marked with profound natural-dreams of the collectivity even more than most of social art of the urban society. Further, it has been marked with profound naturalness, sincerity, and spontaneity. This is in contrast to the urban art which is either commercialized and, therefore, caters largely to the emotions of its potential buyers or is super-individualistic (ivory tower art) and embodies the individualistic caprices and momentary emotions of the artist. Further, rural art has expressed the sentiments and life experiences of countless generations. It has been, therefore, also more organic and durable than most of the urban art.

Rural art was non-commercial. In agrarian societies based on self-sufficient economies, products have not the character of commodities. Thinkers and artists create their intellectual and artistic products not for the market but for the direct consumption of the village rural aggregate that looks after their needs. Rural art, hence, is not commercialized. Since the rural artist is not motivated by the urge to make profit through his art creations, his artistic activity is urged on only by the artistic aim. The urban artist, in contrast to this, is torn between two urges; one, the urge for artistic self-expression and the other, the need to make livelihood in a competitive economic environs by producing for the market and hence by adapting his art to the tastes of those who can buy it. This dualism disrupts his artistic personality and tends to distort his art. The rural artist does not suffer from these contradictory motives and his art is, therefore "harmonious." Here we must strictly guard ourselves against the danger of idealizing rural art and the self-sufficient society which generates that art. In such a society, the individual is not still differentiated from the collectivity, be it the joint family, the caste, or the village community. The individual is subordinated to these groups. The structure and environment of such a society do not, therefore, provide freedom for the development of the creative individuality of its members or scope for them to strike out new unconventional paths of thought and craftsmanship. This puts a limitation on the rural art though its collective spirit should be properly noted and valued. The competitive socio-economic environs of the modern society, on the other hand, while differentiating and liberating the individual from the pressure of the collectivity on his free development, tends to weaken his social urges. Most of the urban art is, therefore, individualistic. It mostly portrays the struggles of the individual against the stifling forces of the unplanned competitive society. Excepting for a growing minority art current which mirrors the dream of, and struggle for a higher co-operative society, the existing urban art is, largely, socially sterile, morbid or escapist.

Artistic craftsmanship and culture were transmitted from generation to generation orally. This was due to the fact that there existed no printing press which would produce literature on art. Further, there did not exist any schools or academies of art in self-sufficient societies. Hence, they were mainly the family elders who trained the youngsters in the knowledge and execution of arts like folk songs, folk dances and others.

We have referred elsewhere to the process of the transformation of the old rural society into the new modern society.

Social Shift

We will briefly summarize the most striking features of this transformation in the sphere of rural aesthetic culture. Art gradually became a specialized activity of the artist. The village population increasingly became differentiated into artists and the rest. Individual artist or a group of artists sang and danced on festive occasions, the rest of the village people constituting the audience. The technique of art also slowly altered, became more complex, thanks to the ability of modern industry to produce complex art instruments. Above all, since commodity production extended to the village also, art itself became a commodity and the artist, a seller of the artistic goods. Pecuniary gain became the main motif of artistic creation.

Art, moreover, became gradually separated from life. Its thematic content changed. It began to draw its themes and imagery from new sources such as the travails of the individual struggling against the pressures of a competitive socio-economic environment. Formerly, it dealt with the vicissitudes of the life of the village collectivity; now it concerned itself with the fate of the individual. Thus art increasingly ceased to be a collective activity of the village group as a whole dealing with its collective life processes and became the individual activity of the artist dealing with the problems of the individual struggling in a competitive world. Further, the traditional practice of handing down art from generation to generation also began to decline since the printing press made it possible to perpetuate art techniques and art creations like folk songs and village tales in the printed form.

The modern cinema with its film songs and film stories, the gramophone with its song records, together with the radio, slowly began to penetrate the rural zone and became new means of aesthetic delight for the rural population.

These developments led to the increasing urbanization of the rural aesthetic culture. Thus under the impact of the technical and economic forces of modern society, not only did the socio-economic structure of the rural society undergo a single transformation but its aesthetic culture with its specific characteristics also suffered an increasing change.

The Indian rural society, for the last one hundred and fifty years, has been experiencing a historical change. The change has not, however, advanced to the same extent as in some other countries since a foreign power which ruled India during this period retarded the process of rapid industrialization and resultant modernization of our country. In West European countries and the U. S. A. the urbanization of the old rural society and its aesthetic culture have advanced to a far greater degree than in India. It must, however, be noted that even in those advanced countries the aesthetic culture of the rural society possesses a number of specific characteristics which distinguish it from the aesthetic culture of the urban society.

It is essential for the Indian rural sociologist to study the aesthetic culture of the contemporary rural Indian people and the transformation it is undergoing. Such a study will enable him to comprehend the transformation of the life of the rural people and their struggles, dreams and aspirations. Art reveals life through more subtle nuances and often provides a more authentic picture of life than what even history books can give. The French society of Balzac's period is more vividly and truthfully laid bare when viewed through the prism of his great realistic novels than as revealed by the French historians in their works.

"To a superlative degree the arts express the qualities which an age prizes, the human actions which it cherishes, and the ideals which it ennobles..... In the aesthetic attitude, a culture can be captured and held, not as a set of bare facts to be statistically tabulated, but as a function of the travail of human minds."

The aesthetic culture of the rural people should be next studied from the standpoint of (1) its content and (2) its form.

Aesthetic Culture

The rural aesthetic culture, a rich complex of myths, legends, folk songs, folk tales, riddles and proverbs, dances, dramas and pantomimes, and graphic and plastic arts, transmitted from generation to generation, embodies directly or symbolically the world outlook, social conceptions and ethical norms of the rural people as they emerged and changed across ages. It can serve as a very valuable source material for a rural sociologist of imagination and insight to build up a concrete vivid picture of the technical, economic, social, religious, moral and cultural life of the rural aggregate in various periods. Since the rural aesthetic culture was always anchored in the life of the rural people, was fused with it and, further, artistically mirrored it, it would reveal what technique they employed in material production in a particular period, what weapons they used in warfare, what ornaments and costumes they wore, what houses they built and lived in, what socio-economic system prevailed during that period, what social classes comprised it, what social conflicts rent it, what type of family and other social institutions then existed, what customs ruled the people, what views and attitudes they held on diverse problems, what norms and criteria determined their social conduct. It will thus not only lay bare the social structure and life of the people in a past period but will also disclose their social, ethical and religious conceptions as well as their material and ideal aspirations and aims. It will also reveal the story of their brave social endeavour, also of their reverses and victories.

The enormous rich material comprising the rural aesthetic culture has to be first assembled, analysed and classified. The next task for the rural sociologist is to interpret it with deep historical imagination and sociological insight. This alone will help him to achieve a living objective picture of the rural society and the rural life as they existed in the past. This is specially necessary because no detailed written history is available.

The Indian rural society is divided into a number of regional rural societies.

A comparative study of the contents of the aesthetic cultures of these units will disclose elements common to them such as a number of common, folk songs, folk tales, myths, proverbs, riddles and other, though generally to be found with regional variations.

Such a discovery will help to comprehend the process of the diffusion of culture which had taken place in various rural zones of India in the past. It will also help to get an adequate picture of the historical process of the contacts and collisions, amalgamation or even assimilation, among numerous tribes and communities which lived in India in past epochs. A veritable past history of the Indian rural society and the Indian rural humanity can be composed through such a comparative study of the various rural aesthetic cultures of the various rural zones today.

Such a history of the Indian rural society is indispensable for evolving the history of the Indian society as a whole.

There are various means of deciphering the past history of the Indian people. The study of the variegated and massive content of the aesthetic cultures of the regional agrarian groups and its evaluation will serve as perhaps one of its most fruitful means for that purpose. Nevertheless, all the varied means should be utilised in mutual co-ordination.

After studying the content of the rural aesthetic culture, it is necessary to study the specific forms in which this culture is expressed.

There exists an organic relationship between the content and the form of art. It consists in the unity of its form and content, the content determining the form.

The specific content of the rural aesthetic culture outlined previously determines the specific forms of that culture. It determines the styles of painting, engraving, sculpture and architecture; the designs of costumes and ornaments; the tunes of folk songs and the rhythms of folk poetry; the structures of folk tales, dances and dramas. Further, a good proportion of that culture is marked with symbolism and it is the task of the rural sociologist to penetrate through the symbols and uncover the hidden significant ideas conveyed in an art work.

The Indian rural aesthetic culture comprising various regional rural cultures exhibits a variety of styles, patterns and modes. For instance, we have such varied forms as Sorathas, Dohas, Chaupais, and Chhappas, Kirtans, Bhajans, Abhangas, Pavadas,

Deshis, Horis, Kajaris, Kawalis and others in the domain of poetry and song; Rasas, Garbas and others in the sphere of dance; and Bhavais, Ramlilas, Tamasas and other in the field of drama. Similarly the words of other rural arts also reveal a rich diversity of forms.

The study of different forms of the art cultures of different regional rural communities will help us to distinguish them as distinct cultural units. Further, since the agrarian life possesses certain common characteristics, though with local and regional variations, such a study will also reveal how basically the same life content has been variously handled in the sphere of art by different agrarian communities.

A considerable amount of specialization is found in the agrarian arts mainly because the art is fused with concrete activities like sowing, reaping, harvesting and others or with such articles of utility as ornaments and earthenware. Again, since the art creations maintain a thematic continuity, the arts dealing with them are enriched from generation to generation. There is this continuous improvement of agrarian arts, their forms, styles and patterns.

A study of the forms of various regional aesthetic cultures discloses the significant fact that a number of them are essentially the same with regional variations only. This would assist the rural sociologist to resolve the problem of the diffusion of art forms, and of the migrations of a number of rural arts.

The Indian rural people have a long and rich history of aesthetic culture. Musical concerts and dramas were a feature of the rural life during the Maurya period and have been, as A. S. Altekar states, described as "Preksha," by Chanakya and "Samaja" by Ashoka. They were an integral part of the celebrations of religious festival such as Ram-Navmi, Gokul-Ashtami, Dushera, Ganesh Chaturthi, and Holi. They were also organised at village and inter-village fairs which were great social occasions in pre-modern times.

Cultural Trends

Since the advent of the British in India, as previously seen, a process of the fundamental alteration of Indian society began. As a result of this the psychology of the rural people also changed. The old aesthetic culture began to decline. The process is still continuing. The old arts have been gradually declining though the new modern ones have not been replacing them with the same tempo.

The rural sociologist is confronted with the problem of a renaissance of the rural aesthetic culture. He has to resolve a number of problems germane to a programme of such a renaissance. What will be the nature of the new aesthetic culture? What will be its content and form? Will the new rural arts be fused with the new rural life? Will the organic unity of art and life, the basic characteristic of the old aesthetic culture, be preserved in the new art? Will the new rural art retain the sincerity and the spontaneity of the old one or will it be sophisticated as a good section of the modern urban art is? What will be the ideology informing it? Will it be a mass art in which the people participate or will it be a distinct domain of the professional artists? Will it be a commercialized art produced by artists who subordinate their self-expression to the needs of the market or an ivory tower art where the artists create solely for their own satisfaction, or an art which is social and still provides free self-expression for the artists? These are some of the vital problems which the rural sociologist has to investigate.

Further, modern humanity has at its disposal an advanced technology which can create a complex and multifold technique of art. The material means and resources available today for such arts as painting, music, drama architecture and others are simply astounding. They can serve as the material prerequisite for the creation of a rich and variegated artistic mass culture which can express profound social ideas and portray individual and mass emotions in all their complexity and variety. The new art by means of the material technique accessible to it can work up not merely a few simple collective ideas and emotions as the old rural art did, but also the multifold and complex collective as well as individualized ideas and emotions which the modern rural humanity even today conceives and feels under the impact of a changing agrarian world. With the steady transformation of the rural society, the social relations are being constantly recast engendering new conceptions and feelings, new social passions, dreams and aspirations.

The existing rural aesthetic culture is in a state of increasing disorganization. This, in the final analysis, is the result of the increasing disorganization of the rural society itself of which it is the aesthetic reflex. The crisis of culture is the product of the crisis of society.

The problem arises whether the process of increasing disorganization and dissolution which the present rural aesthetic culture is undergoing will culminate into the emergence of a new historically higher aesthetic culture.

It depends on how the crisis of the present rural society is resolved. If the present rural society is replaced by one materially and culturally more advanced and based on co-operative social relations; a higher aesthetic culture will spring as a beautiful flower on the tree of such a higher type of society.

As mentioned before, the rural aesthetic culture has been declining and some of the rural arts even disappearing. From the standpoint of the history of the evolution of the Indian art, it is necessary to preserve the knowledge of the present rural aesthetic culture. Further, this is also necessary because, in absence of the written history of the early phase of the Indian society and insufficiently recorded history of subsequent phase, the rural aesthetic culture with its myths and legends, folk tales and folk songs, dances and dramas, paintings, engravings and statues, can provide a clue to the life of the Indian people in past epochs.

Modern technical means such as printing press, gramophone, camera, film and others can be made use of for preserving the rural songs and stories, statuary and architecture, fables and legends, through printing, recording and photographing.

For all these reasons a careful study of the rural aesthetic culture is indispensable for the student of the rural society.

Six

Social Dimensions

In the earlier phases of the development of Anthropology, tribal societies of far-off lands, isolated from the main links of modern civilisation, were the subject-matter of its study. This led to a rather unfortunate assumption on the part of common man that Anthropology is the study of tribes. But "Anthropologists are no longer concerned primarily, or even mainly, with the study of tribal cultures; in increasing numbers they are now operating nearer home in village communities where they have discovered challenging possibilities of theoretical and applied social science research." (Dube, 1958.) Basically Anthropology studies Man—and He should be studied at all levels of cultural development. Keeping this aim in view, Anthropology has extended its frontiers to include not only the rural studies, but also urban societies, determination of national character, and analysis of complex cultures. "Today all over the world, Anthropology has embraced the whole human society." (Ishwaran, 1960:5.) It studies "just every thing human". (Redfield, 1956.)

The tools of research that were sharpened in the microcosms of little tribes could be used for the study of the "village" communities, easily and most effectively, with only slight modifications, and quite in consonance with the techniques of other social sciences. The concept of "Ideal Folk-society" developed by Redfield was tried out in analysing the cultures of Latin America, but there it was found almost non-operational. While re-examining it Redfield thought that there was nothing wrong in the concept itself. The communities that one wanted to fit into the conceptual framework were remote in several of the characteristic traits from the ideal type. The later studies proved that the folk societies tend to lose increasingly their basic traits when they come into contact with other advanced cultures. Folk societies, thus, gradually transform themselves into village communities and isolate themselves from the ideal types, say, the one constructed by Redfield. As a result of the processes of culture-contact it is today hardly possible to get any pure, unaffected, and completely isolated "primitive" community. The culture-contact gives rise to a continuum, technically known as the "Folk-Urban continuum". The intermediate category between the two polar types presents the "peasant society" or the village-community.

Thus, the processes of change initiated and accelerated by contact have opened new vistas of study. They presented new problems of analysis and research methodology. It was apparent that the holistic approach that could be successfully employed in the study of isolated and remotely situated small tribal communities was not possible here. The 'whole' of the village community was not complete. It was a part of a wider 'whole' of a greater society. In order to apprehend the village in its totality, it was deemed essential to take cognizance of extraneous forces and factors that affect the life-ways and work-ways of the community.

In the past few years, the programmes of directed and planned change in the underdeveloped countries have immensely increased the possibilities of modifying the form and structure of the village communities. It was therefore considered desirable to record the existing structure of the rural society which would later help the evaluation of the impacts of the development programmes of planned culture change. Some "challenging possibilities" of applied social science research were easily discernible and they provided enough incentive to the social scientist to undertake such studies.

Typically Indian

In the Indian context, there is one more factor. Indian society is caste-structured. Knowledge about caste was nothing but "Book-view" and the "Upper caste-view" (Srinivas, 1955). What type of caste organisation is prevalent today? Which of the frontiers have had the largest impact of changes, and in which part of the country or which section of the society (rural or urban)? These were some of the pressing problems of theoretical interest and practical significance which demanded a more thorough and intimate enquiry in specific and limited fields in the different parts of the country.

In brief, following factors may be listed which have facilitated inclusion of a new dimension of study in Anthropology:-

1. Attempts to redefine Anthropology as the Science of man at all levels of cultural development;
2. Recognition of the fact that simple, isolated tribal folks are only an ideal construct and that culture-contact has already broken their isolation. Some writers go to the extent of saying that "they were never isolated";
3. The fact that the majority of world population is rural and it demands attention for systematic study;
4. Attraction toward research possibilities of the new field of study;
5. Facilities for research in terms of proximity, easy accessibility and therefore involving comparatively lesser expenditure than in the study of Tribes;
6. Need for the systematic and scientific study of Indian social structure as it exists today to provide authentic, factual material for the posterity, to reconstruct the past, and to enable the planner in his formulation of plans and projects;
7. Need for the study of changing situation in the village communities brought about by external agencies directly or indirectly, planned or non-directed; and
8. Applicability of the traditional anthropological methods of research to the analysis of rural society.

Economists and Sociologists have been engaged in the study of rural society and it could be said that the entrance of Anthropology in this field is an encroachment or an undesirable intrusion upon others' fields. But this is rather an overstatement. Neither Economics nor even Sociology attempts to intensively study any particular village community. Whatever is being written on rural society is only an outcome of the shuffling of data obtainable from official records like the Patwari Registers, census reports, etc. They give their generalised statements for the country as a whole without caring to go into the intricate details which lay hidden and remain unnoticed to the superficial observers. "Survey research of the extensive type does yield certain data that conform to the rigid tests of validity and reliability but its coverage must of necessity be limited. In its very nature it cannot explore the depths and covert aspects of behaviour ...." (Dube, 1958:2.) To the advantage of the planner they can yield general data but the analysis of human factors is beyond their scope. Thus, although the field is common, methods and techniques of study are different. Keeping this difference of techniques in view, if Rural Sociology has to be differentiated from anthropological studies of village communities, it is proposed that the generalised analysis on national level based on books and statistics be designated as Rural Sociology and the intensive study of particular village communities based on anthropological techniques of research be known as Rural Anthropology. Fortunately in India there is no need for such a distinction. Both Sociologists and Anthropologists are jointly exploring the Village Community with a largely common methodology. Rural India provides a good meeting ground for the two disciplines. This effective communication is indeed a healthy trend and one should welcome this happy "merging".

The year 1955 was of immense significance for Indian anthropology and sociology. In that year, for the first time four books and several papers on Indian Village were published. These studies were made by Indian as well as American and British social scientists. Dube's Indian Village, Majumdar's Rural Profiles (ed.), Marriot's Village India (ed.), and Srinivas' India's Villages (ed.) were the major publications of the year. The same year a conference was also held under the Chairmanship of Dr. (Mrs.) Irawati Karve at Madras, in which Professor Robert Redfield also participated. The much-discussed concept of Sanskritisation proposed by Srinivas in Religion & Society in Coorg was reiterated by him who thought the discussions had reinforced his belief in its validity. The proceedings of the conference have been published in a book entitled Society in India. Later, Twice Born (Carstairs; 1957), India's Changing Villages (Dube, 1958), Caste and

Communication in an Indian Village (Majumdar, 1958), Caste and the Economic Frontier (Bailey, 1957) and Village Life in Northern India (Lewis, 1958) were added to the Library of Indian rural studies. Albert Mayer's book Pilot Project, India (1958) summarises the main achievements of the Etawah Project. An Introduction to Rural Sociology in India, an anthology edited by A. R. Desai, appeared in a revised and enlarged version in the year 1959. Recently Adrian Mayer's work "Caste and Kinship in Central India (1960) has come out. Besides these major publications, several research papers based on field work in rural areas have appeared in various journals. The yearly sessions of the Indian Sociological Conference have also included discussions on varied and important problems of Rural Analysis. University departments of Anthropology and Sociology have been and are undertaking various projects for conducting researches in the rural areas. The Research Programmes Committee of the Planning Commission, Government of India, is also promoting rural research through such centres.

The study of Indian Rural Society has helped in developing certain analytical categories. Srinivas has pointed toward a social process, which he christened as Sanskritisation, through which the lower castes try to bring about changes in their life-ways to obtain greater ritual purity, and thereby attain a higher status in the ritual hierarchy of castes. He has also analysed the process of Westernisation which simultaneously operates in a society. N. Prasad has tried to elaborate the concept and suggested the term Kulinisation for the same. Majumdar through Desanskritisation suggests a reverse process by which the Brahman castes also try to identify in some matters with other castes. Ishwaran considers the concept of Sanskritisation as "misleading" and asserts "A thorough understanding of the Hindu culture could only be had by referring to Brahmanisation but not sanskritisation. (1960:9.) Chauhan (1959) while suggesting the limitations of the concepts of sanskritisation and Westernisation mentions the other processes which are simultaneously at work. Efforts have also been made to analyse the hierarchical aspects of caste and the factors leading towards the dominance of a caste. The very concept of caste has been re-examined in an effort to make it more precise, less open-textured so to say. Marriott discovered the processes of Universalisation and Parochialisation (1955) which explain the complexity of Indian civilisation and the communication channels that exist between the Great and Little traditions of the country. To avoid the limitations of the polar distinctions, Dubey is busy in conceptualising the total realm of Tradition into a five-fold division. According to him, "In our study of Indian Village communities ...it may be useful to consider the contextual classical and local traditions as well the regional (culture-area), western (ideological-technological), and emergent national (nativistic-reinterpretational-adaptive) traditions." (1958:10.)

Major Problems

The most significant problem which has attracted the attention of a number of social scientists is that of the representativeness of a village. Can a village represent the whole nation? It could be said that as every one who is a resident of India is Indian so also is every village in India an Indian village. But the problem is not so simple. Every village has a distinct "personality" of its own. It has its distinctive structure, network of kinship-affiliations, caste-composition and dominance, and leadership patterns. The south Indian village is different in many respects from a north Indian village. Even in north or south India no specific homogeneity in the village organisation is to be discovered. In Marriott's Kishangarhi, "Marriage... . is oriented to flow in a single direction only." There is no possibility of "marriage by exchange" there. But in Rajasthan this practice is observed and is locally known as "Anta Santa". The system of Seem Seemna Bhaichara found in villages around Delhi is peculiarity of this region alone. In the villages of Mahakaushal, it was found that it is the parents who will touch the feet of their daughter as a mark of respect. Similarly the brothers would respect their sisters irrespective of age-considerations. The elder sisters, in the same vein, touch the feet of their younger sisters. But in Rajasthan, it is always the daughters who would touch the feet of their parents. Similarly the younger sister has to bow down to her elder siblings. These instances prove that while in Mahakaushal sex of the child or the sibling has an important role to play in commanding respect, in Rajasthan it is not so relevant as the factor of Age is. To give another example, the Telis are oil pressers and traditional confectioners in Mewar. Their `pakka' preparations are acceptable even to high caste Brahmans. But in Mahakaushal the idea of Telis being confectioners will be abhorred. In Mewar, the role of midwifery is traditionally assigned to the Barber woman (Nain). In Mahakaushal two different castes have their role at the time of delivery. The Basor woman performs the surgical operation, and after the preliminary purificatory rites, the Nai-woman takes over. Similarly, differences in dialects, in dressing-patterns, in details of ritual observances, in kinship terminology and usages and in the economic sphere could be located. In such situations, when a village in the neighbourhood of Delhi is compared with that of Mexico, the utility of such a comparison is uncertain and the representativeness of the compared villages very much open to question. From this point of view the very title of the book viz., Village Life in Northern India is dubious.

In spite of all these considerations one moot question still remains: Is the significance of a village study confined only to the village studies or can the results of the research be used for a wider area? To put it in other words, whether the village represents its own confines or a region (or area) bigger than that? In the fifth session of the Indian Sociological Conference held at Lucknow (1960) Brij Raj Chauhan raised the same question in a different manner. According to him, the question as "to what extent any village in India can be considered as representative of the country ... can lead to four facts

1. Any village selected at random represents the nation;
2. There are various types of villages in the country and one village may represent other villages of its own type;
3. A village happened to be studied may be only selectively representative with reference to the item selected for study;
4. It may be possible to find a representative village for the country.

On the basis of Census of India — 1951, Chauhan created a Hindupur village. In terms of size of the village, sex-ratio, distance from a city, and availability of modern means of transport (bus and rail) Hindupur represents the Indian village. "Hindupur is the name given to the village that is 18 miles from the rail, 6 miles from pucca road, 4 miles from Kachcha road and 33 miles from a city. With 269 males and 260 females it is inhabited by 529 persons." When some of the Indian villages reported on in Anthropological literature were compared with this "Ideal type" or, Averagė Type of Hindupur, the following facts emerged in regard to the size of the village.

1. All the villages so compared "fall above the category of small villages thereby excluding 68% of the villages in India";
2. Villages of Mohana (Majumdar), Namhalli (Beals), Kishangarhi (Marriott), Kasandra (Steed) and Rani-khera (Lewis) having a population between 575 and 1,100 "are fairly near the mark of Hindupur and these villages represent 18.5% of the villages in India".
3. Rampura (Srinivas) and Madhopur (Cohn) of the population of 1,523 and 1,852 respectively, "represent 10% of villages".
4. Shamirpet (Dube) village of the size of 2,454 represents only 3.5% of the villages in India.

Similarly these eight villages were compared with Hindupur on the remaining three counts.

Here it is necessary to mention that Hindupur is Chauhan's own creation. He "has not visited this village and in fact does not know whether such a village exists at all". This is the magic of Census figures and statistical computations. Chauhan, however, believes that " for every region perhaps a picture of villages like Uttarpur, Madhyapur, Bangpur, Rajput, etc., will aid in furthering our knowledge and ignorance (sic) with regard to the efficacy of studies of single village communities for making nationwide conclusions."

Reactions in Different Manner

Social scientists have reacted differently towards this effort of constructing an Ideal type in terms of limited factors, based on methods of statistical computations alone. There are certain theoretical difficulties in accepting Hindupur as a representative Indian village. The selection of the four factors on the basis of which this Ideal village was invented has been governed by the considerations of convenience and personal preference. The village as a socio-cultural entity cannot be deduced from quantophrenic rhapsodies. Possibly Asiapur (Asian village) and Vishwapur (universal village) can also be constructed as ideal types for Asia and the world in the same manner as Bangpur for Bengal and Hindupur for India. It is quite possible that the ideal village of Australia or Iraq may have closer identity with Hindupur or Rajpur. In that situation what would remain specifically Indian in Hindupur to justify the prefix "Hind"?

Secondly, where the suggestion for making 'purs' for Rajasthan, Madhya Pradesh etc. is offered, probably it is overlooked that the provinces are organised for administrative purposes and their boundaries are defined mainly geographically. But cultural boundaries do not necessarily coincide with the geographical.

It also appears that Chauhan wants to conceive of Indian Village as a concept. It has happened in the history of Anthropology earlier also; it is implicit in the effort of persons like Tylor, Morgan and Frazer to make anthropology the study of culture and not of cultures. Relevant data suitable enough to be fitted into the scheme of the cultural construct were collected from different cultures "torn out of their cultural context with little reference to their meaning". They were all in search of an ideal pattern of culture which, in extremist hands, split up into the schools of evolutionism and diffusionism. The number of village studies done so far in India is quite meagre and not quite adequate to yield nation-wide generalisations." In order to avoid a mechanical and overly schematic approach to the study of regional similarities and differences in the country, it is most desirable to continue with the anthropological tradition of single village studies." (Dube, 1958: 3.)

However, if we want to understand Indian village as a concept, we have to get hold of those points of comparison which are significant and distinctive of Indian culture. The factors that are analysed in establishing Hindupur as the Indian village do not give any idea of village as a culture-bearing entity. Their Indianness is accidental, and by no means refers to the specificities of our villages.

In spite of all this, the Hindupur proposal has certainly provided stimulation and food for thought. Perhaps, it serves to point out that thinking in terms of the Indian village, or talking about the nationwide representative character of a single village is fruitless. Statistical calculations alone cannot offer any answer. Although Shamirpet, Rampura, Mohana, Ranikhera, Namhalli, Kasandra, Kishangarhi, etc. are different in more ways than one, from the Ideal type Hindupur, they nevertheless represent the tradition of Indian villages in many respects. In every village in India, there is something which distinguishes it from the villages of 'the other countries of the world. If the two village studies of different countries are to be examined, at least this could easily be said that both these villages do not belong to the same country or culture. It, therefore, is implicit that each village has a certain measure of representativeness; the difference may be a matter of degree in which, and the area that it represents.

And moreover, representativeness is always relative. When Man is related to the Animal Kingdom he is supposed to have those characteristics which are found even in a protozoan. But the similarity in the characteristics would go on increasing as he is classified as a vertebrate, a mammal, an eutherian, a primate and ultimately a Homosapien. He would be having all the characteristics of his species and, therefore, would truly represent it. But nonetheless he also represents other subdivisions to which he belongs in degrees that go on reducing as he departs from his station in the scheme. In the same way the village would represent in many respects its own region, then its province, then the nation, the continent and the world.

Traits in Culture and Tradition

Representativeness should be based on similarities of cultural traits and complexes, and aspects of social organisation. Size of the village, distance from the city etc., should be given a secondary importance. It is apparent that proximity to the city in terms of communication may not be coexistent with physical distance. It should not be difficult for the social scientist to assign relative significance to sociological contexts over biological and geographical ones. Thus, caste-system, concepts of ritual purity and pollution, agriculture, hereditary occupational-specialization, temple worship and polytheistic beliefs may be some of the factors on which the representative type may be constructed. Of course, this would necessitate undertaking of more village studies and developing an elaborate methodology of comparative approach. The villages and institutions of the same and of different culture-areas will have to be investigated in order to assess the range of similarities and differences.

The following hypotheses are proposed for determining the representativeness of an Indian Village:-

1. The language (or dialect) of a village can most adequately represent the linguistic area to which it belongs;
2. The ritual hierarchy of castes in a village could be representative of the culture-area or sub-culture-area to which the village belongs. However, it has to be remembered that it would only represent the ritual hierarchy of those castes which are found in the village.
3. In the same sub-cultural and the linguistic-area, social behaviour, ritual belief, customs and traditions, peculiarities of economic organisation, dressing and decoration patterns would tend to be similar;
4. From the point of view of caste-dominance, there could be wide-range differences between the village and the region. The caste which is regionally dominant may not necessarily have the same degree of influence and dominance in all the villages of the region;
5. Along with regional similarities in a social institution found to be present in all the villages of a given region, local variations are also associated. The complete understanding of the structure and functioning of that institution is only possible when all its variations and ramifications are recorded. This requires the study of the institution in more than one village. In such a situation, the very fact of the presence of an institution

in the village is not sufficient to justify its regional representativeness.

If, on the basis of these and other similar hypotheses, new researches are directed the regional ideal types could possibly be formulated. Once the problem of regional representation is solved, we shall be better equipped for the national Ideal type. It has to be specifically pointed out here that the concepts of "region" and "area" are also not sociologically well-defined. Attempts towards defining these concepts will facilitate proper examination of the issue of representativeness. Once good research data from Rural India are accumulated for comparative purposes, the ground will be prepared for thinking in terms of Indian Village as a concept.

The Social Fabric

The social structure of Indian village communities, list some of the important factors of change, and attempt a broad analysis of the major trends of change.

For an understanding of the structure and problems of Indian village society we have to view the village both as a distinct isolable entity, and as a link in the chain of a wider inter-village organization. An individual village derives some of the characteristic features of its organization from the great national tradition of India, while the traditions of the region or the culture area in which it is located also contribute substantially toward shaping its value-orientation, ethos, and general pattern of life. Notwithstanding these national and regional influences, there is much that is individual to the village; its pattern of inter-group adjustment gives a certain degree of distinctiveness to the village. The Indian village is thus sufficiently isolable, but it is not an isolate, and has therefore to be viewed as a community within a larger community.

The interplay of several different kinds of solidarities determines the structure and organization of Indian village communities. Kinship, caste, and territorial affinities are the major determinants that shape the social structure of these communities. An individual belongs to a family-nuclear, compound or joint; and the family belongs to a lineage as well as to a large group of relatives having kin or affinal ties with it. These units belong to an endogamous sub-caste or caste; in some instances we find a number of endogamous sub-castes grouped together as a caste. Non-Hindu religious groups in villages tend to function as separate castes. Most of the Hindu castes are fitted into one of the four major divisions of Hindu society, called varna. Solidarities provided by kin and caste tend to merge, but those of territorial affinity belong to a different level. An individual and his family belong also to a village, which is often multi-caste in its composition. The village itself is a part of a network of neighbouring villages, the region, and the nation. The structural model of Indian peasant communities can be presented in the following diagram:

In the following diagram dotted circles show the comparatively less effective units of social structure. Non-Hindu groups also fit this scheme. In Diagram A, rather than being described as a "sub-caste" or "caste", they should be called "religious group", and of course they are outside the varna organization of Hindu society.

Principle for Organisation

Caste is perhaps the most important single organizing principle in these communities, and it governs to a very considerable degree the organization of kinship and territorial units. In this system of segmentary division of society the different segments are kept apart by complex observances emerging from an all-pervading concept of ritual pollution. The caste divisions are regarded as divinely ordained and are hierarchically graded. The difference between the different segments is defined by tradition and is regarded as permanent. In inter-group relations the caste structure works according to a set pattern of principles: hierarchy and social distance manifest and express themselves in rules and regulations that are calculated to avoid ritual pollution and maintain ritual purity. Marriage, commensality, and physical contacts particularly are governed by strict rules. It has been pointed out earlier that castes are endogamous. Matrimonial alliances outside the caste are viewed with disapproval and are forbidden by tradition. Complex rules of commensality specify the castes from which a particular caste may accept different kinds of food. Foods are classified into several categories, depending on the degree to which they are susceptible to pollution. Everyday interaction between the different castes is also governed by caste rules: persons from some castes should never be touched, while physical contact with some others should be avoided under special conditions, such as a state of ritual purity. Caste largely determines occupational choice: with the exception of a few "open" occupations which may be pursued by anyone irrespective of caste, a large number of crafts and occupations are caste monopolies and can be practised only by certain castes. In its functioning an individual caste generally illustrates a distinctive way of life, for different castes have different sets of prescribed norms of conduct and expectations regarding standards of behaviour. These norms and expected standards of behaviour cover such aspects of life as observance of rules of purity especially those of bathing and washing (at appropriate hours) public conduct, and even dress and speech. Another important feature of caste may also be noted in this connection. In new situations demanding group decisions and group action in recent years, caste has shown its dormant strength and has proved itself a cohesive force. Most local, and even some state and national elections were fought along caste lines, and in these the contestants depended to a great extent on the support of their caste fellows. Within a village the caste system manifests itself as a vertical structure in which individual castes are hierarchically graded and kept permanently apart and at the same time are linked and kept together by some well-defined expectations and obligations which integrate them into the village social system. The horizontal ties of a caste, too, are important, for a village caste group has strong links with its counterparts in other villages, and in several spheres of life they tend to act together. In order to be able to discharge the control functions implied in the complex norms associated with the system, castes have local and regional organizations and associations which have the authority to enforce the rules and customs of the caste.

Forms, Diversified

The great diversity of forms in the family and kinship organisation of Indian peasant communities makes the task of presenting a general account of them somewhat difficult. Contrary to common belief the basic unit of social organization in these communities is not the large joint family, but the nuclear family and the smaller joint family in which only a part of those who should have constituted the ideal larger joint family live together, and even the latter generally breaks up when minors attain maturity and a degree of economic self-sufficiency. Recent village studies have shown that large joint families are relatively few in number and they too are largely confined to the upper, i.e., the priestly, trading, and agricultural castes. In some parts of north Indian plains it has been observed that a house is shared by a number of people having close lineal ties, who live not as one family, but as distinct nuclear families organized as separate hearths or chulhas. However, very special ties are recognized between a family and the local group of near kin, i.e., all other families lineally related to it up to the third generation. The solidarity between this cluster of families expresses itself on ceremonial occasions and in times of stress and calamity. In the hour of need they must support each other, and mutual consultations among them in regard to all major decisions are regarded as desirable. Informally the local group of near kin functions as an effective agency of social control. The larger circle of relations has more or less the same functions, though physical distance between the different constituent units naturally makes its functioning less effective. The outlook of the people has been distinctly kin-oriented, and in an hour of need or stress they almost instinctively look to their kin for sympathy and support.

The village as a unit of social structure cuts across the boundaries of kin and caste and unites a number of unrelated families within an integrated multicaste community. Structurally the village communities can be divided into three main groups: the "single settlement" village, in which the community shares a common and compact settlement site, the "nucleated" village which has a central settlement as the nucleus around which there are a number of smaller satellite settlements, and the "dispersed" village community, in which the community consists of a series of dispersed homesteads having well-defined ties with one another. Both have a number of common features. They are stable populations generally, with a common past and a number of shared values. They recognize and emphasise their individual identity, and in certain situations act as one unit. Their economy is built largely around agriculture; economically and socially the agricultural castes are the most important, while the non-agricultural occupations are subsidiary to agriculture. Land is greatly loved and valued, and the community as a whole shares some common problems and acculturative influences. Being largely caste-structured, the community finds itself integrated in terms of traditional patterns that define the interactions between the different segments of the community in the fields of economy, socio-religious life, and village administration. Operating under traditional arrangements, artisan and other occupational castes render services to the agriculturist in their respective fields of specialization; in return the agriculturist gives them a stipulated share of the crops when they are harvested. Socio-religious life, especially ceremonials and rituals connected with birth, puberty, marriage and death, are so organized that they require participation by a large number of castes at various stages. As the rites progress, at different points small fees have to be paid to the castes that are assisting. For these purposes there are established patron-client relationships under which families of occupational castes are affiliated with families of agriculturists; for services-in the socio-religious field even non-agriculturists are covered by these traditional arrangements. Among the occupational castes themselves there is often a barter of their traditional services. A similar integration of various castes and their functions is seen in the organization of village administration and village rituals, in both of which the different castes often have well-defined position and functions. A common organized authority of the village gives it a still greater unity, and besides maintaining law and order tries effectively to secure observance of village norms. This invariably consists of influential and responsible members of different castes living in the village.

Seven

Development of Villages

Now, we attempt to make a sociological analysis of the Community Development Projects which have been sponsored by the Government of the Indian Union to assist the reconstruction of the agrarian economy and the rural society.

The Planning Commission in its First Five-Year Plan has described the Community Development Projects as the method through which Five-Year Plan seeks to initiate a process of transformation of the social and economic life of the villages. It is, according to an U.N.O. report, `designed to promote better living for the whole community with the active participation and, if possible, on the initiative of the Community, but if this initiative is not forthcoming, by the same use of techniques for arousing it and stimulating it in order to secure its active and enthusiastic response. The Community Development Projects are of vital importance, according to Pandit Nehru, not so much for the material achievements that they would bring about, but much more so, because they seem to build up the community and the individual and to make the latter the builder of his own village centres and of India in the larger sense.'

The word 'Community Development' itself is a novel nomenclature in India. As the Report of the Team for the Study of the Community Projects and National Extension Service (popularly known as the Balwantrai Committee Report) states, 'We have so far used such terms as rural development, constructive work, adult education and rural uplift to denote certain of its aspects. The word "Community" has, for the past many decades, denoted religious or caste groups or, in some instance, economic groups not necessarily living in one locality; but with the inauguration of the community development programme in this country, it is intended to apply it to the concept of the village community as a whole, cutting across caste, religious and economic differences. It is a programme which emphasises that the interest in the development of the locality is necessarily and unavoidably common to all the people living there. It is sociologically significant to note that to renovate the agrarian economy and the rural society through the active participation of millions of villagers, the sponsors of this movement could not find an appropriate term in any of the State languages of India to symbolize this vast process. We will examine the postulates underlying this new connotation of the term " Community " subsequently.

Motivating Factor

The Community Development Projects emerged as a result of inspiration from the following earlier experiments

(i) Intensive rural development activities carried out at Sevagram and the Sarvodaya centres in the Bombay State; (ii) The Firka Development Schemes in Madras; (iii) Experiments to build up community centres for Refugees at Nilokheri and other places; (iv) And more particularly from the Pilot Projects at Etavah and Gorakhpur in the U.P. under the inspiration of Albert Meyers.

Cooperative Way

This idea also arose out of a realization that various efforts made by the Government departments such as Agriculture, Animal Husbandry, Co-operation, Health, Education and others which were carried on separately, should be co-ordinated to make them more effective. Further, according to the sponsors of the movement, this programme was launched with a view to changing the very philosophical basis of rural reconstruction. Most of the other institutions approached the village and rural reconstruction work in a philanthropic spirit. The Community Development Movement 'wants to create a psychological change in the villagers... It aims at inculcating in the villagers new desires, new incentives, new techniques, and a new confidence so that this vast reservoir of human resources may be used for the growing economic development of the country'.

The Community Development Programme was inaugurated on October 2, 1952. Fifty-five Community Projects were launched. Each Project Area comprised about 300 villages, covering an area of 450 to 500 sq. miles, i.e., about 1,50,000 acres with a population of about 2,00,000 persons. A project area was divided into three Development Blocks of hundred villages, each with a population of about 65,000 persons. Each Block was divided into about twenty groups, each containing five villages. Each group of villages was being served by a Gram-Sevak (the village level worker). Of the five villages, one generally became the headquarters of the Gram-Sevak.

The programme launched in 1952 was extended to wider areas at the end of the First Five-Year Plan. There 603 National Extension Service Blocks, and 553 Community Development Blocks covering 1,57,000 villages and a population of 88.8 million persons were created. Nearly one out of every three villages in India was brought within the orbit of this Programme.

The Second Five-Year Plan proposed to bring every village in India under this scheme, 40 per cent of the area being brought under a more intensive development scheme. In all 3,800 additional Extension Service Blocks will be set up, 1,120 of these being converted into Community Project Blocks. The ambitious scheme has, however, been subsequently modified.

The Community Development Programme is broadly divided into three phases, viz., the National Extension phase, the Intensive Community Development Project phase and the post-Intensive Development phase. Of course, it is not laid down that everywhere the first two phases must follow each other, the National Extension phase in some areas having been skipped over to usher in the Intensive Community Development Project phase. Usually, the period of the first and the second phase is to last for three years each.

In the first phase, the areas selected are subjected to the method of providing services on the ordinary rural development pattern with a lesser Governmental expenditure. In the intensive phase, the blocks selected are subjected to more composite and more intensive development schemes with larger Governmental expenditure. In the post-Intensive phase, it is presumed that the basis for self-perpetuation of the process initiated during the earlier phases has been created and the need for special Government expenses reduced. Slowly the areas are left in the charge of the Departments for the development.

In 1952-53 series of community projects, the provision per block was Rs. 22 lakhs for a period of three years. This was reduced to Rs. 15 lakhs for the 1953-54 series. The present provision for the N.E.S. stage of three years is Rs. 4 lakhs and for the Community Development stage is Rs. 8 lakhs, making up a total of Rs. 12 lakhs for six years. In other words, the annual expenditure per Block was reduced first from Rs. 7.3 lakhs to Rs. 5 lakhs and now to Rs. 2 lakhs.

An imposing list of activities has been prepared by the sponsors of the Community Development Projects. They include various items connected with the following eight categories of undertakings

(1) Agriculture and related matters; (2) Communications; (3) Education; (4) Health; (5) Training; (6) Social Welfare; (7) Supplementary Employment; and (8) Housing.

The fourth Evaluation Report of 1957 adopted different criteria for classifying activities undertaken by the Community Development Projects. They divided the programmes of activities into the following major categories: (1) Constructional programmes; (2) Irrigational programmes; (3) Agricultural programmes; and (4) Institutional and other programmes. The detailed list of the various activities undertaken under each of these programmes is as under:

Constructional programmes: 'Kutcha' roads, 'Pucca' roads, culverts, drains, pavement of streets, school buildings, community centre buildings, dispensary buildings, houses for the Harijans and drinking water sources.

Irrigation programmes; Wells, pumping sets, tube wells and tanks.

Agricultural programmes: Reclamation, soil conservation, consolidation of holdings, improved seeds, manure and fertilizer, pesticides, improved methods of cultivation and improved implements.

Institutional and other programmes: Youth Clubs, Women's Organisations, Community Centres, 'Vikas Mandals,' co-operative societies, distribution stores, maternity centres, dispensaries, veterinary dispensaries, key village centres, panchayats, adult literacy centres, primary schools, 'dai' training centres, cottage industries, production-cum-training centres, demonstration plots, soakage pits, smokeless 'chulha'.

An elaborate organization has been created to implement Community Development Projects; it is known as the Community Project Administration. Originally functioning under the Planning Commission, it is now under the charge of the newly created Ministry of Community Development.

The entire administration is composed of four major types-the Central administration, the State administration, the District organization and the Project administration. The power and the control flow from top to bottom making it a hierarchic bureaucratic organization. At every level there is an Executive Officer, functioning with the aid of a Development Committee and helped by an Advisory Board. At the Centre, there is an Administrator, at the State level there is a Development Commissioner, at the District level there is a District Development Officer of Collector's grade and at the Project level a Project Level Officer equipped with a staff of some 125 supervisors and village level workers.

Tasks Finished

We will now survey the achievements of this programme. It is extremely difficult to give a total quantitative assessment of these achievements for a number of reasons. First, to the best of present writer's knowledge, such overall data have not been compiled. Second, it is not very easy to separate the achievements of the Community Development Projects from those brought about by other agencies. Some observers have pointed out that a number of activities attributed to the Community Development Project movement should, in fact, be credited to other agencies. We shall, however, accept for the purposes of evaluation, the achievement data in regard to constructional, irrigational, agricultural, institutional and other activities as collected by the Fourth Report of the Programme Evaluation Organization. It is a data carefully collected from seventeen Project units from different States studied by the Project Evaluation Organization.

The impact of the Community Development Projects has been subjected to analysis and evaluation by a number of scholars and organizations. Prof. Wilson, Prof. Carl Taylor, Prof. Oscar Lewis, Prof. Opler and his team, Prof. Dube, Prof. Mandelbaum and many others have attempted to assess the nature of the impact of the Community Development Projects on the life of the rural people. The Programme Evaluation Organization has also been doing assessment continuously and their Reports are valuable documents. The Bench Mark Surveys also provide insight into the working of the Community Projects. The popularly known Balwantrai Committee Report on the subject is one of the latest authoritative evaluation. Prof. Dube's India's Changing Villages is the latest comprehensive and systematic analysis of Community Projects, although based on a very intensive examination of only two different types of villages in U.P. it will be very difficult indeed to adequately indicate here the main findings of these studies and reports separately. However, a certain general pattern of evaluation emerges which deserves our careful attention.

Significant Trends

It should be noted at the very outset that all the scholars and organisations who have evaluated the Community Development Projects, fundamentally accept the major postulates of the economic policy of the Government of India and of the Five-Year Plans. Further, all these evaluators have assumed that the Community Development Movement is both desirable and appropriate as a technique of reconstructing the agrarian economy and society of India. Not one of them has even raised a single query or attempted to critically examine the major postulates of the Movement. It is, therefore, necessary to make explicit the major assumptions taken for granted by others. As Prof. Carl Taylor remarks: " The whole concept and plan of Community Development-Extension Programme is that local self-help village groups will mobilize their natural and human resources for local improvements of all kinds and all technical agencies of Government will aid them in this undertaking." It implies, according to him (i) initiative of people in both formulating and executing the programmes. (ii) therefore the schemes of generating and organizing a large number of voluntary associations almost of primary group nature and also a wide variety of local institutions, (iii) reliance upon group work techniques, (iv) active participation of people in all the stages of implementation, resulting in local leadership, (v) governmental administrative machinery which acts as an assisting body. The personnel of the administrative machinery, at all levels, should not merely be equipped with administrative and other technical skills but must be fairly well-versed in social skills of evoking voluntary association and community participation.

The philosophy under-laying this Movement, in the context of the Indian agrarian society, therefore, implicitly accepts the following major sociological assumptions: (i) the individuals, sections, groups and strata forming the Village Community have a large number of common interests, sufficiently strong to bind them together; (ii) the interests of the various groups and classes within the village are both sufficiently like and common to create general enthusiasm as well as a feeling of development for all; (iii) the interests of the different sections of the community are not irreconciliably conflicting; (iv) the State is a super-class, impartial, non-partisan association and that the major policies of the Government are of such a nature that they do not further sharpen the inequalities between the existing social groups; (v) people's initiative and enthusiasm and active participation are possible in the extant village communities because they have common interests.

None of the scholars or the committees have critically inquired as to whether these assumptions about both the Village Communities in India and the Indian State and its governmental policies are valid or not.

However, we will review at present only the major findings of these scholars and committees regarding the operation of Community Development Projects and their impact upon the life of the rural people.

Prof. Taylor and most of the scholars feel that the Government machinery, though staffed by intelligent, hard-working and conscientious persons, has not still assimilated the true spirit underlying the entire programme. The Community Development-Extension Programme is operated more as an executive assignment. According to Prof. Taylor, the administration of the programme is predominantly based on aid from and reliance on the Government. The initiative of the people is still lacking. The Government machinery relies more on propaganda and spectacular results rather than on group work and voluntary creative participation. According to Prof. Taylor, a certain amount of active governmental participation was inevitable in a country like India during the earlier phases of the movement. But if that earlier phase was not crossed over and if the movement did not elicit active participation and initiative from the people, the very basis of the Community Development Programme would crumble. The danger has been slowly raising its head.

Prof. S. C. Dube also comes to the same conclusion. "Planning so far appears to be from the top down ... It is necessary to examine the implications and results of the present trends in planning. Because of the unique curbs on Projects autonomy its officials hesitated to demonstrate much initiative. What was worse they tended on the official level to accept orders from above, i.e., from the State headquarters, without question or comment, and this despite pronounced private reservations. As an outcome of this trend the officials were oriented less towards the village people, and more towards the pleasing of their official superiors." And further, "A large number of Project-sponsored activities are directed along the lines of traditional government `drives' rather than according to the proved principles of extension work. Visible accomplishments under such pressure and stimulation and completion of physical targets are greatly valued, and too little attention is given to the question of finding out if the movement is really acquiring roots in the village society." According to Prof. Dube, government servants function as bureaucrats and have not become agents of change with an active social service mentality.

The Balwantrai Committee Report is critical of the structural foundation of the Community Administration. According to the Report:

"admittedly, one of the least successful aspects of the C.D. and N.E.S. work is its attempt to evoke popular initiative. We have found that few of the local bodies at a level higher than the village panchayat have shown any enthusiasm or interest in this work; and even the panchayats have not come into the fields to any appreciable extent. An attempt has been made to harness local initiative through the formation of *ad hoc* bodies mostly with the nominated personnel and invariably advisory in character. These bodies have so far given no indication of durable strength nor the leadership necessary to provide the motive force for continuing the improvement of economic and social condition in rural areas. So long as we do not discover or create a representative and democratic institution which will supply the `local interest, supervision and care necessary to ensure that expenditure of money upon local objects conforms with the needs and wishes of the locality,' invest it with adequate power and assign to it appropriate finances, we will never be able to evoke local interest and excite local initiative in the field of development."

The report suggests that the elected Village Panchayat at village level and an elected Panchayat Samiti at the block level act as agencies to execute the Community Development Programme and the present Block level and Village level bureaucratic machinery be wound up.

In short the major criticism offered by scholars and Evaluating Committees boils down to the following major points: (i) its bureaucratic nature; (ii) absence of elective principle at any level in the machinery; (iii) decisions taken at the top and communicated below, almost like executive fiats; (iv) considerable confusion in the overall administration of the country, expressed in the relationship between the Project Administration and other Government departments; (v) considerable confusion and conflict with regard to powers and duties, and relative position and seniority within the staff of different departments as a result of their being interlocked with the Project Administration; (vi) duplication of work for a section of the administrative personnel and resultant overworking and the problem of divided loyalty towards functions; (vii) absence of social service mentality; and (viii) lack of social work skills among the staff.

In regard to the actual achievement of the Projects, within the cluster of villages operated by a Gram-sevak, his headquarters-village receives more benefits. Further, it has been found that bigger villages get greater benefits. Similarly, commercial belts receive more facilities than the non-commercial agrarian belts. As the Evaluation Report points out

"There is wide disparity in the distribution of the achievement and therefore of the benefits of the community project programmes. This disparity exists as between different blocks in the project areas. Within the blocks it exists as between the H.Q. villages of Gram-sevaks, the villages easily accessible to them, and the villages not so easily accessible. Within the villages, it exists as between cultivators and non-cultivators; and within the cultivating classes, it exists as between cultivators of bigger holdings and larger financial resources and those of smaller holdings and lesser financial resources. This is a matter of serious concern not only in terms of regional and social justice but also in terms of the political consequences that may ensue in the context of the increasing awakening among the people."

Though this disparity of benefits is recognised, none of the scholars or evaluation organizations has made a systematic analysis of its consequences; its ecological repercussions are not even seen by them. The Indian rural society is undergoing transformation under the impact of numerous forces today. Government's programmes of industrialization electrification, land reforms, major irrigation works, export and import plans, taxation, commercialization and monetization of various sectors of economic life, and unification of the country through development of means of communication, are producing important changes in the agrarian areas also. The impact of urbanization and industrialisation upon the pattern of rural life are being studied by a number of scholars. Unfortunately, however, none of the evaluators has analysed the impact of the Community Develop-ment Project upon the rural life from this wider perspective. Nor have these evaluators indicated the significance of this uneven growth of various regions, blocks, and villages.

The Positive Side

The advantages of the improvement, as pointed out by the Community Evaluation Reports, are taken by larger cultivators. As Prof. Dube points out

"Although the ideal of the Community Development Project was to work for the many-sided development of the entire community, from the foregoing account of its work ...it is clear that its significant and best organized activities were confined to the field of agricultural extension and consequently the group of agriculturists benefitted the most from them. A closer analysis of the agricultural extension work itself reveals that nearly 70 per cent of its benefits went to the elite group and to the more affluent and influential agriculturists. The gains to poorer agriculturists were considerably smaller .... For the economic development of this group, as well as for that of the artisans and agricultural labourers, no programmes were initiated by the Project."

Similar observations are made by all Project Evaluation Reports as well as by scholars like Mandelbaum. This impact of the Community Development Project is fraught with serious consequences. It sharpens the gulf between the rich and the poor cultivators. It makes artisans and agricultural labourers relatively more handicapped than the cultivators and therefore generates greater inequality and wider chasm between the affluent farmers, the agrarian capitalist class on one hand and the poorer strata, composed of poor peasants, artisans and agricultural labourers on the other. It implies that in the context of the economy which produces for market and profit, the poor farmers and other strata are made weaker in their competitive strength against the richer strata.

The organizations for rural change are dominated by the upper sections of the rural population. As pointed out by the Programme Evaluation Report, " When one considers the pattern of membership in village organizations, be they Co-operative Societies, Vikas Mandals, Gram Panchayats or Nyaya Panchayats, one clearly finds that the membership is confined to the large cultivators and that the smaller cultivators as well as landless agricultural labourers, have practically no stake in the organizations of the village." As Prof. Dube has pointed out

"The Community Development Project sought the co-operation of the existing village institutions such as the village panchayat and the adalati panchayat schools and co-operative societies. Persons holding offices in these bodies or otherwise prominent in the activities were regarded as ` Village Leader', and the development officials made a special effort to work closely with them. Some others who had contacts with politicians and officials were also included in this category and were consulted in matters connected with the project .... Thus a group of village people having contacts with the world of officials and politicians largely came to be viewed as the local agents of change .... The first mistake was in assuming that these people were the leaders .... Because of their association with the officials and the urban ways of life these leaders as a group had come to possess a special status within the community, but the average villager did not trust them without reservations. Some of the common stereotypes regarding government officials applied in a modified form to these village officials who were recognised as having a semi-government status .... Among others included in the category of ` traditional leaders' were the important and influential people in the village. Naturally most of them were from the dominant landowning group. In identifying power and status with leadership, an important and emerging aspect of group dynamics was ignored ..... The undue emphasis in working with ` traditional leaders' was construed by villagers as an effort on the part of the Government to maintain a status quo in the internal power relations within the village communities and indirectly as a step to support the domination of the landowning groups."

The same conclusion is drawn by almost all the evaluators. This reliance on the upper stratum of the village population by the Government has sociological significance which cannot be underestimated. Nay it has serious social implication in terms of the dynamics of rural society. It implies not merely a hold over the economic resources in that area by a small upper class, but also a hold over the political, social and cultural life of the community. It further means that in agrarian area, as a result of the functioning of the community development programmes, a stratum becomes strengthened economically and politically, and utilizes various institutions for its own end. It also means that in agrarian area, the Community Development Projects are creating an institutional and associational matrix wherein the Government buttresses the economically dominant classes, and in their turn, the economically dominant classes strengthen the power of the present rulers of the State. This development has dangerous significance for the all-round development of the rural society and also for the unprivileged strata of the agrarian area which constitute the bulk of the rural people. It is very unfortunate that the implication of this developmental tendency in terms of class polarization in agrarian area, and the role of the state as an agency of the upper stratum is not fully appreciated.

Almost all the evaluators have recognized that the contributions to be made by the village people are felt very burdensome by the lower sections of the people. Shramdan is the technique by which masses were asked to make contribution to the Community Development. Prof. Dube's observations on Shramdan as a voluntary movement of village self-help deserves attention

"From a close observation and analysis of four Shramdan drives ...certain points emerge that explain differences in reactions to Shramdan. The village elite, as well as the upper status groups have, on the whole, welcomed the Shramdan drives, and through them the construction and repairs of roads. They gained from it in two ways. First, the repaired and newly built roads facilitated the transport of their sugarcane and grain. Secondly, in these drives they could assert their position of leadership and prestige in the village .... because of their status they assumed supervisory roles in this work, and left the hardest and less desirable part of the job to be done by the people of the lower status and lower income groups. Even this token participation won the praise and acclaim of the officials and outside political leaders. The poorer groups, on the other hand, had no practical and visible gain from these projects. Few among them owned bullock carts, and most of them did not have large quantities of sugarcane or wheat to be transported to the urban markets. Their work did not win much praise from outsiders. All that they got often was a formal acknowledgement from the lower officials and some village leaders. They not only had to work hard, but they also lost the wages for the day, which they otherwise might have earned. This explains why many of them viewed this thing as a revival of *begar*, a practice under which influential landowners and government officials compelled the poorer people to work without wages or at nominal wages and which is now prohibited by law."

New Attachments

New associations have been launched or some of the old associations performing those functions have been claimed to be revitalized. Youth clubs, women's organizations, community centres, schools, libraries, adult education classes and social education centres form the predominant type of institutions. These organizations have emerged only in a very few areas. Excepting some institutions like Bhajan Mandalis or Akhadas at some places, very few institutions have taken roots in the villages. A large number of these institutions are operating more as paper organizations. Almost all the evaluators have indicated the failure of this section of the Community Development Programme.

Almost all critics including Taylor, Wilson, the Balwantrai Committee, Dube and V. K. R. V. Rao indicate these trends. They criticise one aspect of the programme or the other. They suggest some symptomatic remedies to cure the ills. Prof. Taylor wants thousands of trained officers, equipped with social skills to make this programme a success. The Balwantrai Committee makes certain proposals for making Village Panchayats and Panchayat Samitis the instruments for operating the Community Development Programmes. It also wants to abolish two-phased division in the form of N.E.S. and C.D. with unequal financial allocations and creation of six-year unit with larger financial allocation. Further, it wants the C.D. Programme to concentrate more on select items like increase in production rather than cultural improvements. According to them, there is nothing wrong with the major premise of the Community Development Projects, nor is there any fundamental fallacy in the postulates of the Five-Year Plans. According to these evaluators, the failure of the C.D. Projects in essence is due to one or more of the following factors: ignorance, lack of will on the part of the personnel, faulty organizational principles, fatalism of the vast bulk of the people, lack of technical and social skills, or wrong choice in selection of items. According to Prof. Dube, the main obstacles are: " (i) the general apathy of a considerable part of the village population, (ii) suspicion and distrust of officials and outsiders; (iii) failure on the part of the Project to evolve effective and adequate media of communications; (iv) tradition and cultural factors."

Are these costly projects, which do not fulfil their proclaimed major objectives, worth continuing? Are they not becoming agencies which do not merely defeat the very purpose for which they are ostensibly launched, but are actually playing the harmful role of strengthening the richer strata in the agrarian society?

In spite of the fact that considerable factual material has been collected which indicates the class structure of the agrarian society, and which also points out how the agrarian proletariat, a large number of uneconomic holders, and an enormous group of ruined artisans constitute the bulk of the rural community, none of these evaluators confronts the question, viz., how can a programme which essentially supports the upper strata of the rural population and which primarily benefits this minority in strengthening it institutionally, be called a Community Development Programme? The very name, to say the least, is deceptive.

Sociologically, the Community Development Programme is not merely proving futile in its acclaimed goals, but is becoming harmful.

Social Fabric

The large-scale development plans which are now under way in India are, in the main plans for technological and economic change. As these plans become realised, they cannot but have effect on social organization and be affected by it. Such reciprocal influence is now being felt in various spheres of Indian society. Certain broad trends of this interaction can be stated, as they are seen in the joint family, in caste structure, in village organization and in relation between villagers and government.

The joint family has long been the common form of family organization in India, sanctified in scripture and sanctioned in secular law. It consists typically of a set of men, related as fathers and sons, or brothers, together with their wives and children. The several nuclear families thus grouped together form a single unit of consumers and often also a single producing unit. The property of all is held in common under the trusteeship of the senior male; every male child is entitled to a share of the joint family property. All in the joint family are fed from a single kitchen and receive money from the family purse. Among cultivators, all in the joint family work together for the family's crop.

Formation and fission go on now as they have before but the regular tendency is toward smaller joint families. Many factors are involved in this, among them the increased chances for a man to earn a living as an individual rather than as one of a joint family team, and the decreased willingness to be subservient to the head of the family or to pool both effort and income. An added impetus toward splitting the larger joint families has come about in those areas where land reform measures have been introduced.

Features in General

A common feature of these measures is to set a limit to the amount of land which any family may own. Hence in these circumstances the men of a large joint family hasten to split up into nuclear families when such reform measures are brought about lest they be restricted to a holding uneconomical for a large family group. With formal separation there tends to be separation in fact also, at least in so far as the joint family is a producing unit. But in many cases the larger family group is a much more efficient producing unit than is the small family group. This is especially true where continuous work is required, as where ripening crops must be watched against animal and human predators and when field labour must be quickly mobilized and intensively worked, as at harvest. The larger joint family is also more apt than the smaller to be able to raise the capital necessary for implements and animals. Thus one rather unforeseen, though by no means inevitable, consequence of land reform may be a hastening of the push toward smaller families with some consequent decline in agricultural efficiency.

Caste structure has close ties with village economics. In the classical system of relations among castes in a village, the *jajmani* system, the various non-cultivating castes provided specialised services for the cultivators and received foodstuffs in return. The economic interdependence is strictly regulated by social and religious patterns which both keep the caste groups segregated in certain respects and require communication and interchange in other respects. Caste ranking and economic status were, and for many villages still are, closely linked. Caste rank is particularly manifest through ritual symbols: a group which was economically well off could acquire ritual hallmark to raise its relative position in the hierarchy.

The results of the development programmes of the last century in the fields of transportation and communication, in the spread of Western education, in the frequent switch from subsistence crops to cash crops, have all had consequences on village caste relations. But the criteria of ritual rank are not greatly changed the eating of meat and the performance of menial services are still stigmas of lower rank and ritual rank remains a main concern in the village. While there may be some relaxation of the taboos on interdining among castes there is no easing of the prohibition of intermarriage.

As the newer development programmes take effect there often is some levelling of economic differences among the villagers. The less high castes, newly advantaged, jockey for higher ritual rank and may attempt to use their new political franchise to gain both economic and ritual prerogatives for their caste.

One exception to the levelling effect of the newer development programmes must be noted. The lowest caste, those who are mainly landless labourers, often gain nothing at all from the irrigation projects and the redistribution of land. They have nothing to begin with, nothing which can be improved, no means of getting an economic start and so they remain economically as well as socially disadvantaged. The gap between them and the other villagers frequently widens rather than diminishes on account of development projects.

The changing nature of caste has effect on village social organization and on agricultural output. The social and economic systems were both relatively stable over many centuries partly because they reinforced each other. Now that both are being modified though still closely connected, changes in one may accelerate changes in the other. Thus the *jajmani* system of traditional, personal, exchange relations is being replaced by contractual, impersonal, pecuniary relations. Many cultivators who could summon sudden aid if quickly needed from among their traditional associates of other castes now can hire labour only if they have the cash. This process is a familiar one and has been going on in India for a century or more. But in recent years the full effect of the change is being widely felt.

The Departure

As the rights and obligations of one village caste to another tend to lapse, so does the whole village drift away from the ceremonial order within which these reciprocal patterns were organized and reinforced. The traditional caste system provides for a division of labour, the traditional ceremonial order stipulates how and when the various divisions co-operate and are rewarded. With the loosening of the system of economic cooperation under religious auspices there is not usually available as effective a plan of village co-operation under purely economic or political auspices, and agricultural output may decline for this reason.

Governmental agencies, of both the central and the state administrations, have attempted to encourage the growth of a new social organization in the village which would be able to cope with modern problems and could make the transition from the old order to some new procedure. Legislation has been passed in some provinces and funds provided to enable village councils, panchayats, to be formed and to function. In name, these are the same as the traditional councils which have for centuries adjudicated disputes among villagers. In manner of composition, in function, they are very different. The members of the new panchayat must be elected, must electioneer; in the old, they were accorded place by universal respect and could hardly keep that respect if they pressed their claims. The old councils were arbitrary, conserving agencies whose prime function was to smooth over or settle village friction. The new panchayats are supposed to be innovating, organizing bodies working for changes rather than conserving solidarity.

Where they have been installed, the new panchayats seem generally to be off to a shaky start. There is some tendency for them to become the battle-ground of village factionalism. Factionalism has long been a frequent disrupter of joint village action. The traditional ceremonial order provides opportunities for the healing of factional breaks by mandatory co-operation towards common ceremonial goals. With the passing of the old ceremonial order, there is not the same rejoining of those whom factional disputes have rent asunder. And village elections may become little more than ways of crystallizing each opposing and non-cooperating faction. In some villages the new panchayat is less a forum for factionalism than it is an empty form set up for the satisfaction of visiting officials. In such villages the older panchayat continues to function much as it has before.

But as a social form, it is not felt adequate by many villagers to deal with the new economic and technological influences-the procuring of irrigation water or of fertilisers, for example-and these influences reach even to relatively remote villages. Hence there is widely in Indian villages today a process of social change from the traditional forms and orders to some other forms. The newer forms may not be those proposed by legislators and planners but they are also not, it seems probable, a mere recasting of the older social system.

Status Structure

We have made sweeping generalisations regarding rural life and its problems. We have depicted village life as if the pattern was similar in all parts of the country. We have ignored the facts of alien invasions, different governments, varying religions and multiple levels of culture, as if they had little or no effect on our rural life. It is true that all parts of the country were not equally touched by social upheavals, invasions or conquests, but today we are becoming more and more aware of specific differences in different parts of the country. We know, however, the basic similarities in all villages and the personalities of villages as well. We know the common problems, and we also know the rough and ready prescriptions for our rural ills. What is needed in rural studies, today, is the shaping of effective scientific techniques of rural analysis to understand the problems of rural life in their wider contexts.

The status structure of our villages is in a fluid state. While still clinging to the traditional ways of eking out an income, the villager is today experiencing the impact of technology and competitive economy. Land is not in abundance, while the size of the family is on the increase. The artisan castes, no longer can secure a minimum level of living, out of their traditional occupation in the village and from the *jajmans* whom they still cater to. They either migrate to centres of greater opportunities, or live a precarious existence. More people today are in the grip of the money-lender than ever before and co-operative societies cannot as yet size up the want and poverty of the villages. The channels of rural finance have changed their course. The abolition of the zamindari has dimmed the halo around the heads of the high caste men. They are nervous about losing their rights-which they have enjoyed from time immemorial-and they are not prepared to give in without a struggle. Fighting tooth and nail they are trying to maintain their hold on the village. If they have lost some rights, they still have wealth, and that means power. Why should they not use their wealth in new ways to strengthen their position of importance? So that many of them have adopted money-lending as their profession, which till now was the much-maligned monopoly of the village-Bania. The breakdown of the status relations has deprived the artisan elements of the village of concessions in kind which helped now and then to relieve their chronic distress. They still yoke themselves to the village economy but they have been caught in deep furrows.

The relationship of status factors to the acceptance of innovations in dress, food and farm practices is important in the context of social change. A number of investigations carried out in various parts of the world on farm practices, for example, 'have highlighted farm-ownership, education, income, size of the farm and social participation as being associated with the adoption of improved farm practices.' Contacts with urban centres, and improved communications are helping adoption of innovations. Leaders in community affairs are not useful in dissemination of new farm practices. On the other hand innovators are not likely to be leaders in community affairs. This is an area of study that must be given due consideration in planning and action research.

We are apt to isolate village leadership in its traditional setting. In the Indian villages of the past, leaders were born, but now in the new setup it is not so. The frequency of leadership from sections or castes other than the dominant one, requires evaluation. Goods, today, are not necessarily delivered through the traditional leaders. The new leaders may not even be from the status groups, neither have they jumped into the scene by the spin of the coin. The social awareness of the people is the medium which fashions new leadership.

We have simplified the social structure of our country by equating it with the magic word 'caste'. Caste is no doubt a complex structure, but it is also a dynamic one. Three significant periods in caste history are worth mentioning. Caste as it was in the time of Manu, a fluid structure, flexible and mobile; vertical as well as horizontal features characterised caste as is understood in the context of anuloma and pratiloma marriages, i.e., marriages prescribed and those forbidden. This was the formulative period of the caste constitution. Caste in the medieval period became rigid and stereotyped. The rigidity encouraged fission, but circumscribed the chances of fusion. The challenge of the rigid caste system was met by religious revivalism in which sectarian and other types of castes emerged to accommodate deviants and aspirants after social status. A critical evaluation of the caste structure at this period would show the caste system as a cross between 'feudalism' and, the 'schism of the soul' to use a Toynbean phrase. Today caste-structure is fighting a battle of survival, as it were, and is mobilising forces and factors, that were once dormant or unintegrated. The saving factors are the not-too-clear lines of demarcation among the castes, between the higher and intermediate and between the latter and lower castes. The intermediate castes most of whom are artisans, usually bridge the disparities between the two ends of the caste ladder. The new trend in caste dynamics today, is a concerted move on the part of the backward and socially non-privileged castes to rearrange themselves on a horizontal plane instead of pressing their claims for accommodation in the hierarchical ladder. The hitherto voiceless castes are becoming articulate, even vocal, and are not prepared to accept the status differentials. The new orientation in the attitude of the non-privileged castes has already made social distance ineffective in many ways. If the trend continues, and it is likely to continue, it certainly augurs well for the future of the Indian caste structure.

Eight

Village Economy

Since economic production is the basic activity of a human aggregate, the mode of production (productive forces and social relations of production) plays a determining role in shaping the social structure, the psychology and the ideology of that human aggregate.

Rural society is based predominantly on agriculture. Village agriculture is sharply distinguished from urban industry by the fact that it is based on direct extraction from Nature by man.

Significance of Agriculture

Land is the basic means of production in the countryside. Land is a part of Nature, though made arable by human labour. From land, the rural people produce, by means of technique and their labour power, such a variety of agrarian products as food, cotton, jute, tea, coffee, tobacco and others.

Urban industry only transforms the products of agriculture into industrial products. In city factories and mills, such agricultural products as cotton, jute and sugarcane are transformed into cotton and jute cloth and sugar respectively.

This basic difference between agriculture and industry plays a significant role in shaping the social institutions, the psychology and the ideology of the rural and urban populations.

Further, the level of production and the way in which the products are distributed among the different strata of a society, determine the level of the material prosperity of the society as a whole and of the various socio-economic groups comprising it.

They also, to a very large extent, mould the institutional set up of that society as well as the cultural life of its people.

For instance, in India, the primitive nature of agriculture, the resultant low level of agricultural production and the specific types of land relations which determine the differing shares of agricultural products among the social groups composing the rural society, explain the general poverty of the rural people, their hierarchic gradation into a pyramidal system of socio-economic groups and, further, their distinct social institutions and cultural backwardness. They also largely fix their customs, conceptions, and social mores.

Production Motives

The rural sociologist should find out whether, in the given society agricultural production has for its objective the direct satisfaction of the subsistence needs of the rural aggregate or is carried on for the market and profit of the producers who do not themselves consume their products. This means whether the agricultural economy is a subsistence or a market economy.

For instance, in pre-British India, village agriculture mainly produced for meeting the needs of the village population. This subsistence village agricultural economy was transformed into a market economy during the British period. This was due to a variety of causes. The British Government created private property in land in the form of ryotwari and zamindari. In the ryotwari area, it introduced the system under which the peasant producer had to pay to the state land tax in cash instead of in kind. The land tax grew progressively heavy resulting into the increasing indebtedness of the agriculturist. In the zamindari area, the burden of increasing rent imposed on the tenant producer by the zamindar impoverished the tenant and saddled him also with the ever expanding burden of debt. Largely due to the necessity for cash for the payment of land tax, rent and debt, the agriculturist, the peasant proprietor or the tenant, was more and more constrained to produce for the market. Thus village agriculture increasingly ceased to produce for directly satisfying the needs of the village population and began to produce for the national and subsequently even world market.

There is a third and new conception of the objective of agricultural production. According to it, not only should agriculture produce to meet the needs of the community but also it should be adapted to the consciously assessed needs of the total community. The exponents of this view argue that this will not only eliminate the competitive market intervening between the producers and the consumers but will also transform agriculture into planned agriculture, a planned sector of the social economy conforming to the needs of the community. They further declare that planned agriculture together with planned industry will transform the entire social economy into a planned economy which alone would make the maximum use of the natural, the technical and human labour resources of the community possible with the result that the material wealth of society would enormously increase and hence the standard of life of the people would rise higher and higher. The rural sociologist needs to devote greater attention to this aspect of the study of agricultural production. This is because not only the technique of agriculture but also the motif of agricultural production determine the level of that production and the resultant wealth of the agrarian community and, therefore, its standard of life.

Production Techniques

The history of agriculture reveals that a variety of implements have been employed by rural communities. Generally speaking, we can divide the rural technical cultures into the following three types:

(1) *Hoe culture*: During this phase of mankind's existence, even the plough had not been invented. It was the early stage of agriculture when it was carried on only through the hoe operated by the human hand.

(2) *Plough culture*: During the next historical phase, man invented the plough. Being technically superior to the hoe, the plough enabled the agricultural community to produce more with the expenditure of the same amount of human labour power. The plough culture implied the use of animals in agricultural operations. Though our country has advanced beyond hoe culture centuries

ago, the hoe still lingers in the existing phase of plough culture in some agrarian areas.

(3) *The higher technical cultural phase of tractors and fertilizers*: The invention of power-driven machinery in modern times resulted into the production of such amazing labour-saving agricultural machines as tractors and fertilizers. Though this new agricultural technique is used on a large-scale in a number of advanced countries at present, it has not yet displaced the plough to any appreciable extent in our country.

The productivity of the labour of the agriculturist and hence the volume of agricultural products have increased in proportion to the advance of agricultural technique. The extent of the material wealth of rural society, therefore, depends mainly upon the technical basis of agriculture.

It may be noted that the power basis of agriculture has also changed in history. As pointed above, the hoe excludes the use of draft animals or any kind of power. The plough is worked with the aid of draft animals. The tractor eliminates even the necessity of draft animals and is propelled by oil power.

The technique of production also determines the division of labour among the members of a society actually engaged in the production process. It gives rise to a definite number of functions in the production process. This results in the emergence of various working groups, each of them attending to a particular function in production.

Thus we have a greater division of labour where the technique employed in production is higher. Correspondingly, we have a greater number of working groups.

Where agriculture is based on the plough, the division of labour is limited. The whole process of agricultural production in various stages is carried on by a peasant family on the basis of the simple and restricted division of labour among its members. In contrast to this, where agriculture is carried on by means of tractors and fertilizers, we have not only a larger physical unit of agriculture (land) but also a greater technical division of labour. We have then such working groups as engineers, electricians, chemists, tractor drivers and others.

The rural sociologist requires to study the various working groups determined by the technique used in agriculture as a part of the study of the rural population.

Value of Land

Next, in the course of the study of the economic life of the rural society, it is vital to understand the land or property relations within the framework of which agricultural production is carried on.

While technique strictly determines the techno-economic division of labour and the resultant number of specific working groups, it does not, as we find from our study, of history always lead to the rise of the same property relations. For instance, the plough was the technical basis of agriculture carried on within the framework of such different land relations as existing in slave and feudal societies. It has also remained the technical basis of agriculture, in modern times, in underdeveloped capitalist societies of countries like India, Burma, Indo-China, and others. Again we find that such advanced techniques as tractors and fertilizers are used in agriculture within the framework of such diametrically opposite types of land relations as capitalist and collectivist which exist in the U.S.A. and Soviet Union respectively.

Thus, while techno-economical relations based on functional division of labour correspond to the existing technique of agriculture, land relations or socio-economic relations of production do not always conform to the technique in the form of a single pattern. Hence even when agriculture is carried on with the same plough, we find such varied socio-economic groups as serfs and barons, zamindars and tenants, peasant proprietors, and labourers and others. And, further, when it is worked by tractors and other kinds of modern machinery, even then we observe such diverse groups as wage workers, capitalist landowners, agriculturists who are members of state-owned collective farms and others.

(1) The nature of land relations determines the share of various socio-economic groups associated with agriculture in the total agricultural wealth. For instance, in the zamindari area, the zamindar receives by far the

larger share of agricultural income than the cultivating tenant. The staggering disparity between the colossal income of the former and the meager income of the latter is basically due to the zamindari type of land relations. Further, the agrarian economy based upon a specific type of land relations has its own logic, its own law of development. Hence we find that the general tendency of the agrarian economic development in the zamindari zone is to accentuate the economic contrast. The cultivating tenant, in spite of a series of reforms, is being increasingly impoverished.

To take another instance, where full-fledged capitalist agriculture exists, a wage worker gets from the capitalist owner of land a wage determined by the state of the labour market.

Thus land relations determine the mode of distribution of the agricultural wealth among the various sections of the rural population just as technique determines the volume of that wealth.

(2) As a consequence of the above, land relations determine the degree of enthusiasm and interest of various groups bound up with agriculture, in the process of production.

For instance, in zamindari area, the cultivating tenant has meagre incentive to work since he has to surrender a big share of the crop, the fruit of his labour, to the zamindar and his agents. This is in contrast to the peasant proprietor in the ryotwari area, who feels appreciable incentive since he retains the whole product of his labour. However, even in his case, if he feels the burden of land tax and debt too heavy, his enthusiasm for agricultural effort would decline.

(3) Land relations play a decisive role in determining the degree of homogeneity or heterogeneity of the rural population.

In the zamindari area, the rural society is mainly divided into such groups as zamindars, non-cultivating tenants and sub-tenants, and finally cultivating tenants. In the ryotwari area, there are generally peasant proprietors of various grades and landless workers. In the case of large-scale capitalist agriculture, there exist such groups as agrarian capitalists, farm managers, technicians, wage labourers and others.

(4) The nature of land relations which determines the share of material wealth of various sections engaged in agriculture thereby also determines the respective specific weight of those sections in the social, political and cultural life of rural society. The class of rich zamindars or capitalist landlords, by virtue of its wealth can have leisure and material means whereby it can establish its hegemony over the life of rural society in all spheres. The mass of poor cultivating tenants or land labourers can hardly have any say in shaping it.

(5) The nature of land relations will also decide the degree of stability and social harmony in the agrarian area. For instance, in the zamindari area, due to the extensive contrast between the wealth of the zamindars and utter poverty of the cultivating tenants, there will exist a permanent condition of bitter struggle between the two classes. If poverty becomes unbearable, the struggle may even take forms which would undermine the stability of the existing rural society. In fact, contemporary India is rapidly becoming an amphitheatre of such struggles.

If we survey the past and the present history, we find that the rural society has been the arena of numerous struggles which had their genetic cause in the existing land relations. During the French Revolution the serfs wanted to abolish feudal land relations and become free peasant proprietors. The success of the communists in China is also largely explained by their skilful solution of the land problem.

The question of land relations has become the crucial question in all backward countries of the world today.

Thus the degree of stability or instability of the rural society is largely determined by the nature of extant land relations.

(6) Wealth is the material means to get access to education and culture specially in modern commodity society.

Land relations, by basically determining the share of various agrarian social groups in the total agricultural wealth, therefore, also decide how much scope each of these groups will have for education and culture. Land relations, thus, play a big role in determining the degree of the intellectual and cultural development of various strata of the rural people and their individual members since this development largely depends upon the education they have received and the culture they have assimilated.

The points mentioned above reveal and emphasize the great significance of land relations in moulding the economic and hence the social, the political, the intellectual, and the cultural life of the rural people.

Living Levels

The standard of life of a village community and its sections will indicate the amount of wealth at its disposal and the manner in which it is distributed among those sections. The volume of wealth of the rural community depends primarily on agriculture, and in final analysis, on the technique used in agriculture since the higher is the technique, the greater is the productivity of agriculture. Land relations determine, as we saw above, the share of various groups comprising rural society in the total agrarian wealth. Yet even where they engender sharp contrasts of wealth among these groups, the absolute share of even the lowest group will be at a high level if the total wealth of the rural aggregate, due to advanced technique of agricultural production, is considerable. For instance, in the U.S.A. where agriculture is mechanised and, therefore, creates great agrarian wealth, in spite of the fact that agrarian capitalists make millions, the income of the wage workers on land is on a much higher level than that of the agriculturist in India.

The problem of the standard of life of the rural population has been keenly studied by eminent sociologists like Sorokin, Zimmerman, Sims, Kirpatrick and others. The criteria and methods laid down by them for such a study can serve as a useful guide to the students of rural society in India.

It is observed by these scholars that the standard of life of the rural people on an average is lower than that of the urban people. This is because the income of the rural people on the average is lower than that of the urban people. "Further, the standards of living of the rural population and its various groups (owners, tenants, croppers and labourers) are more homogeneous than those of the urban classes."

It has also been noted that the standard of life of the farmers approximates more to that of the lower strata of the city population.

Though income is the primary factor determining the standard of life of a social aggregate, there are other factors also which influence it. "To be sure, income may be chiefly responsible for the existence of classes; but wholly apart from material possessions, there are class norms and values dictated by tradition." For instance, in India, the Middle class strives to adopt a standard of life according to its own specific conception of life. This is reflected in their choice of food, dress, recreations, cultural amenities and other things. Their standard of life is thus determined not merely by their economic position but also by their specific group outlook, temperament and taste. The role of caste in India as a determinant of the group standard of living demands special study.

It has been further observed that the degree of civilization existing in a society also influences the standard of life of the people. For instance, such institutions as well-furnished libraries, cultural and sport clubs, radio, telephone, cinema and theatre, swimming pools, restaurants and others, do not generally exist in the rural zone of India. Hence the standard of life of the rural people is not affected by them unlike that of the urban people.

However, due to the interaction of the rural and urban societies and the resultant growth of mutual contacts, the rural people are slowly but inevitably influenced by the urban. They begin to develop a predilection and craving for such amenities. They also tend to adopt the food and dress habits of the urban population. Bicycles, modern footwear, games like cricket and football, school's libraries, cinema, and other things associated with urban life, begin to penetrate the village. This results in gradually modifying the mode of life of the rural people.

In his study of the economic life of the rural people, the rural sociologist needs to study the impact of the more powerful influences of urban life on the rural society and hence on the standard of life of the rural people. Further, he should not take a static view of their standard of life. Human needs are not an immutable entity. They grow from phase to phase.

The Have-nots

A very big section of the rural population has been living in varying states of poverty in all countries. Even in the U.S.A., the most prosperous country of the world today, the poverty of a large stratum of rural society has become a crying problem. As Sims remarks, "Although students of rural conditions have long been aware of the existence of country slums and of disadvantaged or submerged classes, such as the share croppers of the south (U.S.A.) no one fully realised how precarious the lot of a large part of the country population was and how quickly millions could be plunged into a state of destitution until the industrial depression revealed the true situation," and further, "all in all, it is estimated that more than one-third of the rural families of the nation have suffered poverty."

When, as seen above, a large section of the rural population of even such an economically advanced country like the U.S.A. suffers from poverty, it is no wonder that chronic poverty is rampant among the agrarian population in India, an economically much less developed country.

The immense poverty of the Indian agriculturist is proverbial and presents the fundamental problem of the programme of national economic reconstruction.

The principal causes of the rural poverty in India have been, in general, laid bare by eminent Indian economists and sociologists. Primitive agricultural technique, insufficient irrigation system, land fragmentation, uneconomic holdings, overpressure on agriculture, alarming rural indebtedness and, above all, the existing land relations are some of its principal causes.

It is necessary to study the problem of poverty not merely of the rural people as a whole but also of its different strata and, that too, in detail.

Poverty adversely affects not only the health and vitality of the rural people but also explains their backward social and cultural conditions. If the rural people are ignorant, superstitious, uncultured, it is mostly because they are abysmally poor and cannot afford to pay for education. They, thereby, remain excluded from any access to scientific knowledge of the natural and social worlds imparted by educational and cultural institutions.

Economic prosperity is the basic pre-requisite for a flourishing social and cultural life. Hence the problem of rural reconstruction at a high social and cultural level is organically bound up with the problem of the eradication of rural poverty.

Participation in Politics

One of the vital problems which requires to be intelligently studied by the rural sociologist is the political life of the rural people. Writers on rural problems as well as social workers in the rural area have generally paid insufficient attention to this aspect of the rural life. They have often presumed that the agrarian population is politically almost an inert mass and have attempted to evolve and work out schemes of better villages on that premise. However, nothing is more unreal in modern times than the hypothesis of the political inertness of the rural people. When we study modern history, we find that the agrarian masses, predominantly composed of farmers, have participated in mighty political movement in a number of countries. For instance, in India, large sections of peasants and artisans supported and joined the great National Revolt of the Indian people against the British rule in 1857. Subsequently peasant struggles like the Deccan Peasant Riots and others directed both against the moneylenders and the government broke out in some parts of the country. In more recent times, increasing sections of the peasantry participated in a series of national political movements like the Non-cooperation Movement of 1919-24, Civil Disobedience Movement of 1930-34, a number of political satyagraha campaigns in different districts, Quit India Movement and others. After 1934 the peasant masses even started building their own class organizations like kisan sabhas and launched a number of struggles against the government and landlords. During and immediately after the partition of India, the peasant discontent and restlessness found a distorted political expression in bloody communal clashes which occurred in a number of provinces.

Various Dimensions

Recent history also records such peasant struggles as took place in Telangana and in portions of Bengal and Assam.

In other countries, too, the agrarian masses have taken part, sometimes even decisive, in political movements. Tens of millions of peasants participated in such world shaking revolutions as the Russian and the Chinese. Large sections of Indonesian and Burmese peasantry also took part in a series of political struggles having national independence as their objective. Peasant masses constituted the preponderant social force of the resistance movements in France, Yugoslavia, Poland, Hungary and other European countries which developed during the period of occupation of those countries by Nazi Germany. Also in recent decades, the agricultural populations of Spain, Italy, Latin American countries and others have exhibited considerable political awakening, formed sometimes their own political parties and have launched numerous political struggles.

These events explode the misconception that agrarian population is politically a passive force.

In fact, the growth of political consciousness among peasant populations and their increasing political activity are striking features of the political life of mankind today.

The agrarian areas of a number of countries have been transformed into storm centres of militant political activity of the rural people.

Typical Indian Problems

The following are the two main reasons why it becomes imperative for the rural sociologist in India to study the political life of the rural people to-day.

(1)The Constitution of the now independent India has provided universal adult suffrage to the Indian people. Tens of millions of peasants who constitute the majority of the population thereby acquire a political status. Their will expressed through the ballot box would now considerably influence the political life of the nation. This is a unique event in the long history of the Indian humanity, for, it is for the first time that the people including the rural masses have secured the democratic right to determine who will rule them. The theory of the divine right of the king or a "providence ordained "imperialist power to rule the people has been ousted by that of the democratic right of the sovereign people to determine their political destiny. Universal adult suffrage serves as a powerful ferment in the life of the rural people making them politically conscious to a phenomenal degree. It is a momentous event in the history of the rural society.

The new situation has posed a number of fresh questions for the rural sociologist. How will the rural people, illiterate, ignorant and superstitious in the main, exercise their franchise? What social, economic, and ideological influences will determine their voting? What types of political organisations will the peasant masses throw up for implementing a programme embodying their conception of a good society by legislative means? What political parties will emerge in the rural area, corresponding to various layers of the existing stratified rural society? What repercussions will take place in the sphere of social and ideological life of the rural people due to the mass-scale growth of political consciousness and activity among them due to their acquisition of adult suffrage? How will this political equality affect caste and other social as well as cultural and economic inequalities?

The study of these new problems will form an integral part of the study of the Indian rural society.

(2) A proper understanding of the political life of the rural people is necessary also for another reason. Unlike in the pre-British period, the modern state plays a decisive role in determining the life of the rural society. During the pre-British phase, the village, as we have seen previously, was an autarchic and almost autonomous unit. During the British period, it experienced a basic transformation. Its self-contained subsistence economy based on self-sufficient agriculture and artisan industry was undermined.

Further, the British Government established a centralized State with an administrative machinery which penetrated the hitherto autonomous village. This basically changed the political physiognomy of the village. It became a unit of the countrywide political and administrative system.

The consequences of this economic and political transformation were far-reaching. The village population no longer lived an almost hermetically seated existence but was drawn into the wider whirlpool of the national and international economic and political life. Thenceforward the economic, political, and other problems of the rural community had to be considered in the wider context of national and world politics and economy as well as of the policies of the Central Government.

Major Issues

A systematic study of the rural political life may be made on the following lines:

(a) The study of the governmental machinery in the rural area.
(b) The study of the non-governmental political organizations in the rural area.
(c) The study of the political behaviour of the rural people and its various sections.

A few observations on each of these are made below

(a) Governmental Machinery

The study of the governmental machinery can be divided into two parts:

(i) the study of the structure of the administration and its functioning within the village and
(ii) the study of the administrative machinery of larger units like Talukas Districts, Regions and States.

In the pre-British period, when the state did not interfere in the life of the village beyond claiming a portion of the village produce as land revenue and occasionally levying troops, the village administration was carried on by the village panchayat composed of elected or customary representatives of various castes, generally elders of the castes, or by village headman with the panchayat as the consultative body. The village panchayat was the link between the village population and the higher authority. The panchayat and the headman maintained peace in the village, settled disputes among the villagers, looked after the sanitation and other matters of common concern of the village population, determined and collected the share of the farmer family in the collective land-revenue to be paid to the State on behalf of the village, and also regulated the use of collectively owned pasture land and forest area in the periphery. Thus from the standpoint of administration the village was autonomous.

The administrative, judicial, policing, and economic functions of the village were, as seen above, performed by the village panchayat and the headman. So far as the personal, social and religious life of the village people was concerned, the customary law governing it was operated by various caste councils which regulated the behaviour-patterns of respective castes.

The disintegration of empires did not affect the administrative autonomy and general internal life of the village. This was because the State, even the Imperial State, restricted its intervention in the internal affairs of the village to the mere gathering of the tribute and the levying of the troops generally in war time. The State or the king looked after the inter-village administration and other vital matters affecting the people of the kingdom as a whole such as coinage, irrigation, and the maintenance and development of the network of roads.

With the advent of the British rule in India, as we have stated before, the Indian society began to experience a fundamental economic and political transformation. The new administrative machinery evolved and organized by Britain in India supplanted the old one which had functioned for centuries with little variation. The new state, the organ of British rule in India, stationed its own revenue, judicial, police and other officials in the village. The village lost its administrative autonomy and the caste councils, their penal powers. In the new political set up, the village became the basic administrative unit of a hierarchically graded countrywide administrative system.

The local village officials were independent of any control over them by the village population. Thus if the forest had to be cleared, wells to be dug or roads to be built in the village, it was not now the village panchayat which independently and of its own will evolved a scheme and mobilized the village population for implementing that scheme. It was the new village administration, itself a unit of the national administrative system and subject to the latter's control, that decided those questions.

Henceforward the social, political and economic life of the rural people, was largely determined by the State. Village problems became an integral part of the total problems of the nation and could not be solved in isolation by the initiative of the village community.

The character and policies of the government appreciably determined how those problems would be solved and hence what type of life the rural people would live.

After independence, the Indians retained the centralized State apparatus elaborated by the British in India. The rural sociologist needs to study the working of the administrative system inherited from the British in the new national situation. It should be noted that this administrative system had been devised by them as a lever to suppress or restrict the initiative of the people. A critical evaluation of this system from the standpoint of the solution of such problems of the rural population as their general economic advance, universal spread of education, cheap expeditious justice, awakening and play of the local initiative within the framework of the national plan, and others, has, therefore, to be made and a scheme of reconstruction of the existing administrative system evolved.

The study of the administrative system raises the following problems

(i) How far the administrative machinery is responsive to the opinions and wishes of the people.

(ii) How far the people are associated with it and participate in its functioning.

(iii) How far it is cheap, efficient, and sensitive to the problems of the people.

(b) Non-Governmental Political Organizations

It is further necessary to note that the governmental activity is only one aspect of the political life of the village population.

Non-governmental political organizations also have emerged and are functioning in the rural area in modern times. Political parties thrown up by the rural people are principal among them.

It is very essential to study the various political parties operating in the rural area. These parties express the specific interests and aspirations of various classes and socio-economic groups composing of rural people such as landlords, tenants, land labourers, peasant proprietors and others. They voice their desire and determination to secure political power and use it to modify or overhaul the existing social system in consonance with their own interests and social objectives. The rural area becomes the arena of struggle between these parties. To have a concrete composite picture of the political life of the rural people it is, therefore, vitally necessary to study closely the ideologies, the programmes and the policies of these political parties and trace their roots. The general elections recently held in our country on the basis of the new Constitution have revealed the extensive growth of political consciousness among the rural people, the expansion of the old political parties and the emergence of new ones in the rural area and, above all, large scale participation of the rural people in the elections. Paradoxically enough, voting in some rural areas even exceeded that in urban zones. Further, large sections even of illiterate peasant women registered their vote, an event of great political significance.

The student of rural society should also study the changing political moods of the rural people and the resultant increase or decline in the influence of different political parties among them. He should further investigate, by means of a sociological analysis, the causes which bring about the rise and fall of political parties in the rural area. He can predict on the basis of such a study the tendency of the development of the political life of the rural people. Such a study is very vital since the victory of a political party in a country implies its capture of government machinery which it intends to use as an instrument to alter or replace the existing socio-economic structure of society in the interest of the class or the group which it represents. For instance, in India, the Socialist or the Communist Party desires to win political power so that it can use it to abolish capitalism and establish socialism. The Hindu

Mahasabha aspires for political power to establish the Hindu Raj and reconstruct Indian society in conformity with the Hindu ideals. The Indian National Congress, the ruling party in India is working for a society based on a mixed social economy with two sectors, private and state owned, and Secular democracy.

(c) Political Behaviour of Rural People

Another aspect of the rural political life deserving study is the political behaviour of the rural people. The study must be made from two angles.

Welfare Programmes

First, the rural sociologist should study the various programmes which various strata of the rural people or the rural people as a whole are striving to fulfil.

These programmes will disclose the basic social aspirations and the immediate needs of the rural people and its various sections. The nature of these aspirations and needs will also disclose the psychologies and ideologies of the rural people and its constituent groups at a given historical moment.

For instance, some decades back, the cultivating tenants in the zamindari tract considered the zamindari system as immutable and merely desired and asked for a humane treatment from the zamindars. Subsequently, increasing sections of them questioned the zamindari system itself and put forth the demand for the abolition of landlords and transfer of land to themselves. They also aspired for a workers' and peasants' Raj which they previously did not even conceive of.

The rural sociologist is required to concentrate special attention on the study of the programme and the political behaviour of peasantry since it constitutes the major section of the rural people and, therefore, would exert decisive influence on the future of the rural society. The peasant movements in a number of countries in recent times have been transforming the entire social, political, and economic landscape in the agrarian area.

Secondly, the rural sociologist should make a thorough study of the methods which the rural people have been adopting to realize their aims.

Programme Implementation

Different sections of the rural people make use of different methods to implement their programmes at various times.

Indian rural society provides a classical laboratory for the study of a rich variety of these methods. The following are the principal among them.

1. Petitioning.
2. Voting.
3. Demonstrations and marches.
4. Hijrats or mass emigrations.
5. Satyagraha, passive resistance.
6. No-rent and no-tax campaigns.
7. Spontaneous elemental revolts.
8. Organized armed struggles.
9. Guerilla warfare.

Peasant populations in different countries in the present epoch have been employing diverse methods to implement their programmes. In India, too, as previously stated, these varied methods have been used in varying degrees by the agrarian population in different parts of the country in different periods. In the second half of the nineteenth century a section of the Maharashtrian peasantry took to spontaneous armed struggle known as the Deccan Peasant Riots against moneylenders and the government. Mahatma Gandhi organized a number of no-tax campaigns of the peasantry in various parts of India. Subsequently a series of peasant demonstration and marches have been organized by the Kisan Sabhas and the Socialist Party of India. In Telangana, a combination of the methods of open armed struggle and guerilla warfare was adopted by the peasantry led by the Communist Party only a few years back.

In the two General Elections held very recently, the rural population including millions of peasants, men and women have utilized the method of the ballot box and elected representatives to the State Assemblies and the House of the People.

Thus the rural people have used at various times parliamentary as well as extra-parliamentary methods of struggle to achieve their aims and demands.

A sociological analysis of the programmes of the rural people as a whole and its constituent strata as well as of the varied methods employed by them specially becomes necessary when the agrarian society is in a state of deep crisis and is simmering with great discontent of the rural masses in the major part of the world including India.

Effect of Land Relations

Since agriculture is the pivot of the rural economy and land is the most important means of production in agriculture, the struggle between the various groups of the rural society has mainly revolved round the question of the ownership of land. As has been almost universally recognized by sociologists and statesmen all over the world, the problem of land relations is the basic problem in all backward or semi-backward countries of Asia and even of some countries of Europe like Spain and Italy. The peasant movements in those countries have had as their basic objective the abolition of feudal or semi-feudal forms of land ownership and transfer of land to the actual tillers.

Struggle over the question of land has, in fact, provided the main dynamic to the political life of the rural society in the present period.

Different sections of the rural people hold different views on the land problems which are determined by their differing specific position in the socio-economic structure of the rural society. The view-points of the landlords, the tenants, the land labourers, the peasant proprietors, and the moneylenders and the merchants to whom the peasant debtors have mortgaged their land, vary widely. The divergence of views which expresses divergence of material interests of these groups, is the genetic cause of the economic and political struggles between them, struggles which now-a-days form an essential part of the political life of the rural people.

This inter-group struggle among the various sections of the rural people revolving round the land problem has not been adequately and scientifically studied hitherto by the student of the rural society. A historically progressive solution of the land problem is a crucial need since the future of the rural society, its retrogression of further advance, depends upon it.

The Caste Factor

In the Indian rural area where the occupational homogeneity of the caste is not still seriously undermined and where caste consciousness among the people remains stronger than in the urban centre, caste influences the political life to a much greater extent than it does in towns and cities. In recent times, however, due to the growth of class consciousness among various groups into which the rural population is divided on economic lines, the influence of caste on the political life is slowly diminishing. For instance, non-Brahmin landlords will politically ally with Brahmin landlords rather than with his non-Brahmin tenants since both the Brahmin and the non-Brahmin landlords stand for the defence of landlordism, their common economic interest. Similarly, the Brahmin and the non-Brahmin tenants will more and more come together and form a Kisan Sabha or a peasant party with the programme of abolition of landlordism and transfer of land to the tillers of land, both Brahmin and non-Brahmin.

In India, where the old caste system of the Hindus still exists and is strong, special attention should be paid to its role in determining political life. Often even when a caste is not occupationally homogeneous and does not, therefore, correspond to a socio-economic group, the caste allegiance among its members is so strong that they may politically support caste leaders who belong to another socio-economic group.

It should, however, be noted that, due to historical reasons, the caste and the socio-economic group often correspond to a great extent in various parts of the country. For instance, a good proportion of the farmers-tenants in Maharashtra happen to belong to the non-Brahmin caste while a good proportion of the landlords to the Brahmin caste. Due to this the party of the peasantry has an overwhelmingly non-Brahmin social composition. This often blurs the fact that, judged from the standpoint of the basic aim and demands of the organization, it is the party of a socio-economic group, a class. Caste in this case obscures the class content of the party. The specific weight of caste in the political life of the rural people is still great and the rural sociologist has to assess it carefully.

Nine

Agriculture Sector

Until recent decades, agriculture in India had seldom been regarded as a business enterprise. It has been looked upon merely as a source of meager livelihood for the mass of petty peasants, who carry on production chiefly for subsistence and largely with family labour. They are of course known to be working under severe handicaps since the classes of landlords, moneylenders, and traders oppress and exploit them brutally and claim all their produce beyond a bare subsistence for the family and the cattle, often not even that. But they are generally regarded as insulated against the operation of the laws of the free market, and beyond the orbit of economic processes of commercialization and monetization, since they are believed to have little to sell in the market for money or invest in agriculture except on the fringes.

Old and Simple

This view of Indian agriculture has conjured up a rather simplified image of Indian agrarian society. On the top are seen only the layers of intermediaries, moneylenders, and traders, and at the bottom a mass of small peasants, more or less equal and homogeneous in their land and produce and suffering from the burdens of rack rent, usurious interest rates, and middlemen's profits in trade. The solutions derived from this image also have an appearance of naivete. It is perhaps believed that if only the intermediaries are eliminated rent-burdens reduced, interest charges regulated through co-operatives and middlemen's profits brought down through co-operative marketing, there will prevail a regime of social and economic harmony in Indian villages. And this harmonious mass of small peasants, aided with improved seeds, fertilizers, irrigation, credit, and extension services, and somehow persuaded to join the farming co-operatives, would be able to march forward smoothly towards economic prosperity and socialism.

This image of Indian agriculture might have been close to realities at some remote time in the past. But it holds sway over most minds today as if these realities have remained unchanged. However, in recent years, for the first time, ample data have become available which provide an altogether different picture of contemporary realities in Indian agriculture. These data show that this view of Indian agriculture is at best facile, and partial. The realities are far more complex. An attempt has been made in this paper to present these data and discuss some of their implications.

All recent studies about Indian agriculture strike at the root of the mythical harmony and homogeneity of Indian agrarian society. They reveal that it is composed not merely of intermediaries, money-lenders, and traders or of a mass of petty peasants, more or less homogeneous in their social and economic conditions, but of a peasant mass, characterised by a wide hetero-geneity, and bitter mutual strife. They show that the conditions of life of peasants, vary widely not merely from region to region or village to village due to natural factors but even from farm to farm and peasant to peasant within the village, due to socio-economic compulsions.

The farming community of an average Indian village in these studies is found to be composed of several strata of cultivators, highly differentiated from each other in respect of the size of land owned or cultivated, number of draught and milch cattle possessed, nature and amount of capital invested in farming, types of tools and implements used, amount of family or hired labour employed, techniques of cultivation practised, extent of surplus produce sold in the market, amount of gain or loss from farming business and the volume of savings or deficits made. Moreover, the studies also reveal that these strata are no longer the 'parallel social strata' of H. S. Maine's times which were scarcely distinguishable from each other except in the length of time over which they had been absorbed in the village community. On the contrary, they are today very much unlike each other in almost all aspects of their economic and social life. They present the curious spectacle of being engaged in a bitter economic and social strife which affects not only their mutual social relations but also their economic fortunes, standards of living and social welfare. And if one has to grasp the essence of contemporary developments in Indian agriculture, which often appear to pull into contrary directions, one has to look upon Indian agriculture not as a sector aggregate of small, uneconomic and subsistence peasant units of production but as one in which production units of different types and sizes with wide differences in their character of farming, techniques of cultivation, forms of employment of labour power, profitability, saving, investment and consumption, compete with each other and in which laws of the free market operate sluggishly but as ruthlessly as in the other sectors of the Indian economy. The following paragraphs illustrate these aspects with data.

The first and the foremost basis of differentiation amongst the peasants which causes differentiation amongst them even in other aspects, is the ownership and cultivation of land. The distribution of owned land in present day India is 'extremely concentrated with a small minority owning most of the land'. During last few years, three nation-wide surveys, viz. the National Sample Survey, the First Agricultural Labour Enquiry and the Census of Landholdings, have thrown up a mass of data on the pattern of land ownership in India. All these surveys reveal a high degree of differentiation amongst present households in respect of their ownership holdings, as shown in the following Table.

Distribution of Ownership Holdings amongst Rural Households According to size-groups Crop Season (Percentages)

	Household Ownership Holdings			
Size-group (acres)	P.C. of holdings to the total	Cumulative P.C. of holdings	p. c. of area to total area owned	Cumulative percentage of area
0.00*	23.09	-	-	
0.01—0.99	24.17	47.26	1.37	-
1.00—2.49	13.98	61.24	4.86	6.23
2.50—4.99	13.49	74.73	10.09	16.32
5.00—9.99	12.50	87.23	18.40	34072
10.00—24.99	9.17	96.40	29.11	63.83
25.00—49.99	2.66	99.06	18.63	82.46
50.00 or above	0.94	100.00	17.54	100.00
Total	100.00	-	100.00	-

* Includes households owning an area of .005 acres or less

Thus, while at the bottom about three-fourths of all rural households own less than 5 acres of land, and hold less than one-sixth of the total area owned, on the top, one-fourth of all rural households hold 83.68 per cent of the total area in size-groups above 5 acres. Even amongst them, 12.77 per cent of all the rural households hold as much as 65.28 percent of the total owned area in size-groups of more than 10.00 acres. And in the collection of data, ownership of land was defined as 'the right of permanent heritable possession with or without right to transfer the title' which means that even secure tenants of the State or of private individuals, who enjoyed rights, of permanent heritable possession, have been included as owners.

The data of household ownership holdings pertain to the year 1953-54, when the abolition of intermediaries in most parts of India was either in progress or almost completed. Thus ownership of land has remained so concentrated despite the abolition of intermediaries. This may be due to an aspect of ownership which may be noted. Before the abolition of intermediaries, ownership of land was generally vested in a heterogenous class of intermediaries and was very uneven and highly concentrated. It is usually thought that these ownership holdings were almost entirely cultivated by tenants, and the intermediaries were merely a class of functionless parasites. While it was true for the large bulk of land of the intermediaries, they also held some land as their Sir and Khudkashtland unevenly distributed on which they could carry on cultivation with their family labour or hired labour, and in which no tenancy rights could arise, even though a small part of these lands were let out to tenants. The bulk of these lands was cultivated by the zamindars personally with family labour or hired labour.

The average size of Sir and Khudkasht land varied widely between different zamindars. For instance in U. P. it ranged over 1.09 acre to 280.05 acres per zamindar. With such wide differences in the extent of Sir, it was natural that the Sir lands also should have been let out especially when there were no restrictions on leasing. Nevertheless, it may be emphasised that most zamindars engaged in direct cultivation on their Sir and Khudkasht lands with their own family labour or hired labour, in addition to realising rents from their tenants. Confronted with the prospect of abolition of their privileges as landlords a couple of years before the advent of Independence, the zamindars took measures to expand the area under Sir and Khudkasht cultivation to retain the maximum possible area for personal cultivation, and not let it become the property of the State. The age-old struggle of the land-lords and tenants for land was thus left by the government to be fought between themselves for some years before they enacted and implemented legislation taking over the intermediaries' lands.

As a result, while the State acquired a substantial area in ownership, the zamindars also retained large areas, as unevenly distributed as before. And not many tenants acquired ownership rights by paying compensation. Consequently, no significant change in the distribution of owned land took place after the zamindari abolition.

However, an important result, generally unnoticed and scarcely written about, has been that the ex-zamindars have been forced into a new way of life, and are on their way towards changing their character as a class. Deprived of the sources of land rent and prohibited from leasing out Sir lands, they are obliged to take even more interest in direct cultivation of land, and gradually convert themselves into peasant proprietors or capitalist farmers depending on the size of their holdings, and their social and economic position.

Observation and Scanning

A close examination of the laws relating to abolition of zamindari in most States suggests that the governments have gone out of their way to provide for their gradual conversion into cultivators of their own lands by making special provisions for resumptions, evictions, by leaving numerous loopholes and gaps in the land laws, and by delaying implementation. Provision of compensation is also a means to provide them with capital for investment in agriculture. Measures for imposition of ceilings and the manner of their implementation are also devised to compel them to take up farming by leaving only as much land with them as may be cultivated with hired labour on the basis of the technology in vogue, and insufficient for being leased out.

Of course, all intermediaries have not responded alike to these measures. Nor have they all been affected alike since the majority are only petty intermediaries with small holdings. But the bulk of the land retained for self-cultivation is in the hands of a small minority and their conversion into entrepreneur farmers depends on a host of factors, such as the availability and extent of non-farm sources of income, caste prejudices and attitudes towards cultivation, and personal competence to take up various tasks of agricultural enterprise. And for these reasons, variations arise in different regions of the country in the extent and manner in which this small minority takes to self-cultivation.

However, several careful observers of the Indian rural economy have drawn attention to the change in the position of the ex-intermediaries since their abolition. For instance, Daniel and Alice Thorner write:

> ...there are cases where these ex-landlords have used the money paid them as compensation for the taking over of their lands to buy tractors and go in for modern-style agriculture.

Dr. A. M. Khusro, summarising the group discussion held at the Annual Conference of the Indian Society of Agricultural Economics at Pilani, observed that:

> In Punjab and U. P. a substantial fraction of ex-zamindars who became bhumidars or resumed their lands is known to have taken to managerial type of cultivation and a new brand of farming, often termed 'capitalist farming', seems to have been emerging.

Similarly Dr. Otto Schiller has remarked that:

> ...the number of tractors in India has increased many of them are being introduced by big landowners who have become aware of the great possibilities offered by modern techniques. With the help of tractors, they have started to farm land which previously was cultivated by tenants. As a result some of the tenants have had either to work for the landowner on a hire basis or to look for other employment unless they could find other land which they could lease.

Conversion Procedure

This process of conversion of erstwhile intermediaries into 'capitalist farmers' has developed unevenly and at varying speed in different regions of the country. But it has created pre-conditions for vital changes in the agrarian economy and its functioning. By narrowing the gap between ownership and cultivation of land, it has considerably diminished the scope for rack renting of the tenants in future, except covertly under the law, and provided them a sense of security. But, at the same time, it has helped the distribution of total cultivated area remain highly unequal and aggravated the differentiation of peasants in respect of the size of their cultivation. The following Table shows the distribution of cultivated area in India.

Distribution of operational (cultivated) holdings amongst Rural Households according to size-groups Crop season (Percentages)

	Household Operational Holdings			
Size-groups (acres)	Percentage of holdings to the total	Cumulative percentage of holdings	Percentage of area the total	Cumulative to percentage of holdings
0.00*	10.96	-	-	-
0.01—0.99	31.12	42.08	1.20	1.20
1.00—2.49	14.07	56.15	4.38	5.58
2.50—4.99	15.08	71.23	10.02	15.60
5.00—9.99	14.19	85.42	18.56	34.16
10.00—24.99	10.36	95.78	29.22	63.38
25.00—49.99	3.12	98.90	19.54	82.92
50.00 and above	1.00	100.00	17.08	100.00
Total:	100.00	-	100.00	-

It is evident that the distribution of cultivated area also is concentrated in the hands of a small minority. At the bottom, as many as 71.23 per cent households cultivate only 15.60 per cent of the total cultivated land in size-groups of less than 5 acres, while at the top, a small minority of 14.48 per cent households operate upon 65.85 per cent of the total cultivated area in size groups of 10 acres and above.

The pattern of distribution of operational holdings is quite close to that of the ownership holdings. And the bold fact emerges that concentration of ownership in land signifies simultaneously a concentration of the operated area. How little has been the change in this pattern as a result of zamindari abolition is shown by the data regarding distribution of cultivated area prior to and after abolition of zamindari in some sampled villages of Western, Central and Eastern U. P. as follows:

Percentage distribution of cultivating households and cultivated area according to size of holdings before and after zamindari abolition in sample villages of U.P

Before Zamindari Abolition				
Size-group	Percentage of house-holds	Percentage of area	Cumulative percentage of house-holds	Cumulative percentage of area
Less than 5 acres	51.53	16.95	51.53	16.95
5 — 15 acres	37.27	40.17	88.80	57.12
15 acres and above	11.20	42.88	100.00	100.00

After Zamindari Abolition				
Size-group	Percentage of house-holds	Percentage of area	Cumulative percentage of house-holds	Cumulative percentage of area
Less than 5 acres	51.89	18.25	51.89	18.25
5 — 15 acres	37.39	43.55	89.28	61.80
15 acres and above	10.72	38.20	100.00	100.00

Cultivation Practice

Let us examine whether cultivation on such a highly differentiated pattern of operational holdings would really be with family labour and for subsistence, and how far, so long as this pattern remains substantially intact, the objectives of agrarian policy laid down by the Congress Agrarian Reforms Committee can be really achieved. The extent of use of family labour on different size-groups of holdings largely depends upon the number of household members. The following Table shows the relationship between the size of operational holdings and the average household size in the respective size-groups.

In the following Table, the average household size shows an increasing trend with the increase in the size of household operational holding. But the increase in household size is much less (only a little more than twofold) relatively to the increase in the size of household operational holding (about 50 fold).

Average household size by size of household operational holdings

Size of Operational Holdings (acres)	Average Household Size
0.00	3.91
0.01- 0.99	4.14
1.00- 2.49	4.81
2.50- 4.99	5.24
5.00- 7.49	5.76
7.50- 9.99	6.16
10.00-14.99	6.34
15.00-19.99	6.76
20.00-24.99	6.86
25.00-29.99	7.15
30.00-49.99	7.23
50.00 and above	8.30
Average	5.01

If we assume that the proportion of family workers in an average household size of 5.01 is 2-0 and apply this proportion uniformly to all size-groups and compute the operated area per family worker in different size-groups dividing the average size of household operational holding by the number of family workers, we get the following result :-

Average size of holdings, Average number of workers and operated area per worker according to size-groups of household operational holdings

Size-group (Acres)	Average size of holding*	Average number of family workers per household	Operated area per family worker
0.00	-	1.56	-
0.01- 0.99	0.21	1.65	0.13
1.00- 2.49	1.69	1.92	0.83
2.50- 4.99	3.62	2.09	1.73
5.00- 7.49	6.12	2.30	2.66
7.50- 9.99	8.68	2.46	3.53
10.00-14.99	12.18	2.53	4.81
15.00-19.99	17.29	2.70	6.40
20.00-24.99	22.21	2.74	8.11
25.00-29.99	27.40	2.85	9.61
30.00-49.99	37.98	2.89	13.14
50.00 and above	83.54	3.31	25.24
Average	5.43	2.00	2.71

It is evident that the availability of cultivated land in different size-groups of holdings varies widely between 0.13 to 25.24 acres per family worker. In the higher size-groups of holdings, it is so large that family workers would find it impossible to cultivate it only by themselves and would necessarily depend on the regular use of hired labour. Moreover, if the family workers of households with large operational holdings prefer to abstain from physical participation in agricultural operations for reasons of their traditional status as zamindars, caste, etc, and remain content only with supervision and management, the need for hired labour is further aggravated.

From the data collected in the Farm Management Studies, one finds that the use of hired labour increases with an increase in the size of operational holdings, as, for instance, is shown in the following Table:-

Percentage classification of farm labour into family and hired labour on some sampled holdings in U. P. (Survey Sample).

Size-groups of holdings (acres)	Percentage contribution by		Total
	Family Labour	Hired Labour	
Below 5.0	87.8	12.2	100.0
5.0-10.0	79.2	20.8	100.0
10.0-15.0	68.2	31.8	100.0
15.0-20.0	58.0	42.0	100.0
20.0 and above	47.0	53.0	100.0

Now, if we regard the optimum work unit for an average household-sufficient to provide full employment for all the family workers to be, on the average, between 7.5 acres and 10.0 acres, then, under the present distribution of operational holdings, cultivation on 65.84 per cent of the total cultivated area in India must necessarily be done with the regular use of hired labour, permanent or temporary, on cash or kind wages. And it is no wonder that India had 17.9 million agricultural labour households in 1950-51 which constituted 30.39 per cent of all rural households and whose major source of livelihood was wage-labour in agriculture. Amongst them, bulk of the permanent farm servants were found to be employed on holdings of 10 acres or above in size, as is shown in the following Table.

From the Table, it is evident that 64.3 per cent of total permanent farm servants are employed on farms of 10.0 acres or more, and most of the remaining, employed on farms of less than 10 acres must be usually on holdings of small intermediaries or others who either do not touch the plough for reasons of caste, traditional status as zamindars or personal incapacity, or are engaged in non-farm occupations and get their holdings cultivated by permanent farm workers.

Percentage distribution of households, operated area and permanent farm servants by size-groups of operational holding in India (July 1953-June 1954)

Operational Holding Size (Acres)	Percentage of total number of households	Percentage of total operated area	Percentage of total farm servants
0-00 (a)	10.9	0.0	0.0
0.01-2.49	45.2	5.9	6.5
2.50-4.99	15.5	10.6	9.6
5.00-7.49	8.8	10.1	10.4
7.50-9.99	5.5	9.0	9.2
10.00-14.99	5.5	12.8	13.5
15.00-19.99	3.0	9.7	10.1
20.0 and above	5.6	41.9	40.7
Total	100.0	100.0	100.0

(a) Includes households who operate 0.005 acres or less

1. Total number of households = 63,532,000
2. Total operated area = 335,711,000 acres
3. Total No. of farm servants = 7,523,852

It thus appears that use of hired labour in Indian agriculture is not merely on the fringes or marginal but wide-spread. And the prevailing pattern of distribution of operational holdings makes it impossible for the small minority of farm operators (14.8 per cent) who hold about two-thirds of the total operated area (65.84 per cent) to cultivate their holdings merely with their own resources of family labour and necessitates regular use of permanent hired labour in farm operations.

Now let us examine whether agricultural production on the bulk of arable land is carried on for subsistence or for sale. If we estimate the amount of land (of average productivity) required to produce average foodgrain requirements for the average household in different size-groups holdings, we get the following result:-

Estimates of land sufficient to produce household foodgrains requirements in different size-groups of holding and land producing crops for sale

Size-Groups (acres)	Average size of household operational holding	Average household size	Require-ment of food grains for an aver-age house-hold per year	Average amount of land suffi-cient to produce foodgrains require-ments household.	Amount of land produc-tion on which is likely to be for the market.
0.00	-	3.91	1632	2.36	-2.86
0.01- 0.99	0.21	4.14	1728	3.03	-2.82
1.00- 2.49	1.69	4.81	2008	3-52	-1.83
2.50- 4.99	3.62	5.24	2188	3.83	-0.21
5.00- 7.49	6.12	5.76	2405	4.21	1.91
7.50- 9.99	8.68	6.16	2572	4.50	4.18
10.00-14.99	12.18	6.34	2647	4.64	7.54
15.00-19.99	1729	6.76	2822	4.94	12.35
20.00-24.99	22.21	6.86	2864	5.02	17.19
25.00-29.99	27.40	7.15	2985	5.23	22.17
30.00-49.99	37.98	7.23	3018	5.29	32.69
50.00 and above	83.54	8.30	3465	6.07	77.47
Average	5.43	5.01	2092	3.66	1.77

From this Table certain interesting conclusions emerge. First of all, we find that according to our estimates, 67.0 per cent of an average household operational holding would have to be devoted for the production of the foodgrains requirements of an average size household. And thus an average peasant household would have too little land to produce any substantial amount of crops for the market. But if we look at the estimates for the different size-groups, it is evident that households with operational holdings of less than 5 acres (71.23 per cent of all rural households, and operating only 15.60 per cent of the total operated area) would not have land sufficient even to produce their foodgrains requirements. But house-holds with holdings of 10 acres or more (14.58 of all rural households and operating 65.84 per cent of total operated area) would be devoting more than 50.0 per cent of their total holding to the production of crops for the market. It would thus appear that crop production on about two-thirds of the total land is mainly for the market.

In fact, even on holdings below 5 acres, cultivators of which do not have sufficient land for producing their foodgrains requirements, crop production is likely to be for sale. In the first instance, these households are compelled to make 'distress sale' of their produce to meet their money obligations like land revenue, rent and debt service, and to purchase such necessities of life as salt, kerosene and cloth, and for that reason, it has been estimated that the holders of land below 5.0 acres sell a relatively larger proportion of their produce than the cultivators of large holdings. Moreover, these cultivators, in the absence of adequate availability of foodgrains requirements for the household, try to raise cash crops with the help of which they purchase foodgrains for consumption. Such is the situation in areas like Eastern U. P. where cultivators of lands even below an acre or a half raise sugarcane and purchase paddy from fair price shops. In case they resort to neither of these expedients, they depend on money incomes from non-farm sources, like wage-labour in agriculture or non-farm small jobs outside the village or petty trade. In fact, it has been found in most recent studies that small cultivators generally take recourse to subsidiary occupations. For instance, we read in the Report of the All India Rural Credit Survey:

Not Independent

The smaller the holding he (the cultivator) cultivates, the more is his dependence on other forms of earnings; the small cultivator, for instance, has often to resort to carting or agricultural labour. It appears that it is only a small section of the farming community cultivating 14.19 per cent of all rural households and operating in all 18.56 per cent of the total operated area, and holding lands in size-groups of 5.0 to 10.0 acres that devotes more than half of its operational holding size to the production of its own foodgrains requirements. But on the remaining 81.44 per cent of the operated area, particularly on the 65.84 per cent held in size-groups of 10 acres or more, crop-production is generally for the market.

Thus, it is evident that the character of farming, whether farming is based on family labour or wage labour, and whether crop-production is for subsistence or for the market-depends essentially on the size of operational holding, and that over bulk of the land, operated by a small minority of all rural households in size groups of 10 acres or more, is characterised by regular use of wage-labour and production for the market.

Let us now analyse the economics of the farming business in the light of the differentiation in operational holdings, and the characteristics of farming, analysed in the foregoing paragraphs. So far, only a few studies were available in which farming as a business enterprise was examined. But since these studies pertained only to a few selected holdings in small local areas, and there were wide differences in the concepts used and methods followed for collection, tabulation and analysis of data, they could hardly be used to derive general inferences about the economic efficiency of cultivation in different parts of the country. However, in recent years, a series of investigations with uniform concepts, methods and proformas were conducted into the economics of farm management in 'six' typical regions of peasant agriculture' in the States of U.P., Punjab, West Bengal, Madhya Pradesh, Bombay, and Madras. These have provided valuable and useful data for our purpose. From these studies one can derive a fairly general picture of the economic aspects of farming business in different States of India.

Efficient Economically

These studies strikingly reveal that the economic efficiency of the farming business depends to a considerable extent on the size of the operational holding. In all States, the size of the farm has been found to have a decisive influence on the nature and extent of capital employed, forms of employment of labour, techniques of cultivation, input output coefficients, profitability or remunerativeness of the farming business, savings and consumption expenditure of the farming household and the nature and extent of capital formation on the farm. And the relative economic efficiency on different size-groups of operational holdings has been found to be essentially in a similar direction in all States though there are quantitative variations from State to State. Since our purpose is not to examine the quantitative aspects of these data but only to analyse the data bearing upon the relative economic efficiency of farming business on different size-groups of holdings, and since the findings in all States are more or less in a similar direction, we shall utilize data only for U. P. for the year 1955-56 for illustrating the basic economic relationships that obtain on different size groups of operational holdings.

Per farm resources of land capital and labour on 400 holdings in districts Meerut and Muzaffarnagar of U. P. (Survey Samples) in 1955-56

Size Groups (Acres)	Average Area in acres	No. of draught cattle (Units)	No. of milch cattle (units)	Value of investment on live-stock (Rupees)	Investment on Implements (Rupees)	Investment on Farm Buildings Rupees	Total investment on fixed assets land (Rupees)	No. of Family workers (Units)
Below 2.5	1.5	1.1	0.9	354	116	270	793	1.6
2.5- 5.0	3.7	1.8	1.0	559	246	324	1138	2.0
5.0- 7.5	6.1	2.1	1.4	781	348	501	1713	2.3
7.5-10.0	8.7	2.3	1.7	1008	370	717	2357	2.6
10.0-15.0	12.1	3.0	1.7	1209	564	895	2843	2.7
15.0-20.0	16.8	3.8	2.0	1613	669	1039	3895	2.9
20.0-25.0	22.8	4.2	2.1	1812	569	1281	4539	4.0
25.0 & above	34.8	6.0	3.6	2658	1111	2643	7251	3.5
Average	9.1	2.5	1.5	977	407	690	1963	2.5

The above Table shows the assets structure of the farms according to size groups.

In this Table, some of the important economic relationships essential for the determination of economic efficiency of farming have been shown. Per farm resources of land, labour and capital are obviously necessary for this purpose. And we find that the range of variation of these resources per farm is very wide, as, is also the case for the average size per farm in different size-groups of holdings.

While the average size of farm in the sampled holdings was 9.1 acres, the lowest size farms were as small as 1.5 acres and largest size farms as big as 34.8 acres. On these farms, while the average number of draught cattle per farm was 2.5, and of milch cattle 1.5, the small farms below 5.0 acres had much less than the average number, while farms above 10.0 acres had much more than the average. The farms below 5.0 acres possessed less than even 2.0 draught cattle per farm, which is the minimum necessary for independent and efficient cultivation from an individual peasant's point of view. This means that these farmers must either be sharing bullocks of others on an exchange basis, or hiring them from other farms. This would usually involve difficulties in the timely performance of farm operations like ploughing, sowing and irrigation and consequently even loss of potential produce. It would also mean delays in operations like threshing, crushing of sugar cane, and transport of produce, since they must adjust their operations to the convenience of those who provide bullocks to share or on hire. The farmers in the range of 5.0 to lb 0 acres size-groups would not suffer from such disabilities. And the farmers of 10.0 acres or more would not be handicapped in this respect in any sense.

Same Style

More or less similar pattern of distribution is seen in case of the milch cattle. While the cultivators of lands between 5.0 to 10.0 acres possess only the average number of milch cattle, those cultivating below 5.0 acres possess only 1.0 or even less than 1.0 milch animal and those cultivating above 15.0 acres possess 2- 0 or more.

Data on the value of investment in livestock per farm indicate that while farms below 5.0 acres in size possess livestock of poor quality, much less than the average, and farms between 5.0 to 10.0 acres have livestock close to the average, the farmers of 10 acres have much better quality animals.

The data of investment on implements, farm buildings and fixed assets again shows that while farms of 5.0 to 10.0 acres have made investments on these items more or less close to the average, farms below 5.0 acres show much less investment per farm, and farms above 10 acres show investment much more than the average. In fact, farms of 15.0 acres and above have invested in implements Rs. 1,111 per farm, against the average of Rs. 407, in farm buildings Rs. 2,643 against the average of Rs. 690, and in all fixed assets (including livestock, implements, farm buildings and miscellaneous equipment but excluding land) Rs. 7,251 against the average of Rs. 1,963.

The fact that value of capital investment per farm increased considerably with an increase in the size of the operational holdings suggests that the capital-intensity of large-sized fauns is much more than of the small farms. Ipso facto they also command bulk of the total capital resources employed in farming. And thus, concentration of land simultaneously brings about a concentration of capital resources.

The data in value terms do not bring out the variations in the numbers and quality of capital employed in farms of different sizes. But it has been found that the small farms have generally a much less number of implements and of very poor quality and large farms possess more and better implements. For instance, in the region of U. P. under study, we find the following pattern in the distribution of some' improved implements'.

Percentage of farms possessing various types of improved implements according to size of holdings

	Percentage of farms in various size-groups having				
Size-Groups (acres)	No. of farms in the size-group	Iron-ploughs	cultivators	Bullock operated chaff-cutter	Pneumatic tyred bullock cart
Below 2.5	47	-	-	-	-
2.5- 5.0	130	2.3	3.8	-	-
5.0-7.5	111	4.5	1.8	-	1.8
7.5-10.0	104	4.8	3.8	-	1.9
10.0-15.0	103	6.8	4.9	-	2.9
15.0-20.0	52	13.5	9.6	-	13.5
20.0-25.0	25	16.0	16.0	4.0	16.0
25.0 & above	25	8.0	24.0	12.0	32.0
Total	497	5.5	5.2	0.7	4.4

It is evident that the use of improved implements has been much more on the large-sized farms. And, in fact, large farmers have more of these improved implements per farm. For instance, out of 33 farms having iron ploughs, four had more than one. A farmer in the size-group of 25 acres and above has two iron cultivators.

Family Labour in Action

The resources of family labour per farm also increase with an increase in the size of holding like the resources of land and labour. But the extent of increase even for the highest size-groups of farms is not more than about two-fold, which is much less than the increase in per farm resources of land or capital. Consequently, need arises to employ hired labour in bigger size-groups on a regular and permanent basis. And, we have already seen that the proportion of hired labour to the total farm labour increases considerably on farms of 10-0 acres or more, and about two-thirds of all the permanent farm servants are engaged on those very farms.

However, despite an increase in the quantum of hired labour employed with an increase in the size of farm, since the resources of capital per farm increase more than proportionately to the increase in labour, the value of capital investment per worker increases with an increase in the size of farms. The following Table illustrates this point fully.

It is evident that on farms below 5.0 acres and even on farms of 5.0 to 10.0 acres, investment per worker is less than the average. But on farms between 10.0 acres to 20.0 acres, it is higher than the average, and highest on the farms of 20.0 acres and above. The investment per worker (excluding land) in the highest size-group is more than double of that in the smallest size-group.

From these data, and from the variations in the nature and quality of capital employed on different sizes of farms, it follows that techniques of farming on small farms are labour-intensive and tend to become relatively capital intensive as the size of farms increases. We have already seen that the proportion of hired labour in total farm labour increases considerably with an increase in the size of farms. Thus it appears that increasing employment of hired labour and increasing investment of capital per worker co-exist together. This co-existence suggests that an increase in capital investment per worker with an increase in the size of farm may be due to the efforts of the large farmers to increase productivity of hired labour by providing them relatively more and better capital. Since the large farmers have to pay a wage to hired labour, they like to extract the maximum output from them, and for this reason provide relatively better tools and implements, better means of irrigation and better types of inputs. A small farmer dependent only on family labour has neither incentive nor compulsion nor even resources to economise on family labour since it is surplus and there is no payment of wages. But as the size of farm increases and the share of hired labour in total farm labour increases, the farmer is obliged to consider whether it would provide him sufficient additional output to compensate for the payment of the wage.

Capital investment (fixed and operating excluding land) per worker according to size-groups of holdings

Size-Groups (acres)	No. of workers per farm	Investment of capital (fixed & operating including land) per farm Rs.	Investment of capital (including land) per worker per farm Rs.	Investment of capital per farm (excluding land) Rs.	Investment of capital (excluding land) per worker Rs.
1	2	3	4	5	6
Below 5.0	2.0	4236	2118	1718	859
5.0-10.0	2.8	7077	2528	2059	735
10.0-15.0	2.6	13377	5145	4432	1705
15.0-20.0	3.9	20608	5284	5680	1456
20.0 & above	4.6	37445	8140	9000	1957
Average	2.9	11892	4076	3477	1199

Moreover, since bulk of production on large farms is destined for the market, large farmers are compelled to maximise their net money income by extracting maximum possible work, from their hired workers. In times before abolition of zamindari when the zamindars had almost an unbridled and despotic command on farm labour, the exploitation of the farm worker used to be in the form of being made to work for the longest possible hours under conditions of bondage and servitude and providing forced labour himself and by his dependents. But since after the abolition of zamindari, such bondages of servitude and forced labour have practically disappeared. The zamindars, being obliged to convert themselves gradually into entrepreneurial farmers, have lost their earlier over- lordship of farm labour. They are now also obliged to change or modify their forms of exploitation. Despite persistence of old practices of oppressions on farm labour in some regions, they now generally seek to increase the productivity of the farm worker by employing more and better capital equipment unlike before by keeping him attached to their farm in servitude.

Concentration at Work

Of course, with such extreme concentration of total cultivated land in the hands of a small minority consisting mainly of ex-intermediaries and big peasants, plentiful supply of cheap labour and stubborn persistence of the earlier forms of exploitation of farm labour are bound to remain with us for a long time. Under these circumstances, a rapid or widespread movement for increasing productivity by investment of more capital per worker, amongst the large farmers, is hardly likely to gather momentum since the cost of labour would generally remain lower than the cost of capital until the pace of industrialisation and absorption of surplus labour from agriculture into non-farm sectors of employment becomes very fast. But the prevailing pattern of distribution of operational holdings has made such a development almost inevitable. One witnesses an increasing use of tractors and other farm machines in Indian agriculture. For instance, the number of tractors in India increased from 4,524 in 1945 to 35,000 in 1961 about an eight-fold increase; the number of electric pumps for irrigation from 8,561 in 1945 to 46,930 in 1965, a more than five-fold increase; and the number of oil engines with pumps for irrigation from 12,062 in 1945 to 1,22,230 in 1956, a more than ten-fold increase. These machines are employed mainly by the large farmers, and make their techniques of farming highly capital intensive. They replace farm labour from substantial areas and make surplus labour and unemployment accumulate amongst the lowest strata of the Indian agrarian society.

Turning away from per farm resources of land, labour and capital, let us now examine the relative availability of labour and capital resources per unit of land. Despite an increase in per farm resources of labour and capital with an increase in the size of farms, per unit of land, these resources decline with an increase in the size of the farms, as shown in the Table below.

These data reveal that while small farms possess much less capital and labour relative to the large farmers, they have too much capital and labour per acre, relative to the large farms. One finds that farms below 5.0 acres possess resources of labour and capital per acre much above the average, farms of 5.0 to 10.0 acres a little more than the average, and farms of 25 - 0 acres and above employ the least resources of labour and capital per acre.

Per acre resources of land, capital and labour on 400 holdings in districts Meerut, Muzzaffarnagar of U. P. (Survey Sample)

	No. of draught cattle (Units)	No. of milch cattle (units)	Value of investment on livestock (Rupees)	Investment on implements (Rs.)	Investment on farm building Rs.	Total investment on fixed assets excluding land Rs.	No. of Workers (units)
1	2	3	4	5	6	7	8
Below 2.5	0.70	0.53	233	77	178	523	1.1
2.5- 5.0	0.47	0.26	150	66	87	305	0.6
5.0 - 7.5	0.35	0.22	129	57	83	282	0.4
7.5-10.0	0.26	0.19	116	47	83	272	0.3
10.0-15.0	0-25	0-14	100	42	74	236	0.2
15.0-20.0	0-23	0.11	96	40	62	231	0.2
20.0-25.0	0.19	0.09	80	25	56	199	0.2
25.0 & above	0.18	0.10	76	32	76	208	0.1
Average	0.27	0.16	107	44	76	215	0.4

This aspect of farm structure has an important bearing upon the costs of production, input-output coefficients, and profitability or remunerativeness of the farming business in different size-groups of farms. As a result of this farm assets structure, the inputs of labour and capital per unit of land decline and the costs of production per acre go down with an increase in the size of farm. In fact, the inputs per acre even of other resources such as seeds, fertilizers, manures and irrigation decline with an increase in the size of farm, leading to a considerable decline in total inputs per acre. Evidently, the output-input coefficient is more favourable on larger farms and the profitability of remunerativeness of farming increases with an increase in farm size, despite a somewhat larger gross output per acre on small farms. The following Table illustrates these points.

Input-Output relationships, costs of production and profits or losses of farming on 400 holdings (Survey Sample) in U. P. according to size-groups of farms.

Size-Groups (acres)	Average size of farm	Value of inputs per acre (Rs.)												
		Bullock labour	Human labour	Seed	Fertilizers & manures	Upkeep of implements	Rent & Cess	Irrigation on charges	Interest on fixed capital	Total of inputs per acre	Total of output per acre	Output/Input ratio	Total amount of profit per farm	Net profit or loss as percentage of output
1	2	3	4	5	6	7	8	9	10	11	12	13	14	15
Below 5.0	3.2	137.9	56.8	18.6	8.5	17.4	9.7	9.8	10.9	269.6	291	1.08	75	8
5.0-10.0	7.2	94.3	50.2	17.0	7.4	12.3	9.5	9.0	8.2	208.9	253	1.21	314	17
10.0-15.0	12.1	76.8	45.9	16.0	7.0	11.0	10.0	9.5	6.8	183.4	241	1.31	691	24
15.0-20.0	16.8	74.4	43.8	15.5	6.8	10.1	9.3	8.3	6.7	174.9	216	1.23	678	19
20.0 & above	28.6	60.1	36.8	13.5	5.9	7.6	8.4	5.8	6.2	144.3	190	1.32	1299	24
Average	9.1	84.3	45.9	16.0	7.0	11.1	9.3	8.4	7.5	189.5	234	1.23	407	19

The costs of production per unit of land, as well as per unit of output are lower on large farms, and higher on small farms. The profits per farm and net profit or loss as percentage of total output also increases with an increase in the size of farm. Thus the farming business is more economic and efficient on large farms than on the small farms.

It was further found that 'farms incurring loss are most numerous among those below 10 acres and form about 80 per cent of total number (of farms) showing loss in both samples'. It thus appears that farms smaller than 10.0 acres have not merely made less profits but have also incurred losses, whole larger farms have made much greater profits and relatively suffered much less losses.

The calculation of profitability or remunerativeness of farming business by 'imputing' values to the contribution of family labour at the current wage rate for permanent labour and including it as an input factor for calculating the output-input co-efficient has been criticised recently. This is because, by following this method, much of Indian agriculture appears un-remunerative. In fact, even the authors of the farm-management studies, who have done much to apply and popularise this method of calculating farm profitability, themselves felt the need to develop some other concept of cost which may provide the explanation for continued production in spite of sustained losses' (on the basis of the method of calculation followed). However, no satisfactory concepts of cost, or criteria of economic efficiency have yet been developed. Only Dr. A. K. Sen, in very brief-in fact too brief outline has suggested that since 'there may be no alternative employment opportunities, at the margin' for family labour, the factor that makes the crucial difference is the system of farming viz., whether it is wage-based or family-based, and non-wage family farming has some efficiency advantages, since it would enable family labour to be applied to a piece of land upto the point where net marginal product of labour becomes almost equal to zero.

Even if one agrees that imputation of value to family labour at the prevailing market rate for permanent labour exaggerates the costs of the small farmer, it nevertheless remains necessary to develop a method which may provide a uniform basis for comparison of economic efficiency on different farms, so heterogenous in their assets structure, forms of employment of labour and techniques of cultivation in which it is often difficult to distinguish a purely family-based and purely wage-based farm since all farms make use of both family and hired labour though in different proportions. It appears that if instead of taking into account the profit or loss per farm in this fictional sense, we take into consideration the farm business income, also computed in the farm management studies, which is the measure of earnings of the farmer and his family for management, risk, their labour, and capital investment and is obtained by adding the family labour income, the unpaid interest on owned capital and unpaid rent on owned land, we might bet a better measure of economic efficiency of different farms.

Some other measures of farm efficiency are also available in the U. P. Farm Management study. These measures are not given as alternative criteria of economic efficiency of farm business but have nevertheless been calculated. And we can use them also for a comparative picture of farm efficiency according to the size-groups. These are return per labour-day of family members, output per earner, or return per worker per year (including among workers both family and hired workers).

Economic efficiency of different size-groups of farms according to diferent criteria.

Size-Group	Farm Business income per farm Rs.	Farm Business income per acre Rs.	Farm Business income as p.c. to total output	Output per earner Rs.	Return per worker per year Rs.	Return per labour day of family members Rs.
1	2	3	4	5	6	7
Below 5.0	497	155.3	54	459	136	1.3
5.0-10.0	779	108.2	43	758	245	1.5
10.0-15.0	1396	115.4	47	1074	334	1.6
15.0-20.0	1520	90.5	42	1252	327	1.7
20.0 & above	2302	80.5	42	1359	595	3.1
Average	940	103.3	44	868	304	1.7

In the above Table the relative efficiency of different size-groups of farms is shown according to these criteria.

Thus it appears that even if we ignore the criterion of economic efficiency in terms of profit and loss altogether, we find that large farms yield much larger total farm business income per farm, although the small farms yield more farms business income per acre than the large farms. Similarly, in terms of output per earner, return per labour day of family members or return per worker both family and hired, large farms have a distinct advantage in terms of economic efficiency and productivity of family or hired labour, and yield a much higher income per family member than the small farms, despite the fact that the proportion of hired labour on large farms increases. This means that family members obtain larger incomes for themselves even while employing hired labour and productivity per worker on large farms increases even when a larger proportion of them are hired. This fact dispels the myth that application of family labour in agriculture is inherently superior and more productive than hired labour, because the latter lacks personal interest and requires supervision.

The Bright Side

The only advantage of small farms appears to be their ability to extract more output per unit of land, though not per unit of labour. But since these farms operate within a competitive market mechanism, and compete with the produce of large farms, this advantage would only be temporary. It would last only during the period until the large farms, which are slowly ascending the scale of entrepreneurial agriculture in the wake of zamindari abolition, by investing more capital, employing better tools and implements, using improved methods of farming, and raising the productivity of both hired and family workers outstep the small farms even in output per unit of land. We have seen that in a strictly economic sense, the costs on the small farms are not compensated even by higher gross output per acre. But the small farms continue in production because they do not calculate their profits or losses in the economic sense but only look to their total farm business income. And since the size of their land is extremely small, they try to extract the maximum output. But despite that they have to depress their standards of living to the lowest level and they have little to invest in land or its cultivation. Consequently, in the long-run, they are bound to lose in the race so long as their economic fortunes are determined by a competitive market system. The following data in following Table brings out these aspects.

Living expenses per family and per member and savings per family on (197) holdings (Cost Accounting Sample) in U. P.

Size-Groups (acres)	Average number of family	Living expenses per family	Living expenses per member	Savings per family	
Below 2.5	6.1	772	126	-	302
2.5- 5.0	6.5	941	145	-	132
5.0- 7.5	5.5	1399	154	-	433
7.5-10.0	7.1	1216	171	-	19
10.0-15.0	6.8	1564	230	-	360
15.0-20.0	9.5	1998	210	-	356
20.0-25.0	14.1	2404	170	+	430
25 and above	12.5	2541	203	+	713
Average	7.6	1446	190	-	186

It is evident that living expenses per family as well as per member are much lower in the small farms than on the large and increase with an increase in farm size. And despite such a depressed standard of living, the small farmer is unable to make both ends meet even with his total farm business income, because of his high input costs and high living expenses. Even farmers between 10.0 to 20.0 acres suffer from the same difficulty. And only farmers of lands above 20.0 acres have savings for capital accumulation or investment on land or in cultivation. Thus, despite the initial advantage of higher gross output or farm business income per unit of land, the small farmer tends to lose this advantage in course of time, because the large farms, in the meanwhile accumulate capital and improve farm productivity.

The inability of the small and the medium farmer to make any savings or capital investment is also revealed by the Rural Credit Follow-up Surveys. For instance, we read that:

> The capital formation reported by cultivators resulted in a substantial measure, through the efforts of big and large cultivators. The performance of medium and small cultivators, especially the latter group, was poor, barring one or two districts. It is significant to note that even in the districts in which big and large cultivators found it possible

> to undertake substantial capital formation expenditure, the performance of medium and small cultivators was generally poor. Medium and small cultivators had generally to finance a fairly large proportion of even their small capital formation through borrowings.

And yet another place, we find that:

> The data for the four classes of cultivators clearly show that generally it was only among big and large cultivators that any net investment took place during the year. Medium and small cultivators generally recorded, disinvestments in the districts barring Mandsaur, East Khandesh, and Coimbatore.

And with disinvestments, the small and the medium farmer will not be able to retain their advantage of a higher gross output or farm business income per acre for very long.

Market and Competition

Let us now examine as to how these farming units, with such wide differences in their assets structure, costs of production, input-output coefficients, farm business income, productivity per worker, and savings and investment potential, would fare under a competitive market mechanism. The output of all these production units competes in the market where a given price prevails. And those whose costs of production per unit of output are the lowest, productivity per worker the highest, and output-input co-efficient most efficient, derive the maximum profits. The large farmers are thus very favourably placed in a competitive market for agricultural produce while the small farmers face heavy odds in competition against them. And the middle group of farmers, since they are generally average in all aspects of farming, are in a state of continuous instability and flux due to the uncertainties of the market prices which affect them for the better or for the worse from time to time. The natural tendency of a competitive market is to impoverish the small farmer, enrich the large farmer, and to push the group of average or middle farmers into contrary directions, depending upon the numerous economic group of middle farmers gets drawn gradually into the whirlpool of economic competition, and is unable to remain close to the average and is slowly and gradually split up, some of them rising in the scale to become large farmers, and others, the bulk of them, dwindling into the position of small farmers.

Estimates of the likely amount of output per farm sold in the market according to size groups of holdings (Survey Sample).

Size of the farm	Output per farm	% of actually incurred cash & kind exp. to total output	Living expenses purchases and other payments	% of actual exp. in purchased for the purpose of Col. 3	Account of output exchanged for the purpose of Col. 5	Amount of output exchanged	Total amount of output	% of exchanged output to total
1	2	3	4	5	6	7	(6+7) =8	9
Below 5.0	918	36.7	895	38.9	337	348	685	74.6
5.0-10.0	1818	38.3	1293	40.0	696	517	1213	66.7
10.0-15.0	2904	43.9	1564	40.3	1275	630	1905	65.6
15.0-20.0	3630	39.0	1998	39.1	1416	781	2197	60.5
10.0 & above	5437	42.9	2476	44.2	2333	1094	3427	63.0
Average	2135	40.2	1446	39.6	854	573	1427	66.8

This view of the impact of a competitive market on different types of farming units refers only to a long-term tendency. It is only the abstraction of an extremely complicated and protracted process which passes through complex stages and manifests itself in various forms. For instance, the impoverishment and economic ruin of the small farmer may express itself-and that too after a fairly long time-not in his complete elimination from the farming business but in his increasing dependence on non-farming subsidiary occupations, increasing burden of indebtedness or increasing liquidation of his farming assets. Gradually, he might turn to leasing out his land for a crop-season or a year, and may return to farming again depending upon the regularity and adequacy of his alternative employment. He may also continue to remain in the farming business by depressing his standard of living to the lowest possible level. These processes may also take long to become manifest on a considerable scale in a large country like ours. Similarly, the process of gradual splitting up of the middle group of farmers into small and large farmers may never come to light in the absence of two-point studies of a selected group of middle farmers over a reasonable perioa of time. The enrichment of the large farmers may also proceed slowly over a long period and remain disguised for a long time in the absence of any data regarding the changes in the distribution of land, capital investment, total output, savings, and few capital formation in the countryside. But a competitive market, un-checked by any counter measures, is likely to lead into these directions, is certain and\ well-known. So long as the market remains an effective regulator of the economic fortunes of the farming units, the direction of the movements of the small, middle, and large farmers would be along these lines.

If this view of the competitive process be correct, we should expect a bitter economic strife to prevail amongst peasants. There must exist a movement in opposite directions in India's agrarian society-a process of economic prosperity and ruin, improvement and decay, progress and regress. Some in the rural society, possessed of ample resources of land and capital, and using hired labour for farm operations, would make large profits, accumulate capital and expand output. Propelled by the motive to maximise their net money returns, they would take all steps conducive to economise on costs, enhance productivity of labour and output including the efforts to enlarge the scale of their farming business by taking more land on lease or buying it up from others, subject to the legal maxima. Another group-designated as the middle group-though not having such large resources of land and capital, but only a little more or less than the average, would also be drawn into the process of improving output, reducing costs, and investing capital in farming in order to be able to take the maximum advantage of the competitive market mechanism. And a few who are more skilful, hard-working and enterprising amongst them, by using inexpensive techniques of farming, and improved implements would succeed in expanding their scale of farming, make some profits and accumulate some capital. But because of their limited resources of land and capital and because of the severe competition from the top-group who command the bulk of the land and capital resources and reap much larger profits per farm, most of them would be gradually sliding down the scale of economic efficiency and welfare. And lastly, the vast majority of farmers, having only a small fraction of the total resources of land and capital, and with vast resources of surplus manpower, and suffering from acute pressure of population on their small holdings, would be fighting a losing economic battle against their formidable adversaries and would gradually face economic ruin and impoverishment. Sustained losses in the farm business, and inability to depress their standards of living beyond a given minimum will drive them to seek non-farm sources of income, thus diminishing the importance of cultivation as a source of livelihood for them, even leading them to lease out their small fragments to those who are expanding their scale of farming business.

This contradictory movement is likely to proceed only if there are no counter-checks or hindrances against it. However, in actual situations, numerous hindrances arise, and many counter-checks are applied against this natural tendency. For example, in economies with a large agricultural population, a highly unfavourable man-land ratio and without any alternative avenues of employment, this process does not lead to elimination, of the small farmer from cultivation despite such heavy odds against him but only intensifies his exploitation as share-cropper, tenant-farmer or agricultural worker. Nor is the movement for increasing the productivity of human labour by investment of capital or by improvement of technology very rapid.

In some agrarian economies, conscious counter-measures may be planned against this movement. For instance, the State may guarantee minimum prices for agricultural produce at a level at which most of the small farmers may continue in production despite all the diseconomies of their farming business. Even though it might lead to increasing disparities of income and wealth, since the large farmers would benefit more from the guaranteed prices, it may at least stabilise the small farm economy and arrest the process of its decline and economic ruin. Or limits may be imposed on the expansion of scale or farming by imposition of ceilings on the size of the operational holding, thus preventing complete alienation of the uneconomic farmer from his land, despite all disadvantages. Ad hoc measures like provision of subsidised inputs-irrigation, seeds fertilisers, manures, credit and extension-may be provided which also, to some extent, may check these contradictory processes. However, so long as production is destined for a free market, and the market plays a dominant role in determining the economic destiny of the farming units, the process must tend to assert and manifest itself.

In India, in the context of the present-day distribution of operational holdings, the process is likely to work out with particular severity. The group of large farmers with adequate resources of land and capital consisting only of those having farms of 10.0 acres or more, is extremely small only 14.58 per cent of all rural households, which commands 56.84 per cent of total operated area. Even amongst them, only 4.22 per cent of households hold as much as 38.62 per cent of the total operated area. And this small group is likely to ascend the economic ladder. The next group of middle farmers, holding farms between 5.0 to 10.0 acres which forms about 14.19 per cent of all rural households and holdings about 18.56 per cent of the total operated area, though drawn into the economic strife, is scarcely likely to make much headway, except for a few. And the vast mass of the small peasant households, with lands below 5.0 acres, forming 71.23 per cent of all rural households and possessing only 15.60 per cent of the total operated area, must face economic ruin and utter impoverishment if they are left entirely to the free winds of a competitive market.

Had the pattern of land reforms been different, and the monopoly of cultivated land by a small group of persons was liquidated at the time of abolition of intermediaries, or even later, the impact of the competitive process would have been far more widespread, rapid, and much less iniquitous. The movement for improving production and productivity, improvement of technology and investment of capital in agriculture would have embraced a far larger number of peasants than at present, and some of the anomalous developments currently apace in the countryside could have been avoided. But the path appears to have been laid, and unless it is reversed, must work itself out even though slowly, sluggishly, yet tortuously.

Negative Factors

In recent years, there has been some evidence of these opposite processes developing simultaneously in the countryside. But this evidence is relevant only for small areas since no countrywide impirical investigations have been conducted for this purpose. The data about area and agricultural production, yields per acre, livestock, agricultural machinery and equipment and national income are collected only on an aggregative basis. No serious attempt has yet been made to collect these data according to broad socio-economic groups, or by size of operational holdings, which alone can reveal changes of opposite character in case of different groups. Nor have data been gathered in the decenial census to gauge these changes, even broadly. However, there are some studies, which do reveal some aspects of these contrary processes of growth and decay. We shall analyse them for whatever they are worth.

It is well known that Indian agriculture has shown considerable dynamism during the last decade since 1950-51. The index of agricultural production has risen by 45.5 per cent and agricultural output has risen at the simple rate of about 4.5 per cent per annum, or at about twice the rate of population growth. This rate of increase is in sharp contrast to the rate of growth of agricultural output during the half century before 1950-51 when it was scarcely more than the rate of growth of population. However, it has been estimated that out of the total increase of Rs. 1700 crores in agricultural income during 1949-50 to 1958-59, the share of the upper-income in the agricultural sector (accounting for only about 3.0 per cent of the rural population) in the increase of income at current prices may have been Rs. 600 crores or more (35.3 per cent of the total, increase).

It is already well-known that the benefits of the community projects have chiefly gone to the large landholders. For instance, we read in the Report of the Team for the Study of Community Projects and National Extension Service.

> In nearly all the facilities that have nothing to do with agriculture and animal husbandry one notices that there is a direct relationship between the size of landholdings for a group and the proportion of respondents from that group that derive benefit from the particular facility. Thus we see that 66 per cent of the large owner-cultivators, 46 per cent of the medium owner-cultivators and 22 per cent of the small owner cultivators have derived benefit from the programme of improved seed supply. The same is found to be true about manures and fertilisers, improved methods of cultivation and pesticides. This implies that the better of group of farmers tends to be represented in higher proportion among the beneficiaries of agricultural facilities.

Now, if we relate these observations with the gradual conversion of ex-intermediaries and a few big peasants into entrepreneurial farmers, who seek to raise output and productivity, by employing agricultural machinery, hired labour, etc. It is natural that the large farmers should have more or less monopolised over the benefits of the Community Projects and contributed a major share in the total additional agricultural output. It has been suggested that the percentage increase (of agricultural output per acre) has most probably been greater in the bigger than in the smaller farms. And it should cause no surprise since bulk of the capital investments must also have been made by the large farmers, and bulk of the increased inputs like seeds, fertilisers, irrigation etc., must have also been applied by them. The large increase in the number of tractors, electric pumps and oil engines for irrigation, iron ploughs, bullock carts and other implements during the last 15 years suggests that large farmers, amongst whom there are ex-intermediaries and large peasants, have made considerable capital investment in the farming business. The investments are not only large in amount but also larger in per acre terms as compared to the small farmers. For instance, we find that

Big cultivators, who numbered 10.0 per cent of the cultivating families accounted for more than 40 per cent of the total capital formation reported by cultivators in Ferozepur, Broach and West Godavari. In all these districts the share of big cultivators in the total capital formation was marked higher than their share in the total area of cultivated holdings.

Apart from making capital investment in agriculture, large cultivators have also been taking lands on lease. For instance, the N. S. S. data show that of the total area taken on lease (which forms 21.0 per cent of the total operated area), three-fifth is with households operating farms of 10.0 acres or more, one-fifth with farmers of 5.0 to 10.0 acres size holdings, and only one-fifth with cultivators of holdings below 5.0 acres. Evidently, cultivators of farms of 10.0 acres or more do not take land on lease for eking out their subsistence, for which their own holdings are more than sufficient, but for commercial cultivation.

Similarly, the increasing use of hired labour in Indian agriculture, since 1950-51, is revealed in the data of the Second Agricultural Labour Enquiry. According to the Report, the total agricultural wage paid employment of agriculture since 1950-51 is revealed in the data of the 189 days per annum in 1950-51, to 194.26 days in 1956-57, despite more rigorous norms of working hours and intensity of employment having been used for determining a day of wage labour than in the First Enquiry. Again, wage paid employment for women workers in agriculture also increased during the period from 120 to 131 days per worker per annum. These data show that during the six years period, there has been relatively greater availability of wage employment, even though the level of total employment per worker per annum has gone down. Of course, the extent of increase is not much, but the significant aspect of this fact is that it has taken place only over six years, and within 3-4 years after the abolition of zamindari. As years roll by, its magnitude is likely to increase although in view of the plentiful supply of cheap labour, the increase in the figures of employment per worker per annum may yet be small and may not reflect its full significance.

Taking all these data together, one can form a broad view of the direction in which Indian agriculture has been moving in recent years. It is manifestly a path towards the development of the system of farming, often called, 'capitalist farming', in which a very small group of farm holders are becoming economically more prosperous and socially and politically more powerful in villages.

Unfortunately, not much data are available specifically about the relative performance of the small farmers during the last decade, since attention has been confined only to the new emergent group of prosperous farmers. Yet some symptoms of increasing economic difficulties of small farmers are seen in the N. S. S. data on the leasing out of land. For instance, it reveals that of the total area leased out, 61.38 per cent is leased out by those holding lands below 5.0 acres, which means that the small owners have found it difficult to continue in cultivation because their holdings are too small even to grow a bare subsistence.

A direct corollary of this situation is the dependence of small farmers on off-farm subsidiary occupations. The Rural Credit Survey found a close relationship between the size of landholding and the extent of dependence on subsidiary occupations. Again, in a study into the problems of low-income farmers in Kodinar Taluke (Gujarat), it was found that 83.0 per cent of the small farmers depended on off-farm labour, and a few on sale of subsidiary products. Similar observations have been made in the numerous unpublished village reports of the agro-economic research Centres and other studies.

Another important aspect of the small farm economy is the liquidation of physical assets or net disinvestment over a period of time. For instance, in the Gujarat Study, it was found that during 1948-53, a period of high prices of agricultural produce, small cultivators had sold away land to finance the acquisition of other assets like implements and livestock. Again, comprehensive data about investment and disinvestment was collected in the All India Rural Credit Survey and it was found that in almost all the districts except a few the small cultivators showed a net disinvestment position, while for the medium cultivators this was the position except in respect of a large majority of the districts.

The liquidation of assets or net disinvestment by small farmers only accelerates the process of their gradual alienation from the farming business and increases their dependence on borrowing and off-farm sources of income.

All these symptoms are only aspects of the basic problem, the uneconomic and unremunerative character of small scale cultivation. Since no comprehensive studies over two points on the relative performance of small cultivators in respect of agricultural output, income, capital investment, productivity per acre etc. are available, one has to depend only on these indirect symptoms of a basic malady.

However, recently resurvey investigations have been completed in several villages in different states which are expected to throw some light on the nature and extent of socio-economic changes in the farm economies of different groups of cultivators. The preliminary findings of one of these studies on the relative performance of the different size-groups of cultivators in respect of agricultural output over the years are shown in the Table.

Percentage changes in gross value of output, output per acre, and residual income (total and per acre) from cultivation (net of actually incurred expenses) at constant prices according to size of operational holdings in village Sohalpur Gara

Size-Group (acres)	p.c. Change in the gross value of output over	p.c. change in gross value of output per acre	p.c. change in residual income from cultivation	p.c. change in residual income per acre
1	2	3	4	5
Below 4.1	- 41.2	- 19.8	- 9.9	- 24.8
4.1- 8.2	- 4.1	- 2.3	+ 21.2	- 7.5
8.2-12.3	- 0.6	- 0.3	- 13.2	+ 1.8
12.3-16.5	+ 23.0	+ 12.9	+ 13.1	+ 9.1
16.5 & above	+ 6.6	+ 3.8	+ 34.2	+ 1.0
Average	+ 1.8	+ 1.0	+ 11.0	- 1.0

From these data, it is evident that during a brief period of 4 years, significant changes have taken place in the farm economies in different size-groups of cultivators, and the small cultivators have suffered a decline in gross value of output, (both total and per acre) as well as in residual income from cultivation (total and per acre). And the farmers of lands between 12.3 to 26.5 acres have achieved the maximum increase in gross output as well as residual income. These changes have altogether changed the relative position of small farmers in terms of even gross value of output and residual income per acre, and reduced them to the lowest ladder in the scale, as shown in the Table.

Changes in gross value of output and residual income from cultivation per acre during 1954-55 and 1958-59 according to the size of operational holdings in village Sohalpur Gara.

Size-Groups (acres)	Gross Value	Output per acre	Residual income per acre	
1	2	3	4	5
Below 4.1	203.3	167.1	166.05	124.80
4.1- 8.2	180.0	175.9	137.30	127.02
8.2-12.3	189.2	188.6	138.57	141.03
12.3-16.5	178.4	201.4	127.22	138.77
16.5 and above	175.6	182.2	129.98	131.22
Average	128.7	184.5	135.41	133.20

These data show that changes in opposite directions have taken place in different size-groups of operational holdings and have entirely changed their relative position. They pertain only to one village and are used here for mere illustration of the manure as to how different farms respond to the processes of a competitive market mechanism, and how the gap between the small and the large farmers widens under its impact.

The opposite process of increasing prosperity along with increasing economic ruination has its social symptoms as well. These are reflected in 'the conflict between the rural elite and the rural poor' which, according to an eminent sociologist, 'is bound to grow acute as the latter become increasingly conscious of the fact that they are not benefitting as much as they should from the various development programmes.' This conflict generates social tensions and intensifies caste feuds, mutual rivalries, and the struggle for economic and social power in the village. And these tensions are only the reflexes of a deeper economic process penetrating into the vital pores of our rural economy and society. The whisper about increasing inequalities of income and wealth and the cry about the rich getting richer and poor getting poorer also owe their genesis to the inevitable logic of this process.

For those who are shaping the course of the current agrarian revolution in India, it is necessary first to grasp this vast and complex process, before they can muster the strength and the will to cope with the problems generated in its development.

Ten

Organisational Setup

In a clear, interesting and systematically developed study, under the title of "Social Structure and Change in Indian Peasant Communities" has been presented a general panorama of the Indian population in this century.

The population of an Indian village is united by three different bonds of solidarity: (a) family ties, (b) the caste system, and (c) territorial affinities.

The caste system is the most important and over-rules family and territorial ties; in order to understand the extent and depth of its influence, it is only necessary to know that internal relationships within the castes are subject to rules governing matrimony, meals, physical contact and occupations and that these rules are obeyed because they are considered to be of divine origin.

Castes have remained as exclusive groups throughout the ages, since strict endogamy is observed.

The influence of the castes in social relationships is, accordingly, very great in India, although sometimes of a negative character. "The taboos of the Indian caste system," asserts Max Weber, "inhibit social intercourse much more than the system of Chinese belief in spirits hindered trade." Nevertheless, according to this same author, "the railways will gradually render caste taboos illusory."

The interesting paper by Dr. S. C. Dube on present day India confirms the study made by the great German sociologist at the end of the last century. In effect, according to S. C. Dube, the social structure of India is subject to considerable changes under the impact of Western culture and civilization. Modern systems of transport and communications, modern technology, industrialization and Western type education during the last 10 years have combined to produce the following obvious changes:

(1) The social position of the individual in India is dependent upon his caste; but at present that system of class distinction is being superseded by another rival system by which the individual's position in society is determined on his own personal merit.

(2) This change in class distinction is more apparent when a person moves from country to town since on establishing himself in the city, he has to accustom himself to urban customs.

(3) There is a noticeable weakening in the authority of the individual castes in rural India.

(4) A certain individualism has developed within the family.

(5) Western forms of life and modern technology have been accepted by the upper strata of society as they have the opportunity of acquiring them.

(6) On the other hand the lower strata are, in a way, conservative because of their lack of education and poverty.

(7) Notwithstanding the relative conservatism of the lower classes, it appears that the social structure of the village is in a state of dissolution and disintegration.

The work of Dr. Tarlok Singh of the New Delhi Planning Commission complements the information given by Dr. Dube.

Dr. Tarlok Singh discusses the "Landless Labourer and the Pattern of Social and Economic Change" and explains in detail in this valuable work the effect upon India of what is known as "the impact of the West". This impact is particularly noticeable in the villages and has developed slowly and indirectly.

(a) The products of Western industry introduced into the villages of India by pedlars diminished the demand for home-produced goods. Many craftsmen who used to make such local products became redundant and turned into farm workers without land of their own.

(b) Western ideas on ownership and finance changed the self-sufficient spirit in the village for an acquisitive, profit-seeking spirit, with the exploitation of the weak by the strong under the guise of legality. Wealth and self-seeking replaced the community spirit in the scale of values.

(c) These conditions created an internal capitalism represented by foreigners and by Indian traders and landowners who promoted the feudal conditions by means of latifundism and monetary loans.

(d) New techniques diminished the opportunities for work in a growing population, thus accentuating the effect of Western economic influence and Indian capitalism.

(e) As a result of all this, in the last 60 years, the population dependent upon agriculture has increased. It is calculated that it increased from 193 to 250 million between 1931 and 1951.

(f) Under Western influence, the bonds created by the social castes are tending to decrease, and some castes have disappeared altogether; but this has created the problem of providing work for men who were formerly employed within the strict caste system.

Labour without Land

The increase in the number of agricultural workers in India without land of their own is a problem which requires early solution. For this reason a democratic planning scheme is being put into practice and is founded on various definite points which tend to explain what should be done. Dr. Tarlok Singh is working on this. But can a Sociological Congress embark upon the study of these questions which properly belong to politics? We think not; the role of sociology should be defined as the study of prevailing social conditions for the purpose of obtaining scientific theories capable of serving as a basis for action; but sociology cannot indicate the precise terms for this action since they are dependent upon political conditions and the economic and social potentialities of each individual country.

Dr. A. R. Desai, of the Department of Sociology of the University of Bombay, with his work on "The Impact of the Measures Adopted by the Government of the Indian Union on the Life of the Rural People", confirms the concepts we have just put before you. He describes firstly the changes which took place in Indian society under the influence of Western culture and civilization during the period of British rule and the effects mostly negative of the measures adopted by the present Government of the Indian Union to reconstruct the country on new social and economic bases. The study of the effects of these measures certainly comes within the scope of sociology since they form part of the social structure of India and the failure of many of them shows how daring and dangerous it is to prescribe them.

The study now being made by Dr. Desai of the results of the contact between Western culture and civilisation and Indian culture, under British rule, to a large extent confirms and also complements the information given by Doctors S. C. Dube and Tarlok Singh

(a) Western culture dealt a mortal blow to the rural organization of India, based on an autarchical village community, with common ownership of land.

(b) It destroyed the collectivistic spirit and introduced individualism and competition.

(c) It introduced private ownership, letting out of land and individual cash taxation.

(d) In this way, agrarian economy based on the satisfaction of the needs of the family changed to an economy based on satisfaction of the demands of the market.

(e) It destroyed the self-sufficiency of rural life, at the same time ruining the small village industries by the introduction of machine-made products.

(f) The mass of craftsmen-deprived of their crafts by the articles imported from modern British factories-turned to agriculture, thus increasing the volume of labourers without land and accentuating the pressure of the rural population on the land. The size of small holdings diminished, and uneconomic properties increased in number.

(g) It increased the power of moneylenders, tradesmen and landowners over the poverty-stricken farmers.

(h) It increased the number of tenants and intermediaries (farmer-tenants, sub-tenant, sub-sub-tenants, etc.) supported by those who actually cultivated the ground.

(i) It decreased the power of the caste and reduced the size of the family.

(j) All this produced considerable impoverishment of the masses and internal lack of balance in the rural structure of India. To remedy this situation the Government of the Indian Union has put various measures into practice: (a) measures of a political nature establishing universal suffrage which gave rise "to considerable social and political quickening in rural India"; (b) measures of an economic nature such as irrigation projects, the introduction of better seed and fertilizers, reforms in letting arrangements to protect the tenant and cut out intermediaries, protection of the peasants against abuse by creditors, economic development of rural zones and the creation of co-operative societies and assistance to the small rural industries.

But these and other measures have failed because they only benefit those farmers who are in a sound economic position. No measures have been taken to allocate land to rural workers who have none, or to provide them with employment. The protective measures are easily circumvented; the co-operative societies only favour the clever farmers.

The plans for rural economic development do not favour those who have nothing and, on the other hand, the subscriptions required to put them into operation overburden them.

To sum up, according to Dr. Desai, the governmental measures adopted in India have produced changes in the rural community which tend to intensify the opposition between classes in the rural communities and also between castes, thus causing tension, antagonism and clashes.

Orientations

What sociological conclusions can be obtained from the three studies we have mentioned? What can the sociologist advise in regard to the changes which are taking place in the rural community of India?

The experience of the Indian people, like that of other peoples as history shows, supports the following generalization: whenever peoples of different culture and civilization come into contact, the most advanced tends to dominate and exploit the least developed. When these latter gain their independence, their upper classes who succeed in assimilating the civilization of their rulers, replace them in ruling and exploiting the masses.

The failure of the measures adopted by the Government of India to help the rural working class in the face of the changes in agrarian economic structure brought about by British rule and Western culture and civilization, in the same way as similar failures suffered by other peoples, serves as a basis for this further generalization: the upper classes of a country, who hold the economic power, tend to circumvent all the protective measures devised by the Government to help the working classes or to turn these same measures to their own profit.

From a strictly scientific point of view this is what, in our opinion, the Third World Sociological Congress can prove by way of general conclusions on the interesting studies submitted by Doctor Dube Singh and Desai with regard to the changes in agrarian economic structure in India.

Although it is certain that sociology must study prevailing conditions, it does not follow from this, arms the talented French sociologist, Emile Durkheim, " that we should give up trying to improve them: we would feel that our speculations were not worth the trouble if they had no more than a speculative interest." " Science, " he adds, " can help us to find the road we should follow and to determine the goal towards which we blindly struggle."

With the support of the above mentioned theories the sociologist can recommend, also in a general way, that in all those countries where peoples of different civilizations come into contact with each other, the Governments should not adopt empirical action in favour of the economically and politically weaker rural classes, but action planned on the basis of investigations and research carried out by scientists experienced in the social sciences so that the political action guides the changes in agrarian economic structure efficiently, preventing abuses, social inequalities and injustices.

Petty Farmers

The agricultural reconstruction has proved an achilles hill of planning in India. The official policy of 'betting on rich' in rural areas has only aggravated agrarian crisis in India. One of the basic prerequisites for the revitalization of agriculture is the effective resolution of problems of marginal farmers in rural India. The overwhelming majority of Indian cultivators operate on sub-marginal or marginal units of cultivation. The inadequate appreciation of this vital phenomenon has undermined official endeavours for rural reconstruction. An attempt is made here to unfold the deeper implications of the problems of marginal farmers within the profit-oriented matrix of Indian economy. A proper appraisal of their problems assumes greater significance in the light of the emerging trend among the experts, advocating inherent superiority of marginal farms compared to bigger units of cultivation.

Distribution of ownership holdings amongst rural households according to size groups crop season

	Household ownerships holdings			
Size-Group	P.c. of holdings to the total	Cumulative p.c. of holdings	P.c. of area to total area owned	Cumulative p.c. of area
1	2	3	4	5
0.00** 23.09	-	-	-	
0.01- 0.99	24.17	47.26	1.37	-
1.00-2.49	13.98	61.24	4.86	-
2.50- 4.99	13.49	74.73	10.09	16.32
5.00- 9.99	12.50	87.23	18.40	34.72
10.00-24.99	9.17	96.40	29.11	68.83
25.00-49.99	2.66	99.06	18.63	82.46
50.00 or above	0.94	100.00	17.54	100.00
Total	100.00	-	100.00	-

Major Problems

It is generally accepted that the cultivators whose holdings are below 5 acres, can be placed in the category of marginal farmers in the present state of agriculture in India. The vast bulk of these farmers are deficit cultivators as the farming has ceased to be a gainful occupation for them. The Table reveals the proportion of these farmers in the total cultivating population.

It can be seen from the above Table that nearly three-fourths of all rural households operate on holdings which are below 5 acres, and together own only one-sixth of the total area. In sharp contrast to this, the top one-fourth of households hold 83.68 per cent of the total area in size group, above 5 acres. It can be also further observed from the above figures that, 12.77 per cent of the rural households hold as much as 65.28 per cent of the total owned area in size-groups of more than 10.00 acres. Even after implementation of land reforms the land distribution pattern has not altered in favour of marginal farmers. This fact is also confirmed by the Mahalanobis Committee Report.

We shall now examine how the laws of market economy remorselessly operate against marginal farmers and gradually worsen their plight.

Structure of Prices

The last decade witnessed unprecedented rise in the prices of manufactured articles as well as agricultural products. The recent sharp rise in the prices of foodgrains transcended all past records. This inflation of prices caused primarily by deficit financing, erodes the standard of living of masses and leads to further concentration of wealth in the hands of the richer sections. According to Prof. Gyanchznd, "Rise of the prices in the Second Five Year Plan period has been of the order of 25 per cent and since 1956 the rise has been maintained and even accelerated. This has happened in spite of the increase of 33 per cent in agricultural and 66 per cent in industrial production..... The premise that in a developing economy rise of prices is inevitable is being made a cover for all errors and failings in respect of price policies..... The fact that in spite of the peak of agricultural production of 76 million tons and increase of industrial production of 11.7 per cent during the course of 1960, the average level of prices has risen during the year by 6.5 per cent, of raw materials by 16 per cent. The index number of general price level at the end of war with 1939 as base was 260, the average at 1952-53, when the new base for the revised index number was adopted, was 380, and in January 1961 it was 475. In everyone of these indices are congealed unwanted and iniquitious changes in economic relativities of different income groups, which have been known to exist but have been deliberately left unredressed owing to the extreme difficulties of righting the wrongs created by inflationary upsurge from time to time. The result has been that these inequities have accumulated and their incidence has been severe on agricultural labourers and even industrial labourers, small peasants, small traders and lower middle classes with fixed and relatively in elastic incomes. The whole income structure of the country has been gravely distorted on this account and the increasing national income has not accrued to the benefit of these classes i.e. the vast majority of our people, and they are as a matter of fact distinctly worse off than they were before the war. Any price policy which leaves this cardinal fact of the economic situation out of account follows the line of least resistance and is escapist in the worst sense of the word."

Though it may sound paradoxical, it is still true that high agricultural prices hit the marginal farmers as much as the urban population. The rise in agricultural prices benefits only the rich farmers with marketable surplus. They profit from higher prices and strengthen their economic position, at the expense of the deficit cultivators and agricultural labourers. Nearly 40 per cent of the Indian cultivators have to buy a part of their food requirements from the market and they suffer heavily from the high prices of essential commodities. Thus rise in prices only depresses the already depressed consumption standard of vast bulk of our deficit farmers. Even the exchange equivalents in the countryside are also more unfavourable to the marginal farmers than suggested by the wholesale price indices. The overwhelming proportions of small farmers are still under the firm grip of the village Shaukars, most of whom perform the combined functions of moneylending as well as trading. It is estimated that the 'moneylender-cum-traders' profit over the prices paid to the growers ranges from 30 to 200 per cent whereas in other countries it seldom goes beyond 15 to 20 per cent. Thus the market mechanism within the framework of underdeveloped economy intensifies the process of impoverishment of the marginal farmers. The following Table distinctly reveals the worsening plight of the marginal farmers in terms of the quantity of sales per acre.

Distribution of sales of paddy by farmers in selected villages

Size group of holdings (acre)	Percentage sales of each group to total		Quantity of sales per acre of holdings (in mds)	
	1942-43 1944-45	1955-56 1956-57	1942-43 1944-45	1955-56 1956-57
upto 2.5	3.29	1.94	1.76	0.82
2.5 to 5	12.92	10.91	1.90	1.94
5 to 10	37.99	30.32	3.60	4.57
10 to 20	33.15	28.58	6.22	6.46
Above 20	12.65	28.25	5.14	10.69
Total	100	100	3.94	4.61

It is evident from the above Table that the quantity of sale by small farm registered a fall while that of the big farms relatively increased during the periods under review. Similarly eminent scholars like Prof. Khusro, Dharam Narain and others have also pointed out that marketable produce as a proposition of total produce increases generally with increase in farm size.

It can be seen that the marginal farms possess much less capital and labour compared to the larger farms. In contrast to this they exhibit too much capital and labour per acre in comparison to larger units. "This aspect of farm structure has an important bearing upon the costs of production, input output coefficients, and profit ability or remunerativeness of the farming business in different size-groups. As a result of this farm assets structure, the inputs of labour and capital per unit of land decline and the costs of production per acre go down with an increase in the size of farm. In fact, the inputs per acre even of other resources such as seeds, fertilizers, manures and irrigation decline with an increase in the size of farms, leading to a considerable decline in total inputs per acre. Evidently, the output input coefficient is more favourable on large farms and the profitability or remunerativeness of farming increases with an increase in farm size, despite a somewhat larger gross output per acre on small farms".

Unremunerative and uneconomic character of marginal units of cultivation can be further elucidated from the following Table.

Per acre resources of land, capital and labour on 400 holdings

Size-groups acres workers cattle (units) stock	No. of draught cattle (units)	No. of milch vest-ment on live-stock Rs.	Value of in- imple-ments Rs.	Invest-ment on farm build-ings Rs.	Invest-ment on ment on fixed assets exclud-ing land Rs.	Total invest- (units)	No. of
1	2	3	4	5	6	7	8
Below 2.5	0.70	0.53	233	77	178	523	1.1
2.5- 5.0	0.47	0.26	150	66	87	305	0.6
5.0-7.5	0.35	0.22	129	57	83	282	0.4
7.5-10.0	0.26	0.19	116	47	83	272	0.3
10.0-15.0	0.25	0.14	100	42	74	236	0.2
15.0-20.0	0.23	0.11	96	40	62	231	0.2
20.0-25.0	0.19	0.09	80	25	56	199	0.2
25.0 & above	0.18	0.10	76	32	76	208	0.1
Average	0.27	0.16	107	44	76	215	0.4

Under the circumstances, it is no wonder that the under-utilization of available resources is a chronic problem faced by the marginal farms. This can be better illustrated from the under-utilization of the working capacity of bullocks on small farms. A pair of healthy bullocks is presumed to be capable of work for 8 hours each day for 350 days in a year. On this basis, it can be seen from the following figures that, the utilization of bullocks varies from 13.1 to 43.30 per cent of their available labour on holdings of different sizes.

Below 2 acres	13.14%	5 to 10 acres	36.79
2 to 5 acres	34.12 %	10 to 15 acres	43.35

Distribution of Cultivators' Holdings According to Size-groups

	Under one acre		1 acre to 2-5 acres		2.5 acres to 5 acres		5 acres to 10 acres		10 acres to 25 acres		Above 25 acres		
Census Zones	Number	Area	Number	Area	Number	Area	Number	Area	Number	Area	Number	Area	Average size of holdings (acres)
1	2	3	4	5	6	7	8	9	10	11	12	13	14
North India	14.8	1.4	26.2	8.3	25.1	16.7	20.6	26.4	11.4	30.6	1.9	16.6	5.3
East India	21.4	2.1	24.4	9.1	26.4	20.8	18.4	27.6	8.0	25.1	1.4	15.3	4.5
South India	28.0	2.7	27.1	9.5	20.9	16.3	14.0	21.1	7.9	25.4	2.1	25.0	4.5
West India	11.2	0.5	15.6	2.1	13.9	4.1	20.4	11.9	25.4	32.6	13.5	48.8	12.3
Central India	7.4	0.3	12.3	1.5	16.4	4.5	22.1	12.0	28.4	33.7	13.4	48.0	12.2
North-West India	5.4	0.2	14.4	2.0	16.9	5.1	22.5	13.4	31.0	39.3	9.8	40.0	12.6

It is evident from the above figures that the considerable amount of the working capacity of the bullocks remains unutilized on smaller farms. Dr. C. H. Shah has further highlighted this phenomenon. He observes, 'The field survey in the Kodinar taluka reveals that the central problem of the small farmers is relatively greater imbalance of factors of production. This affects on the one hand farm production and land productivity and on the other affects his income, savings, credit and investment and through them his economic betterment. Since two aspects are interlinked they set into motion a vicious circle which with passage of time brings about deterioration of his economy. Imbalance in factor combination takes two forms. Firstly, since the quantum of family labour is given and the size of holding is inadequate to provide full employment to all working members of the family, his economy has surplus of labour, only a part of which is employed outside. Unemployed labour is a heavy drag on his small income. Secondly, a certain minimum of equipment and housing facilities is necessary but his investment is rather heavy for his size of holding. On the other hand, his equipment is inadequate for efficient farming. Further the low income leaves very little for investment in working capital, with his small holdings, he commands low credit which is inadequate to meet the requirement of working capital." The above observations of Dr. Shah distinctly reveal the paucity of resources and resultant helplessness of the small farmers in a relatively prosperous tract of Gujarat. He also prognosticates decay of small farming with the passage of time.

We shall conclude this paper, by referring to the extent of underemployment that prevails in marginal units of cultivation in the absence of opportunities for gainful employment.

The number of labour days put in per acre is more on the marginal farms. Even if it is assumed that the intensity of cultivation and reliance on mixed farming is greater on marginal units that by itself cannot explain such a wide range of difference in the number of days put in per acre which vary from 133 for the size group of 2.5 acres and below, to 31 for 25 acres and above. Therefore, it can be safely concluded that the labour input on marginal units of cultivation has very low returns. This precisely indicates that there is considerable amount of underemployment of small farms. The unremunerative character of marginal farms becomes evident from the fact that family labour income per acre increases with the increase in the size of farm though the family labour input is much smaller.

The following Table provides some pertinent facts with regard to labour days and family labour income per acre for different size groups of farms in U. P. in the year 1954-55.

Size group (acres)	Labour days (per acre)	Family labour income (per acre)
Below 2.5	133	83.72
2.5 to 5	114	
5 to 7.5	96	119.87
7.5 to 10	67	
10 to 15	52	91.81
15 to 20	49	111.84
20 to 25	40	124.47
25 & above	31	

From the foregoing discussions the conclusion remains irresistable that economically, farming is a unremunerative occupation for the large bulk of marginal farmers. These farms also suffer from under-utilization of available resources and man-power. The input-output coefficient too works unfavourably against marginal farmers. Further the prevailing price structure also affects them adversely. This phenomenon viewed in context of our competitive economy, spells their disintegration, perhaps a rapid one from the Indian agriculture.

Agrarian Stratification

The inequality of cultivators' holdings is considerable in India. While the average size of the holdings was about 7-5 acres, about 70 per cent of the holdings were below this average. Holdings below one acre formed about 17 per cent, those between one and 2½ acres about 21 per cent and those between 2½ and 5 acres another 21 per cent. These accounted respectively for 1.0, 4.6 and 9.9 per cent of the total area. At the other end of the scale, 16 per cent were in the group 10 to 25 acres accounting for 32.5 per cent of the area and another 5.6 per cent above 25 acres covering about 34 per cent of the area.

Holding Distribution

The overall average size of holdings was 5.3 acres in North India (Uttar Pradesh) but the number of holdings upto 2.5 acres in size formed about 40 per cent of the total number of holdings and cover 9.7 per cent of the total area. The largest concentration of holdings, viz., 25 per cent was in the group 2.5 to 5 acres covering 16.7 per cent of the total area; 20.6 per cent were in the group 5 to 10 acres and covered 26.4 per cent of the area, while 11.4 per cent were in the group 10 to 25 acres covering 30.6 per cent of the area.

In East India zone, the overall average size was 4.5 acres. Here also, the largest concentration of holdings, namely 26.4 per cent covering 20.8 per cent of the total area was in the group 2.5 to 5 acres. However, 45.8 per cent were below 2.5 acres and covered 11.2 per cent of the area. The rest were above 5 acres.

In South India zone, as much as 55 per cent of the holdings covering 12.2 per cent of the area were below 2.5 acres, the overall average size being 4.5 acres. About 21 per cent of the holdings occupying 16.3 per cent of the area were in the size group 2.5 to 5 acres, while the rest were above 5 acres.

In West India zone, the overall average size was high, namely 12.3 acres, but 61 per cent of the holdings were below 10 acres and occupied 18.6 per cent of the area. A little above 25 per cent of the holdings covering 32.6 per cent of the area were in the group 10 to 25 acres, while 13.5 per cent covering 48.8 per cent of the area was above 25 acres.

The overall average size of holdings in Central India zone was 12.2 acres but 58 per cent of the holdings covering 18 per cent of the total area were below 10 acres. About 28 per cent were in the size group 10 to 25 acres and accounted for 34 per cent of the area, while 13.4 per cent occupying 48 per cent of the area were above 25 acres in size.

The average size of holdings was the highest, viz., 12.6 acres in North-West India zone. However, 59 per cent of the holdings occupying 20.7 per cent of the area were below 10 acres. About 31 per cent of the holdings was in the size group 10 to 25 acres and occupied 39.3 per cent of the area, while 9.8 per cent covering 40 per cent of the area were above 25 acres.

The above statement gives the percentage distribution of cultivator's holdings according to size groups in the different Census Zones.

Families in Various Categories

The enquiry revealed that besides the cultivating owner families and tenant families the agricultural labour families as also the non-agricultural families were also cultivating holdings, smaller though, as a subsidiary occupation. Of the total number of holdings, about 35 per cent were cultivated by owners, another 35 per cent by tenants, 20 per cent by labourers and 10 per cent by non-agriculturists. The percentage distribution of the total area of the holdings as amongst these categories was 52.4 for landowners, 35.7 for tenants, 7.8 for agricultural labourers and 4.1 for non-agriculturists. While the average size of the holdings of owner families was larger, being 11.37 acres, that of the tenants 7.74 acres approximated the overall average. The average size of holdings of the agricultural workers was 2.86 acres and that of the non-agriculturists 3.10 acres. About 51 per cent of the area of the holdings were occupied by landowners and 37 per cent by tenants, while agricultural workers and non-agriculturists occupied 8 and 4 per cent respectively.

Cattle Heads and their Utility

Small farming requires livestock, implements and considerable human labour since mechanisation is possible only on large farms. Livestock such as bullocks, buffaloes and horses and to a small extent camels, are used as draught animals for ploughing, irrigating and sometimes for threshing. Bullock labour is also used for transport of manure to the fields, agricultural produce to the market, etc. Operations such as preparatory work, sowing, weeding, irrigating and threshing require many implements such as crowbars, spades, hoes, seed-drills, charas and persian wheels, etc. In case the cultivator does not own sufficient livestock or implements, he either borrows them or engages workers who bring their own in return for higher wages.

The number of work animals and ploughs owned are thus closely related to the number of holdings and their size. It is possible to arrive at, broadly, the average work unit for a pair of work animals and a plough in a particular region by dividing the total cultivated area by the number of pairs of work animals and ploughs separately and obtain a mean of the two sets of figures relating to average area per plough and per pair of work animals. This concept of a work unit will have some value in attempting to estimate the labour surplus in agriculture.

During the General Family Survey, data on livestock and ploughs possessed by each family living in the sample villages were collected. The average number of cattle, sheep and goats, poultry and ploughs according to different categories of families.

The families of agricultural landowners had 44.8 per cent of the ploughs, while those of tenants, agricultural workers and non-agriculturists had 38.2, 11.7 and 5.3 per cent respectively. On an average, there were 0.7 plough per family. The zonal figures were almost the same.

The following statement gives the zonal differences:

Average Number of Ploughs per Family

Zones	Number of ploughs per family of Zones				
	Land-owners	Tenants	Agri-cultural labourers	Non-Agri-culturists	All families
North India ...	1.2	1.0	0.2	0.2	0.7
East India ...	1.4	0.8	0.2	0.2	0.6
South India ...	1.5	1.5	0.3	0.1	0.6
Western India ...	0.9	0.9	0.2	0.1	0.8
Central India ...	1.4	1.1	0.3	0.3	0.8
N. W. India ...	1.1	1.2	0.2	0.2	0.8
All India ...	1.2	1.0	0.3	0.2	0.7

On an average, a landowner's family had 1.2 ploughs, whereas a tenant's family had 1.1. The average number of ploughs per agricultural labour and non-agricultural family was extremely small, viz., 0.3 and 0.2 respectively. As stated already, about 50 percent of the agricultural labourers held land. If, therefore, adjustments are made keeping this point in mind, the average number of ploughs per family would come to about 0.6. Similarly, the average number of ploughs per family of non-agriculturists having land would come to 0.7. The average number of ploughs per landowner and tenant family in South India zone was higher than that in other zones. The average was the least in West India zone.

For purposes of the Agricultural Labour Enquiry, the term 'cattle' included oxen or bullocks, cows (over 3 years), he-buffaloes and she-buffaloes. There were, on an average, 2.2 head of cattle per family taking all rural families together. The families of agricultural landowners had 3.8, tenants 3.3, agricultural labourers 1.0 and non-agriculturists 0.9 head of cattle. The zonal details are given in the statement below:

Heads of Cattle per Family

Zones	Heads of cattle per family of				
	Land-owners	Tenants	Agri-cultural labourers	Non-Agri-culturists	All families
North India ...	3.0	3.1	1.2	0.9	2.4
East India ...	4.1	2.5	1.1	0.9	2.0
South India ...	3.8	3.8	1.0	0.6	1.7
West India ...	3.4	3.5	0.8	1.0	2.4
Central India ...	4.3	4.7	0.8	1.1	2.6
N. W. India ...	3.7	4.3	1.2	1.1	2.9
All India ...	3.8	3.3	1.9	0.9	2.2

The average head of cattle per family of landowners and tenants varied between 3 and 4 in all the zones. But the average for agricultural labour families was about 1 and even slightly less in some of the zones.

The average number of sheep and goats per family came to 1.3, the corresponding figures for families of landowners, tenants, agricultural labourers and non-agriculturists being 1.7, 1.1, 0.8 and 1.5 respectively. The statement below gives the zonal details:

Sheep and Goats per Family

Zones	Average number of sheep and goats per family of				
	Land-owners	Tenants	Agri-cultural labourers	Non-Agri-culturists	All families
North India ...	0.4	0.6	0.5	1.1	0.7
East India ...	1.1	0.9	0.7	0.6	0.8
South India ...	2.4	1.2	1.1	0.4	1.2
West India ...	1.4	0.9	0.7	3.7	1.6
Central India ...	2.0	1.2	1.1	3.9	1.8
N.W. India ...	1.9	2.7	1.0	2.2	2.1
All India ...	1.7	1.1	0.8	1.5	1.3

The average number of sheep and goats in each category of family was comparatively small in North India zone. The average for land-owners family was quite high in South and Central India zones. This was due to high averages for Mysore (5.2) and Hyderabad (3.6). The average for tenant families was also quite high (2.7) in North-West India zone. This was due to high average for Rajasthan, viz., 2. 8. The relatively high average for non-agricultural families in West and Central India was partly due to high figures for Saurashtra and Madhya Pradesh and Hyderabad respectively.

Average Number of Poultry per Family

Zones	Average number of poultry per family of				
	Land-owners	Tenants	Agri-cultural labourers	Non-Agri-culturists	All families
North India ...	0.2	0.1	0.1	0.2	0.1
East India ...	3.5	1.8	1.1	1.1	1.5
South India ...	2.1	3.2	1.0	1.0	1.4
West India ...	0.9	0.9	0.6	0.3	0.8
Central India ...	0.5	0.6	0.5	0.5	0.6
N. W. India ...	0.3	0.3	0.3	0.5	0.5
All India ...	1.2	0.9	0.8	0.7	0.9

The average for East and South India zones were much higher than that for any other zone.

The following statement gives the zonal differences:
The average number of poultry per family was 0.9. The average per family of tenants, agricultural labourers and non-agriculturists was almost the same, it being 0.9, 0.8 and 0.7 respectively. The figure for landowners families was, however, relatively high being 1.2. The above table gives the average area of cultivated land per plough and per pair of work animals in the sample villages. In working out the figures, however, it has been assumed that only the ploughs and the work animals owned by the families living in the same villages were utilised for the various agricultural operations, that no ploughs or work animals were brought from outside and that the ploughs and work animals owned by the families in the sample villages were not utilised by others outside the villages. The average area of cultivated land per plough and per pair of work animals in the sample villages worked out to 6.04 and 7.18. acres respectively. The relatively high figures for Saurashtra and Kutch have to be viewed in the context that the average size of holding was high and the soil sandy.

Pattern of Housing

During the General Family Survey, information on housing was collected through a special rubric. The data collected have, however, considerable limitations. In the first place, it is very difficult to have standard definitions especially for purposes of place to place comparisons. Broadly, houses were classified into pucca houses and kacha houses. Pucca houses are those the walls and roofs of which are built of bricks and stones with lime and mortar. If the walls were made of bricks and stones but the roof was made of thatch, the house was called partly pucca and partly kacha. Others were classified as kacha houses. The nature and structure of the house differed from region to region and was determined primarily by the climatic conditions on the one hand and the building materials easily available on the other. Thus, in the hilly regions of Assam, U. P. and Himachal Pradesh the houses were mostly of wooden structure. In regions with hillocks around, the walls were usually built of stones as they were available in plenty. In villages which were situated near rivers, the reeds grown on these river banks were used as thatching material. It was also common for villagers to use dried stalks of maize, cocoanut leaves and palm leaves for making roofs.

Since the construction of pucca houses with bricks and mortar require substantial initial investment, only those who were relatively better off owned such houses. Thus, a few big landlords, merchants and moneylenders had pucca houses and the rest, working classes, the artisans and the marginal cultivators lived in kacha houses with mud wall and thatched roofs.

Data on the floor area of houses and the rent paid either for the house or for the ground on which it was erected were also collected. These are not, however, given here since these were not considered to be quite accurate in view of the difficulty in getting precise information from the villagers.

Types of Housing

In the sample villages about 84 per cent of the houses were kacha houses. Amongst the major States, this percentage was more than 90 in U. P., the Eastern States of Assam, Bihar, West Bengal and Orissa and the Central States of Madhya Pradesh and Hyderabad. It ranged between 80 and 90 in Rajasthan and Madhya Bharat and between 70 and 80 in Punjab, Bombay, Madras and Travancore-Cochin. The position was comparatively better in Pepsu and Saurashtra, the percentage being about 60. This was so presumably due to availability of stones. The following statement shows the percentages in the different Census Zones:

Percentage of kacha houses occupied by important categories of families

	Percentage of kacha houses occupied by families of	
Zones	Agricultural workers	All families
North India	99.7	92.5
East India	97.2	98.5
South India	90.0	78.1
West India	68.5	63.5
Central India	95.6	92.1
North-West India	88.6	76.1
All Sample Villages ..	92.6	84.1

The percentage of partly pucca and partly kacha houses was only 2.1, taking the Indian Union as a whole. Thus the percentage of pucca houses came to 13.8. The percentage of partly pucca and partly kacha houses was, however, relatively high, viz., about 8 per cent in North-West Zone mainly due to existence of such houses in Punjab and Pepsu.

***Ownership of houses*:** The houses were almost all self-owned. This meant that the plot on which the house was erected was also owned by the house owner. However, when ground rent was paid, it generally meant that only the house was owned but not the plot. Such cases were included in the owned houses. Taking all the sample villages, the percentage of rented houses was about 1.7 and varied up to 4 in the major States. In respect of the agri-cultural labour families in particular, this percentage was about 1.3.

***Families per house*:** Generally there was only one family per house. In fact the percentage of houses accommodating a single family was 95.3; those with two families formed 3.2 per cent and those with three or more families only 1.5 percent. The same trend was observed in each of the six Census Zones. The percentage of houses having one family varied from 93.6 in North India to 96.6 in South and Central India, while the percentage of those having 2 families varied from 2.3 in South India to 4.2 in North India, and those having 3 or more families varied between 1 and 2.

Distribution of houses according to number of families living in them

Zones	Percentage of houses accommodation		
	One family	Two families	Three or more families
North India	93.6	4.2	2.2
East India	94.4	3.7	1.9
South India	96.6	2.3	1.1
West India	95.7	3.0	1.3
Central India	96.5	2.6	0.9
North-West India	94.8	3.6	1.6

***Number of rooms per house*:** Houses with a single room formed the largest percentage, viz., 38. Two room houses formed

28 and those having three or more rooms 34 per cent. The average number of rooms per house was 2.3. The agricultural labour families had limited accommodation, the average number of rooms per house being 1.9 and houses with one room formed the largest percentage, viz., 55, while two room houses constituted 27 per cent. The following statement gives the frequency distribution of houses according to rooms in the different Census Zones.

Taking the major States, the average number of rooms per house was 1.3 in West Bengal, 1.8 in Madhya Pradesh, 1.8 in Bombay, 1.9 in Madras and varied between 2 and 3 in the remaining States. The position in important States is given in the statement below:

Percentage Distribution of Houses According to Number of Rooms

	All families			Agricultural labour families		
Zone	1 room	2 rooms	3 or more rooms	1 room	2 rooms	3 or more rooms
NorthIndia	17.7	24.6	57.7	27.5	32.3	40.2
East India	42.0	24.7	33.3	48.8	27.5	23.7
South India	47.9	27.5	24.6	60.6	25.6	13.8
West India	42.7	38.6	18.7	54.7	33.9	11.4
Central India	48.6	30.3	21.1	63.9	27.4	8.7
North-West India	25.9	32.3	41.8	46.0	34.1	19.9
All sample villages	37.7	28.2	34.1	54.8	27.7	17.5

Number of Persons per Room: The number of persons per room depended on the number of rooms per house and the size of the family. Taking all the sampled villages, the average was about 2.3. The average generally varied between 2 and 3 as among the different States and was the highest in West Bengal being 3.6.

Taking the agricultural labour families, the size of the family was generally less than that of other classes of families and still the congestion was higher in view of the limited accommodation. In most of the major States, the number of persons per room was 3 with the exception of U. P., Assam, Bihar, Orissa, Rajasthan and Travancore-Cochin where it was, 2, 1.8, 2.5, 2.2, 2.1, and 2.6 respectively. The following statement gives the average number of persons per room in the different zones:

Average Number of Persons per Room

Zone	Average number of persons per room in the houses occupied by families of: Agricultural workers	All families
North India	2.1	1.7
East India	2.5	2.3
South India	3.0	2.4
Central India	2.6	3.2
West India	2.9	2.8
North-West India	2.7	2.6

Number of Persons per Room

Zones	Average number of rooms per house occupied by families of: Agricultural workers	All families
North India	2.5	3.2
Uttar Pradesh	2.5	3.2
East India	2.1	2.4
Assam	1.9	2.6
Bihar	2.4	3.2
West Bengal	1.2	1.3
Orissa	2.2	2.9
South India	1.8	2.1
Madras	1.5	1.9
Mysore	1.8	2.1
Travancore-Cochin	2.0	2.0
West India	1.8	1.9
Bombay	1.6	1.8
Saurashtra	1.2	1.6
Central India	1.5	2.0
Madhya Pradesh	1.5	1.8
Madhya Bharat	1.5	2.3
Hyderabad	1.5	1.8
North-West India	1.9	2.8
Punjab	1.6	2.4
Pepsu	1.6	2.6
Rajasthan	2.3	2.9
All sample villages	2.0	2.3

Eleven

Farm Products

This subject is usually discussed under the broad heading land reform or agrarian reform. There are many aspects of agrarian reform and I shall deal only with what I consider to be the core of agrarian reform in India, namely, organisation of agricultural production with particular reference to the size and structure of the unit of agricultural production.

The main constituents of the programme of agrarian or land reform currently undertaken by the State in India are classified as follows in the Progress Report for 1953-54 of the Five-Year Plan:-

(1) The abolition of intermediaries;

(2) Tenancy reforms designed:-

  (a) To scale down rents to 1/4th or 1/5th of the produce;

  (b) To give tenants permanent rights subject to the landlord's right to resume a minimum holding for his personal cultivation within a limited time;

  (c) To enable tenants (subject to the landlord's right of resumption for personal cultivation) to acquire ownership of their lands, on payment of moderate compensation to the landlord spread over a period of years;

(3) Fixing of ceilings on holdings;

(4) Re-organisation of agriculture including the consolidation of holdings, the prevention of fragmen-tation and the development of co-operative village management and co-operative farming.

Many of the items included in the above have been subjects of attention and activity on the part of governments for many decades past. However, a number of important elements are of recent introduction and the programme has begun to look like an integrated attempt only within the last few years. An important feature which has received emphasis only since the attainment of Independence is the abolition of intermediaries, popularly regarded as equivalent to the abolition of zamindari.

While emphasising the primary importance of the abolition of zamindari it is necessary to remember that, in India, it affects, in the main, the distribution of the total agricultural product and not the size and organisation of the unit of agricultural production.

This is because, in the first instance, the abolition of intermediaries does not mean the break-up of large farms or farming estates or the redistribution of land and secondly because, even if this had been a part of the programme, there are, in fact, with the exception of a small number of regions, no large farming estates in India. The very description of the reform as abolition of intermediaries, emphasises this aspect of the redistribution of the product and reduction of the burden on the actual cultivator. It is conceived of essentially as establishing, as far as possible, a direct relation between the actual tiller of the soil and the State.

Tenancy reform or tenancy legislation has a much wider sphere of operation than legislation for the abolition of intermediaries.

Various Reforms

Tenancy reform also, it will be obvious, does not affect the size and shape of the agricultural holding. It brings about, in the main, a redistribution of the total produce in favour of the tenant and also gives him a sense of security regarding the future which should react favourably on the economic and technical operation of the tenant cultivator. However, there is one important difference between tenancy reform and the abolition of intermediaries. The latter is, for the most part, a once-for-all operation; the former, on the other hand, has not only continuous effect but has further to adapt itself constantly to a changing situation. In consequence though tenancy legislation may not operate directly on the unit of agricultural production, the framing of tenancy legislation is always influenced by total land policy including policy relating to the size and structure of the unit of agricultural production. In India, tenancy legislation has to concern itself with problems such as those of sub-letting or of the alienation, transfer or inheritance of land; and all of these have relation with objectives of policy relating to the unit of agricultural production.

The fixing of ceilings on holdings is likely to affect the size of the unit of agricultural production much more directly than either the abolition of intermediaries or tenancy reform. Before proceeding further I may note that the omission to distinguish clearly between the ownership holdings and the cultivating holdings leads often to a confusion in thinking and exposition of the subject of land reform in India.

The immediate effect of the adoption of a ceiling for the future, on size of the production unit would, on the other hand, be negligible, except to the extent that it would encourage actual or notional division of existing large holdings among family members so as not to be affected early by the operation of the legislation. The long-term effects are problematical and would depend on the extent to which the existing or future situation otherwise favoured the formation of very large holdings.

Even the comparatively large estate of Kashmir and Telengana do not or did not contain elements of direct cultivation large enough for redistribution to effect sensibly the problem of the small peasant holding, in even restricted areas. Elsewhere the contrasts are much less glaring. The concept of the ceiling, if it is to be used in India must, therefore, be different in content and operation from that in countries with large landlord estates plantations or latifundia.

The concept of the economic holding or a minimum holding called by any name, like the concept of the ceiling, can form the basis of an immediate operation of reorganisation or can be confined to setting a limit to future transactions. In the latter alternative it may act as an effective means of preventing a worsening of the existing situation and may partly even help to improve it gradually in the future. These effects will, however, become apparent only slowly over a series of years and a limit for the future cannot help towards reorganisation, if the existing situation in itself is extremely unsatisfactory. A minimum holding or a floor has not been used in any State in India yet for bringing about immediate reorganisation of production units in lands included in units below the minimum size.

Consolidation as practised in India affects powerfully the internal organisation of a holding, though not usually its total size. The process of consolidation may lead to some saving in the land surface used for such purposes as boundaries or roads and may thus enable formation of a pool of land for specific common purposes. But the saving effected in this way is not likely to yield substantial acreage for distribution among existing holders. Co-operative farming or co-operative village management are yet chiefly in the stage of thought. What little action has been taken is experimental and nowhere has any legislation been formulated or contemplated which bases itself on the formation of co-operative farming units for at least a part of state policy relating to land management.

Land Reforms

Legislation on land reform is essentially a matter for governments of States. Therefore, the programme is usually framed in the context of particular problems of each State. The activity of the National Planning Commission affords the chief occasion and instrument for integrating policies of different State Governments and for formulating a common Indian policy. Considerable importance, therefore, attaches to the views regarding land policy contained in the First Five-Year Plan. The problems of the policy are divided into two aspects; Land Management and Land Reform. It is evidently considered that there is some conflict between the two; for, it is said that "Land Policy should include both elements but should maintain a balance between the two."

The suggested land reform policy is again not uniform; it is evidently to change with size of land owning. The most important result is that the tenants of small and middle owners are recommended much less protection than the tenants of large owners. As middle owners are defined as owners of land upto three times the family holding the field of tenancy, protection is thus seriously narrowed. The main reason given for the maintenance of a large class of tenants-at-will in this way is that otherwise movement of people from agriculture and rural areas into other occupations and towns may be seriously checked. It is fortunate that most State Governments have paid little attention to this recommendation in their legislative programme.

In relation to the landless worker the main concrete reference is to the Bhoodan movement. "It offers the landless worker an opportunity not otherwise open to him." This can be only interpreted as meaning that the State itself considers it neither necessary nor possible to do anything for him. It is added that the problem of the landless worker must be considered in terms of institutional changes which would create conditions of equality for all sections of the population. The essence of these changes is described as a system of co-operative village management. Co-operative village management is referred to in the Plan in other context also. For example, after having formulated the important and unexceptionable proposition that "the basic condition for increase in agricultural production is increase in the unit of management of land" this also is said to be possible only through co-operative management at the village level. With regard to the small and the middle farmers again it is recommended that they should be encouraged and assisted to develop their production and organise their activities on co-operative basis. With this emphasis on co-operation it would be expected that co-operative organisation or cooperative village management would be described in specific detail and a programme sketched out for establishing it. The following extract summarises the ideas of the Planning Commission on co-operative village management.

"Broadly speaking, however, we envisage that the village panchayat should become the agency both for land reform and for land management in the village. In the first place it should be the body concerned with the management of land taken over from substantial owners, and also of village waste lands. The leasing of lands by small and middle owners should also be done through the panchayat and not directly. In this way the village panchayat may be able to provide cultivating holdings of economic size, at any rate for landless cultivators. The exercise of these functions would naturally lead on to the wider conception of the co-operative management of the entire land of the village and the undertaking of activities for creating non-agricultural employment in the village."

It is not necessary to comment on the above except to note that it does not deal with the problem in the comprehensive manner that might have been expected, that it is over-optimistic and also that the working model presented is obviously unsuitable and inadequate in most respects. Moreover, no concrete programme is provided for progress in the direction of co-operative village management even according to ideas contained in the Plan, beyond the Rs. 50 lakhs provided for study, training and experimentation. It would not be unfair in the circumstances, to suggest that the Plan proposes little of importance in relation to land management and that we have at present no effective programme in contemplation for dealing with what the Planning Commission itself recognises as the basic problem, viz., that of " the increase in the unit of management of land".

Not only is the subject treated unsatisfactorily in the Plan but also the subsequent activities of the Planning Commission and the Central Government do not indicate that it is currently held in importance or receives any special attention.

Popular Projects

The Community Projects are supposed to be the special field of the Planning Commission and great reliance is placed on them in relation to agricultural development in the future. Not only do these projects pay no attention to land reform or land distribution but even experimentation in relation to land management appears to find no place in them. The complete absence of any attention to it in the programme of community projects is evidenced by its not having been necessary to devote any attention to the subject in the Evaluation Report on the first year's working of these projects. And the later report of the Evaluation Organization, "Community Projects-First Reactions" contains enough evidence to show how the project authorities completely ignore land management and land reform problems. In regard to co-operative organizations we have the following comment in the Evaluation Report. "While in the very initial stages of the formulation of community plans this aspect of mutual dependence between community development and co-operative organization was not so explicitly stated, during the course of the year increasing emphasis was placed by the Community Projects Administration on promotion of cooperative organizations." (p. 39.) The cooperatives to which increasing attention is reported are still the credit, purchase and sale and other organizations and not experiments in increasing scales of land management. The putting forward more recently of agricultural extension as the panacea for all rural ills is, perhaps, a reflection of the same attitude. It appears to be considered by the Planning Commission, as by many foreign experts, that all that is required to increase agricultural production in India adequately is to arouse enthusiasm and to transfer techniques. The problem as to whether conditions in the field are such as to favour generation of enthusiasm and the acquisition and continued practice of new techniques does not evidently need prior consideration. Finally, it is reported that in some States, the Central Government, presumably acting through the Planning Commission, was responsible for persuading Governments to modify their original ideas regarding immediate operation of a ceiling on holdings. All in all, one gathers the impression that while in its theoretic formulation the Planning Commission may recognize the existence of the problem of land management it is not ready to give this recognition any immediate or in concrete form.

As indicated above, the Planning Commission appears content to operate with the existing unit of agricultural production and does not propose to change in any radical manner the organization of land management and operation. The Congress Agrarian Reforms Committee also formulates its actual programme very largely in terms of the peasant farm and it does not appear to consider that a programme of reorganization involving large numbers of families and a considerable land surface is insistently called for. The experts appear to talk almost exclusively of the peasant unit and their ideas of land reform are confined mostly to abolition of intermediaries and dealing with large estates. In the circumstances, it becomes necessary to examine existing conditions carefully, especially with a view to throwing light on the strength and efficiency of the independent peasant farm as the unit of land management and agricultural production.

Farms, Small and Large

It is generally known that the size of the large bulk of farms in India is very small and that numbers of them cannot be called family farms in any valid sense of that term. However, no attempt is usually made to indicate with figures the dimensions of the problem. I shall, therefore, note certain salient features of the situation very briefly. My concern is with the unit of land management, the cultivated holding, and data relating to ownership of land are not relevant to my purpose. The data required are those relating to size, scale of operations and of investment, receipts and employment, etc., from farming, of the independent farming units.

According to the Survey a little over half of the cultivators reported a value of gross produce of farm business lower than Rs. 400 for the year. This then is a useful starting point of the description, that half or more of the farm units, i.e., independent units of land management in India may have a gross produce of farm less than Rs. 600 a year. The next step is to assess the relative importance of farming activity to the farm family. In the total number of cultivators reporting less than Rs. 400 of value of gross produce during the year two divisions were made representing those with a value of gross produce below Rs. 200 and those with a value of gross produce between Rs. 200 and Rs. 400. The former formed slightly more than 29 per cent of the total cultivators and the latter, group 21 per cent. Those reporting value of gross produce less than Rs. 200 reported total farm expenses which exceeded their value of gross produce and those in the latter class reported total farm expenses that were on an average only about Rs. 60 less than the average value of gross produce. The average reported cash receipts from sale of crops and fodder in the two classes were about Rs. 20 and Rs. 70 respectively and both classes reported cash farm expenses that were more than Rs. 50 on an average than the average cash receipts from sale of crops and fodder. Making all allowances for errors in reporting, etc., it is clear that the cultivators included in these groups earn little, if any, net cash income through their farming activity and the main advantage derived by them from farming is some contribution in kind to family living.

In the main, however, cultivators in the lower strata have much lower values of gross produce than those in the upper. Of the total borrowings of even the middle four deciles more than half represented borrowing for family expenditure items; for the last three deciles the corresponding proportion was almost 60 per cent. The capacity of the average cultivating family to undertake capital expenditure was obviously extremely limited. The average expenditure undertaken on all items such as bunding, reclamation, irrigation sources, implements, etc., including expenditure on repairs, maintenance and replacement was about Rs. 22 for families of the lowest three deciles and Rs. 51 for families of the middle four deciles; the corresponding amount was Rs. 311 for families of the first decile. But if this expenditure is taken together with expenditure on purchase of livestock by the respective groups of deciles and the total calculated on a per acre basis the expenditure incurred actually increases as one goes down the groups of deciles. This means that while the total outlays of the families of the middle and lower deciles are small and are known to be inadequate their burden in terms of per acre costs rules high.

It is not necessary to labour the point further. What I want to emphasise is that the size of farming business of at least half the cultivating families in India is such that it is futile to consider them as independent units of land exploitation in any plan for a developing economy. It is irrelevant in the light of the data cited above to talk in terms of family farms or economic holdings. Even the definition of basic holding of the Congress Agrarian Reforms Committee cannot cover these units. Therefore, a land policy for a developing economy must face up to the serious problem of the reorganization of these units. A vague recognition of these facts is seen in the general comments made in various contexts by numerous experts and committees on the "non-creditworthy" or the "marginal and submarginal" groups. This recognition must become more explicit and must lead on to a realisation of the inability of any supply or credit reorganization to deal with fundamental defects of the small size and turnover of the existing basic units and of the large numbers involved in any scheme of reorganization.

There appears at present general agreement on the nature of the problem and the main approach to its solution. The following statement by the Prime Minister, Pandit Jawaharlal Nehru, may be taken as representative of this.

"As agriculture is the principal occupation of the great majority of our people, it must be the first concern of the State. The abolition of the zamindari system has been the first reform and this must be expedited. But it must be remembered that this by itself is no solution of the problem Even before this abolition a very large proportion of land was self-cultivated. An addition to it, without any further reforms, will not help much. The small subsistence farm makes progress difficult. We have to think, therefore, and think soon, of other and further steps. There should be a diversion of a part of the agricultural population to other occupations. There should be a development of cottage and small-scale industries. But essentially the problem of agriculture needs co-operative cultivation and the application of modern techniques. This does not mean necessarily mechanising agriculture all over India, though some degree of mechanisation is taking place and is desirable. But there is no escape from some form of co-operative cultivation, if we are to make agriculture progressive."

Considerations of production economy do not seem to indicate any particular figures or proportions in this context. However, data from the Rural Credit Survey may be set out to illustrate the relative proportions involved. These data relate to all the cultivated holdings in the 600 villages selected for the survey in 75 districts. The cultivators were arranged, for the purpose, in order of the size of their cultivated holdings. When so arranged it was found that the first 10 per cent or decile of the cultivators held more than 25 per cent of the total land surface in almost all districts and held more than 30 per cent of it in 51 of the 75 districts. The first 30 per cent of three deciles taken together held more than 50 per cent of the land in almost all districts and in 48 districts they held more than 60 per cent; in no district was this proportion larger than 85 but in 6 it varied between 75 and

85 per cent. The middle four deciles held between 25 and 35 per cent of the total cultivated land in the large majority of districts. The holdings of the last three deciles included less than 10 per cent of the total cultivated land in the majority of districts; but in 27 out of the 75 districts they held between 10 and 15 per cent. Taking the broad division of cultivators into the upper half and lower half the relative size of their holdings of total land surface would be approximately 3:1.

The above taken together with the data relating to occupational distribution of families should give an idea of the overall dimensions of the problem. We may assume that about 60 per cent of families in rural India are cultivators in the sense of operating some cultivated land and that of the non-cultivators at least half depend for their support on agriculture and land. This gives about 80 per cent of rural families as interested in land management units and policy. We may, on the basis of data set out before, consider about half of the cultivators as having unsuitable units for independent land management, the proportion cannot at a minimum be put at less than a third of the cultivators. If we take the former figure the cultivating families together with the landless interested in reorganization, will form about half the total number of families in the countryside, and, if the latter, about 40 per cent of them. Working with the data for existing distribution of cultivating holdings and assuming a transfer, because of the operation of the ceiling, of the order of 5 per cent of the total cultivated land, we have the following figures of the extent of land surface and number of families affected by reorganization; if, half the units cease to be independent, about 50 per cent of rural families and 30 per cent of the cultivated land; and if, about one-third of cultivators are so affected, about 40 per cent of the rural families and about 15 per cent of the total land surface. These calculations are so broad as to be almost notional and they have been indulged in at this place only to give some idea of the dimension of the problem.

Basic Measures

The two fundamental steps in reorganization of land management units in India are: (i) redistribution of the land surface and: (ii) formation of the larger consolidated units out of the pooled resources of the uneconomic units and surplus available for redistribution. The first step is an essential preliminary in almost all programmes of land improvement and agricultural development. Its importance is universally recognized in connection with the consolidation of fragmented holdings. It is, however, necessary from other points of view also. One can view the process of consolidation in a wider context as part of the process of a rational layout of the total land surface for agricultural and other utilisation.

This task is no doubt of vast dimensions. But tasks of somewhat similar dimensions have been undertaken in other countries and the total work indicated above is not more complicated or larger than the process of consolidation undertaken currently by many State Governments in India. As I visualise it the first stage in the process will be that of determining the general layout and the second of locating in this layout the independent farm units now fixed in location and made impartible, and the co-operative estates or farms.

The formation of larger units out of pooled land and other resources will have two aspects, one compulsory and the other voluntary. I have assumed that once the floor has been defined independent units of farm management smaller in area will not be allowed to exist. Obviously the enforcement of this must be by some sort of legislation. The measure of compulsion may vary. In the early stages the step may be initiated, as in some programmes of consolidation, only on the motion of a minimum number of families involved.

Both these tasks, that of redistributing the land surface and the formation of a small number of co-operative farms in each village are immense in extent and complexity. I would argue that not only are they a *sine qua non* of any programme of land reform but also that they are not beyond our capacity, if a sincere and concentrated effort is made. Consolidation is already generally accepted as a necessary part of the programme by everybody. The formation and proper functioning of co-operative farms is undoubtedly less generally accepted as part of universal policy and is somewhat more difficult. It is, however, equally necessary.

I shall, without elaborating them, briefly state a number of reasons in favour of this proposition. In the first instance, without cooperatives, collectives or state farms, an economic reorganization for operation of the existing numerous small units is impossible. Secondly, except as member of a co-operative the small farmer can never be in a position to avail himself of technical, financial, or other external aid of which he stands in need, more than anybody else. The findings of all studies; whether, e.g., of the Rural Credit Survey or the Evaluation Organization are that the bigger man gets the greater profit out of everything, government loans, co-operative finance or other financial or technical assistance of any type. One need not go into the reasons for this state of affairs; it is, however, clear from the studies that the scattered, weak units cannot really be helped effectively unless they come together. Also, as long as there is no consolidation of these weak units the balance in rural society will always remain against them. Any close study of the effects of recent land reforms legislation reveals large variations in its results, dependent chiefly on the strength of tenants and smaller holders in a locality or region. In a large number of instances legal protection and other devices prove constantly fruitless because of the strength and ingenuity of the strong. It is sad to record that large deflection of original intentions, brought about by the strong, has been reported even in the working of the Bhoodan movement. The moral is that unless the weak acquire economic strength by joining together they could never stand up and get full advantage of state policy and state legislation. The formation of a small number of co-operative farming societies of the smaller holders and the landless in each locality is a necessary step in this direction. It will be noticed that I consider redistribution as only a part of the process in the formation of the large co-operative farms. I cannot see any virtue in merely tenancy co-operatives which perpetuate the smaller units of management. Leaving scope for allotments or kitchen gardens would be welcome but the main cropping operations must be in terms of the large units. The experience elsewhere, such as with the Ejido in Mexico, emphasises importance of this.

I do not think that widespread formation of such co-operatives is an impossible undertaking. In the initial stages the progress may be slow but once the movement gathers momentum the field could be covered fairly quickly. Wide extension of the activities of State governments in rural areas together with efforts made by the Central Government in directions of Community Development and National Extension already provide comparatively large staffs in the field; the work of this staff would come to have real meaning and purpose only if it is linked to a programme of the formation and operation of such co-operatives. Instead of chiefly conducting propaganda they would find in these co-operatives numerous local units which could prove centres of demonstration and experimentation. All governmental information and propaganda, aid and assistance could be directed towards and routed through these co-operatives. The special terms of assistance, etc., laid down for these co-operatives should combine the features of the programmes envisaged in the draft outline of the Five-Year Plan for the Registered Farms and for the Co-operative Farming Societies. Instead of receiving very little or nothing of government protection and assistance this step would ensure that the most disadvantaged received, as they should, the highest priority and the greatest assistance.

There are following basic propositions. That in relation to land management we are following, in this country today, a policy mainly of drift; that a programme of economic development requires more positive approach in respect of agricultural productive organization and units of land management; that a very large number of existing cultivating holdings are extremely unsuitable for functioning as independent units in a programme of agricultural development and that a rational layout of the land surface for its proper utilisation and a programme for the creation of large consolidated holdings are essential ingredients in any agricultural and land development policy. I may add finally that it would be impossible to deal with this problem except in term of bold steps and very large and strenuous effort. However, these would be no more radical and strenuous than those undertaken by many other countries in analogous situations, as evidenced, for example, by the Mexican Agrarian Revolution which redistributed land in favour of the Ejidos or the transformations brought about in countries of South and East Europe both during the inter-war years and in the period after the Second World War.

Industries in Rural Belt

The weakest spot in our programmes of community development is the development of rural industries for providing employment to the unemployed and the underemployed. From the data available, it appears that only 2.5 per cent of the families have been benefited by our activities in the 80 blocks examined by us. These figures are too generous in that the benefit of employment to one man has been equated to benefit to one whole family; also the employment has been assumed to be full employment. Even so, this additional employment introduced in the village is insufficient to set off the two years' increase in population. The training-cum-production centres have been the main channel of opening new rural industries. Figures available, however, show that more than 50 per cent of the persons passing out of such centres do not take up the profession to which they have been trained. These disquieting facts have to be faced and our present approach to the problem has to be revised radically.

To this end steps have to be taken for:

(i) carrying out a rapid local economic and technical survey in each block in the possibility of specific industries;

(ii) training for improvement of existing technical skills and introduction of new ones in consonance with the findings of (i.) above;

(iii) establishment of pilot projects to demonstrate the technical feasibility and economic soundness of any particular industry or industries;

(iv) co-ordination of cottage, village and small-scale industries;

(v) rural electrification which could equally well serve irrigation purposes;

(vi) provision of credit for rural industry;

(vii) supply of raw material where necessary and of improved designs;

(viii) quality control and facilities for marketing; and

(ix) research, technical supervision and guidance.

Cottage, village and small-scale industries need a very considerable coordination in their working. They have their appropriate place in the rural economy but sometimes are apt to cut into one another. At the all-India level, a number of such individual industries are promoted by all-India boards which sometimes are inclined to work in separate compartments. It should not be difficult to make some effort to pool funds, personnel; agencies of supervision and inspection and marketing arrangements so that inefficiency and waste can be minimised. The all-India boards, themselves should function through State boards nominated by the State Governments in consultation with them. The State boards in their turn should function through the various State departments concerned with the industry and through local representative organisations.

Cottage Industries

Taking up first those difficulties which are special to cottage industries, as distinguished from agriculture, three main items are obvious:

(1) Cottage industries have to face the competition of larger, better organized and technically much more competent units in the shape of the manufacturing industries situated in towns and cities.

(2) The market for cottage industries is much less assured than for the agricultural industry. Fortunately for the latter, food is firstly wanted by all, and secondly is still grown on land and not in factories. For cottage industries, on the other hand, the essence of the problem is to find a market and then not lose it to a more powerful urban competitor.

(3) The other important special problem for many cottage industries is the finding of the raw material. Thus, one of the greatest difficulties of the handloom industry, except perhaps in periods of control, has been that of the purchase of yarn. A number of weavers' co-operative societies, it is interesting to note, are little

more than societies for buying yarn and distributing it among their members.

Apart from these items, all of them grave and all of them important, the nature of the difficulties seems essentially the same for cottage industries as for agriculture when looked at from the point of view of the reorganization and rehabilitation of the industry on a co-operative basis. The main and still largely unsolved problem for co-operative cottage industry is, we suggest, the same that has been faced by co-operative agriculture, namely, how to make a combination of the very weak strong enough in relation to the much stronger. Just as there is the moneylender in the sphere of agricultural credit, so there is the Karkhanadar for each important cottage industry, with the difference that he combines in himself the handicraftsman and the financier. The karkhanadar is himself part of a wider system of private finance. Thus a whole set of private creditors, financing agencies, marketing agencies, etc., deal with the individual small weaver, as do the private traders and private financiers with the cultivator. We would, in this connection, quote from a note which appears in the First Annual Report (1954) of the All-India Handloom Board.

"Since, according to the Fact Finding Committee's Report, the unorganised condition of the industry is responsible for its abnormal high marketing costs and its consequent evils, it is but natural to accord pride of place to the organisation of the industry in all schemes aiming at the stabilization of the ancient industry and thereby ensuring the prosperity of the weavers." According to the Fact Finding Committee, the official agencies have fostered only co-operative organisations which have, speaking generally, suffered from financial weakness, inefficiency of management and inability to cope with fluctuation in yarn prices and with marketing of the finished product. The Committee has also emphasised the age-long social and business relations and, in most cases, ties of caste and creed between the master-weavers, sowcars and mahajans, on the one hand and the weavers on the other, which may have been primarily responsible for the half-hearted support accorded to the co-operative movement. It is also possible that the lack of credit facilities on social occasions such as marriages, pujahs, absence of any effective voice in the management of co-operative organisation and the smallness of the capital invested by him in the society did not evoke the enthusiasm of the weaver who preferred to eke out an existence as best as he could with the aid and support of the master-weaver or the sowcar mahajan. It is also not unlikely that co-operative organizations invited within their fold only the weavers and thus alienated the sympathy of the master-weavers and the mahajans.

Promotion of Sales

"The next question of importance is the question of marketing. In so far as the independent weavers are concerned, they form the smaller proportion of the weaver population in the country; no tangible relief could be possible unless they join either the co-operative or any other organization which may be fostered. Their slender finances, chronic indebtedness and, therefore, complete dependence on the yarn dealer for the supply of yarn on credit leave them no option other than that of selling at the buyer's price. Unless, therefore, they are brought within the fold of such organisation as would supply them yarn on credit and take back the finished product at prices based on standard wages and replacement cost of yarn, they would in due course of time be relegated to the position of mere wage-earners.

"...The numerous types of middlemen and the functions of each has been dealt with fully by the Fact Finding Committee in paragraphs 60 to 63 of its Report, and the Committee has discussed the middlemen's profit in paragraph 124. The Committee has also come to the conclusion that `there are far too many middlemen participating in the trade and that their efficiency and individual turnover are much lower than they should be. At the same time, there are many middlemen who appear to be keeping their heads above water by taking a proportionately higher share of the gross profits of the industry than the weaver himself.' The Committee has emphasised that the cost of marketing of handloom fabrics is 'prohibitively high and that the middleman is largely to be blamed for this.' `The principal problem, therefore, so far as marketing is concerned, is how to reduce the marketing costs."

Twelve

Agro Economy

A little more than a decade has elapsed since this country launched upon a programme of planned economic development. According to the estimates of the Planning Commission, an investment of 10,110 crore rupees has been made in the economy between 1951 and 1961. The Third-Five Year Plan envisages an investment of another 10,000 crore rupees during 1961-65. It is legitimate to expect that all this investment and the organizational effort that goes with it, would not only accelerate the pace of economic development, but, in the process, also alter the structure of the economy. It would be interesting therefore to examine the nature and extent of change in the structure of the national economy during the last decade, by reference to some of the conventional economic indicators.

For the purpose of this Address, I should like to focus attention on the impact of the process of growth on the agricultural sector. The literature on the economics of growth visualizes a certain role for agriculture in the process of economic development, stage by stage, but a little more precisely in the early stage of development. Not that all writers are unanimous on the subject, but most of them agree on the importance or the crucial role of agriculture.

As a background to our main factual analysis of India's experience, it would be interesting to review briefly, first, some of the theories on the role of agriculture in economic development, and then, the thinking of the Indian planners on the subject, as revealed in the successive Five-Year Plans.

Basic Principles

The primacy of agricultural development is emphasized by some writers, because agriculture is not only the most populous but also the most depressed sector of the economy in most of the developing economies. This view is sometimes carried to the extreme of opposition to industrial development. It is argued that "the policy of industrialization will intensify the tendency for savings to be drained from the countryside by making investment in urban industries more attractive", and thus widen the range of inequality between the urban and rural standards of living. "Problems of over-population and unemployment, very low incomes, excessive urbanization, food shortages as well as certain social and political considerations would suggest that the policy of industrialization is premature and undesirable at the present stage of Asian development." The importance of increased supply of food and other wage goods is emphasized by a group of thinkers not merely on welfare grounds, but as a necessary investment in human capital. The `consumption multiplier', it is argued, is not less crucial than the conventional investment multiplier in the strategy of development.

Priority for agriculture is also favoured on the ground that the creation of investible surplus is technologically easier in agriculture and has much shorter gestation period. Increase in agricultural production in the initial period of development can be brought about through the application of resources which have a low opportunity cost and make no inroads on the critically scarce resources necessary for industrial development.

The point of departure comes on the question whether the economic surplus in agriculture should be retained within it for improving the standard of rural living or should be siphoned off for urban, industrial development. Those who advocate the latter are interested in agriculturists either forcibly or through lower prices. The non-violent strategy is expounded thus: "Increase in the output of foodgrains and other agricultural commodities sufficient to lower their price will make the terms of trade unfavourable to agriculture. The fall in agricultural prices will be steep, due to the fact that the demand for food is not infinitely elastic. If agricultural prices are depressed relative to non-agricultural prices, agricultural surpluses will go into the hands of non-agriculturists."

As against the agriculture-first school, those who emphasize the role of rapid industrialization in economic development argue that most of the underdeveloped countries are, in fact, so termed because of the predominance of agriculture in their national economy. The path of progress, therefore, must inevitably lie in the direction of a shift of resources, both capital and labour, from low-productivity enterprises to high-productivity enterprises. Agriculture is admittedly a relatively low-productivity sector even in most of the advanced countries; as such, the strategy of economic development would consist in gradually reducing the preponderance of the agricultural sector in the national economy through a process of industrialization. This, in any case, would be necessary inasmuch as with rising incomes, the community's demand-pattern will undergo a change in favour of industrial products.

International comparisons of shares of major sectors in national product "reveal a negative correlation between the level of income and agriculture's share in it, and a positive correlation between the level of income and the share of non-agricultural commodity production. As the level of per capita income increases, the share of agriculture in national product drops and that of industry rises." Analysis of long-term trends also confirms the results obtained by cross-country analysis. Thus, Prof. Kuznets found that with the secular rise of product per capita and per worker, the share of the agricultural sector in total product declines and the share of the manufacturing sector rises. The analysis in terms of distribution of labour force in the different sectors of the national economy suggests a significant positive association between the rate of growth in per capita and a shift away from agriculture in the structure of the labour force. One is therefore led to argue that "if real income per capita is to grow rapidly, the accompanying changes in the occupational structure of the labour force should be equally large. In the sample of eighteen countries, the total shift in the percentage distribution of labour force (including unpaid family labour) among the three major sectors (agriculture, manufacture, services) tends to be large in countries with high rates of growth of per capita income and vice versa."

These conclusions, however, should not be interpreted to imply that re-deployment of labour force would automatically, so to say, lead to higher per capita income. Kuznets' analysis has also revealed that a mere shift of the industrial structure of underdeveloped countries towards the pattern of developed countries-retaining the contrast between the high, relative, per-worker product in the manufacturing and service sectors and the low one in the agricultural sector-will not reduce the international differences in per-worker product. "To put in simply," he says, "the major source of international differences in countrywide output per worker (and per capita) between developed and underdeveloped countries is not that the full-time labour force of the former and of the latter are distributed differently among the several industrial sectors .... It is rather in the fact that within each sector proper within agriculture, within mining, within manufacturing, within transportation and trade, etc.-the product per worker in the underdeveloped countries is so much lower than in the developed." As a matter of fact, Kuznets himself has elsewhere argued: "Agricultural Revolution-a marked rise in productivity per worker in agriculture-is a pre-condition of the industrial revolution in any part of the world." Whatever be the motive or objective of economic development, welfare of the rural community or its surplus-generating-potential for overall economic development, there appears to be a fair degree of consensus regarding the crucial importance of agriculture in the initial period of economic growth.

Planning for Agriculture

In the light of the foregoing discussion on the role of agriculture in economic development, it would be useful to review briefly the views of the Planning Commission on this question as stated in the successive Five-Year Plans. Writing about the pattern of priority in the First Five-Year Plan, the Planning Commission states: "The conception of priorities over a period has to be a dynamic one, the emphasis as between different sectors shifting as development in those taken up initially prepares the ground for development in others." Having laid down this broad principle, the Planning Commission proceeds to state: "For the next five-year period, agriculture including irrigation and power must, in our view, have the top-most priority. For one thing, this emphasis is indicated by the need to complete the projects in hand, and further we are convinced that without a substantial increase in the production of food and of raw materials needed for industry, it would be impossible to sustain a high tempo of industrial development. In an underdeveloped economy, with low yield in agriculture, there is of course no real conflict between agricultural and industrial development. One cannot go far without the other; the two are complementary. It is necessary, however, on economic as well as on other grounds, first of all to strengthen the economy at the base and to create conditions of sufficiency and even plenitude in respect of food and raw materials." Consistent with this approach, in the total Plan outlay of 2,356 crore rupees, as much as 15.1 per cent was allocated to agriculture and community development and 28 - 1 per cent to irrigation and power (16.3 per cent to irrigation, 11.1 per cent to power and 0.7 per cent to flood control, etc.) as against 7.6 per cent to industry and mining (6.3 per cent for large and medium industries and 1.3 per cent for small industries). It should, however, be mentioned that the Planning Commission, at that stage, held the following view: "The progress in industries, especially large-scale industries, would have to depend, to a great extent, on effort in the private sector, while the State would concentrate on the provision of basic services like power and transportation." Though it was stated that the State had also "special responsibility for developing key industries and heavy industries like iron and steel, heavy chemicals and manufacture of electrical equipments without which development in the modern world is impossible," no significant allocation was made for the development of these key industries in the public sector.

Agricultural production during the First Five-Year Plan increased substantially, though in retrospect it appears that the bulk of it was due to an increase in the acreage and to good weather conditions. At the end of the First Five-Year Plan, food-grain production had increased from 55 million tons to 65 million tons, exceeding the target of 61.6 million tons laid down for the last year of the Plan. Prices of agricultural commodities also declined sharply. The comfortable situation on the agricultural front induced the Planning Commission to shift the emphasis towards industrialization, while formulating the Second Five-Year Plan one of the major objectives of the Plan was stated to be "rapid industrialization with particular emphasis on the development of basic and heavy industries". The other objectives mentioned in this context were a sizeable increase in national income, large expansion of employment opportunities and reduction of inequalities in incomes and wealth, but there was no specific mention of the development in agriculture. Arguing the case for rapid industrialization, the Commission state: "Low or static standards of living, under-employment and unemployment and, to a certain extent, a gap between the average and the highest incomes are all manifestations of basic under-development which characterizes an economy dependent mainly on agriculture. The core of development is thus rapid industrialization and diversification of the economy. But, for industrialization to be rapid enough, basic industries like iron and steel, non-ferrous metals, coal, cement and heavy chemicals as well as industries which make machines for making machines have to be developed rapidly." The approach of the balanced growth was not given up. It was stated that balanced pattern of industrialization requires well-recognized effort to utilize labour for increasing the supplies of much-needed consumer goods in a manner which econonizes the use of capital.

Consistent with this view, the percentage of the developmental outlay (Rs. 4,800 crores) allocated to industry and mining was increased to 18.5 per cent (from 7.6 per cent in the First Five-Year Plan) and that for agriculture and community development was reduced to 11.8 per cent (from 15.1 in the First Plan). There was a similar reduction to 19 per cent from 28.1 per cent in outlay allocated for irrigation and power. The targets of agricultural production for the Second Five-Year Plan were also relatively modest. For example, the production of food-grains was to be increased from 65 million tons in 1955-56 to 75 million tons in 1960-61, an increase of 10 million tons in the five years of the Second Plan as against an increase of 14 million tons achieved during the First Five-Year Plan. Soon after, however, it was realized that the target for foodgrain production in the Second Five-Year Plan was rather low and was raised to 80 million tons, without however, making any addition to the financial allocation for agricultural development.

Outlay in the Public Sector in the First, the Second and the Third Plan.

Head	First Plan Outlay	First Plan Per cent-age	Second Plan Outlay	Second Plan Per cent-age	Third Plan Outlay	Third Plan Percent-age
Agriculture & Community Development	357	15.1	568	11.8	1,068	14
Major & Medium Irrigation	401	17.0	486	10.1	650	9
Power	260	11.1	427	8.9	1,012	13
Village & Small Industries	30	1.3	200	4.1	264	4
Industries & Minerals	149	6.3	690	14.4	1,520	20
Transport & Communications	557	23.6	1,385	29.9	1,486	20
Social Services & Miscellaneous	533	22.6	945	19.7	1,300	17
Inventories/ Miscellaneous	69	3.0	99	2.1	200	3
Total	2,356	100	4,800	100	7,500	100

* Planned, not actual. Source: Five-Year Plans.

Though in the last year of the Second Plan, food-grain production nearly reached the revised target, in the preceding years, shortages were experienced resulting in a substantial increase in food-grain prices. The Third Plan, therefore, restored the primacy of agriculture in its development programme. Unlike in the Second Plan, the achievement of self-sufficiency in food-grains and increased agricultural production to meet the requirements of industry and export, found place in the principal objectives of the Third Plan. It was stated that in the scheme of development in the Third Plan, the first priority necessarily belonged to agriculture. The experience during the period of the first two Plans, especially the Second, had shown that the rate of growth in agricultural production was one of the main limiting factors in the progress of the Indian economy. This, however, did not imply relaxation of emphasis on the development of basic and heavy industries. As a matter of fact, there appears to be a degree of ambivalence regarding the relative importance of agriculture and industry. On the one hand, it was stated: "The development of agriculture based on utilization of manpower resources of the countryside and the maximum use of local resources holds the key to the rapid development of the country." On the other, it was also stated: "There is no doubt that industry has a leading role in securing rapid economic advance." This was sought to be reconciled by the following statement: "The growth of agriculture and the development of human resources alike hinge upon the advance made by industry. Not only does industry provide the new tools, but it begins to change the mental outlook of the peasant."

Allocation of financial outlay to the different sectors in the Third Plan does indicate a slight shift in favour of agriculture. The share of agriculture and community development in the total financial outlay was increased from 11.8 per cent in the Second Plan to 14 per cent in the Third, while the percentage allocated to major and medium irrigation was slightly reduced. The percentage share of organized industry and minerals was stepped up from 14.4 to 20 per cent. It was, however, stated: "In formulating agricultural production programmes for the Third Plan, the guiding consideration has been that the agricultural efforts should not be impeded in any manner for want of financial, or other resources. Accordingly, finance is being provided on a scale which is considered adequate and further assurance is given that if for achieving the targets of production, additional resources are found necessary, this will be provided as the Plan proceeds." During the first two years of the Third Plan, progress of agricultural production was very unsatisfactory and when national emergency was declared, after the invasion of the northern frontier, the National Development Council sanctioned supplementary allocation for minor irrigation and soil conservation.

Investment (Private and Public) in the First, the Second and the Third Plan

Head	First Plan Investment				Second Plan Investment				Third Plan Investment			
	Public (a)	Private (b)	Total	Percentage	Public	Private	Total	Percentage	Public	Private	Total	Percentage
1	2	3	4	5	6	7	8	9	10	11	12	13
Agriculture & Community Development	234	363	597	18.0	210	625	835	12	660	800	1,460	13
Major & Medium Irrigation	250	(b)	250	7.2	420	(b)	420	6	650	(b)	650	6
Power	203	23	226	6.7	445	40	485	7	1,012	50	1,062	10
Village & Small Industries	31	101	132	4.0	90	175	265	4	150	275	425	4
Organized Industries & Minerals	62	392	454	13.5	870	675	1,545	23	1,520	1,050	2,570	25
Transport & Communications	421	78	499	15.0	1,275	135	1,410	21	1,486	250	1,736	18
Social Services & Miscellaneous	359	553	912	27.0	340	950	1,290	19	622	1,075	1,697	16
Inventories	—	290	290	8.6	—	500	500	8	200	600	800	8
Total	1,560	1,800	3,360	100	3,650	3,100	6,750	100	6,300	4,100	10400	100

Note:-Investment should be distinguished from outlay. The former represents expenditure on the creation of physical assets, the latter corresponds to revenue expenditure on Plan schemes.

(a) The break-up of investment in the private and the public sector for the period of the First Plan is not available. The break-up given in column 2 corresponds to the break-up of public outlay. The break-up in column 3 is worked out under the assumption that its pattern was the same as in the Second Plan.

(b) Included under agriculture and community development.

Viewing the three Five-Year Plans together, one can state that the only period during which the importance of agricultural development was not sufficiently appreciated was at the time of the formulation of the Second Plan. It may be perhaps more appropriate to say that during that period, the importance of the basic and heavy industries in national development came to be emphasized for the first time. It was interpreted as 'neglect' of agriculture. In this connection, it is important to mention that the allocation of only 6.3 per cent of the total financial outlay in the First Plan to the development of large and medium industries in the public sector was altogether too meagre and its step-up to 14.4 per cent in the Second Plan was, in a way, a correction of the 'neglect' of industrial development in the First Plan. It is interesting to note that, in retrospect, even the critics of the heavy-industry bias of the Second Plan agree that it would have been worthwhile to have endeavoured to establish a steel mill during the period of the First Plan.

In this connection, it is necessary to emphasize that it is inappropriate to judge the priorities accorded to different sectors, only by reference to the composition of planned public outlay or investment. Apart from the considerable non-monetized investment, particularly in the agricultural sector, so characteristic of underdeveloped economies, the quantum of private investment in different sectors constitutes an important component of the total investment in which the ultimate output would depend. According to the estimates given in the Third Five-Year Plan, during the period of the First Five-Year Plan (1951-56), the private-sector investment came to 1,800 crore rupees as against 1,560 crore rupees of public sector investment. The corresponding figures for the Second Plan period (1956-61) are 3.100 crore rupees and 3,650 crore rupees. It may also be noted that during the period of the Second Plan, private investment in agriculture and community development came to 625 crore rupees as against public investment of 210 crore rupees. In the case of major and medium irrigation, however, as expected, there was no private investment against an investment of 420 crore rupees by the public sector. Further, as Reddaway has rightly pointed out, "The only way of judging whether a development plan is well-balanced is by considering the flow of output of the various goods and services. Investment is simply one means of securing this balance and the character of the development cannot be judged by the way in which this one means is allocated between various industries. "The capital expenditures", he says, "are a very important means of helping to attain this output, but they are not objectives in themselves; if some other method of raising output could be discovered during the Plan period (e.g. by the use of better seeds instead of costly irrigation schemes), then, the essence of the Plan can be fulfilled even if the capital expenditure were far below the original figures."

Professor Reddaway has elaborated this point thus: "A five-year plan normally shows two main sets of figures: targets for the outputs of various commodities which should be attained in the last year of the plan, and plans for capital expenditure to be done in the whole period of the plan. Of these two, the capital expenditure is the thing which calls for direct and immediate action, and it tends, therefore, to be regarded as the essence of 'the Plan'. This is, however, to mistake the means for the objective: the fundamental objective of the Plan is to attain the higher levels of output, and it is these levels of future output which have to be kept in balance as between one product and another, if the Plan is to be a coherent one."

After this rather prolix introductory background, we may concentrate on our main theme: the impact of the growth-process on Indian agriculture. Let us begin with the examination of the relative growth-rates in the agricultural and non-agricultural sectors of the economy. To keep quantitative analysis within a modest limit, ours will be only a two-sector analysis: agriculture-including animal husbandry, forest and fisheries—and the rest of the economy which, for the sake of convenience, has been termed non-agricultural sector, unless otherwise stated.

Several factors influence the relative position of the two sectors in the process of development. Firstly, the growth-rates in the two sectors may vary. The impact of the differential growth-rates on per capita (or per worker) income will be modified by the sectoral transfer of labour-force. The change in the terms of trade will further alter the income-parity ratio of the two sectors. We shall first briefly review the experience in regard to these three dominant factors during the last decade.

Fast Development

A variety of statistical data, not always easily comparable, is available on growth-rates in agricultural production, and productivity.

We have the unadjusted and the adjusted figures of annual production in absolute terms. We have also the Index Numbers of Production, Area and Productivity which claim that they remove the non-comparability due to changes in statistical coverage and methods of estimation. As the measurement based on two specific points (years) would be influenced by seasonal conditions which are important in agriculture, linear growth-rates and compound rates have been calculated. One series is based on the three-year moving-averages of the index numbers for the period 1949-50 to 1961-62 and the other for the period 1952-53 to 1961-62.

All-India Compound Growth-rates in Percentages

Food-grains	3.45	2.46
Non-food-grains	3.57	3.88
All crops	3.49	2.94

The table reveals that agricultural production increased at the compound rate of about 3.5 per cent during 1951-61. If, however, a three-year average centred on 1951-54 is taken, the increase amounts to only three per cent per year.

The better results in the 1949-50 series are believed to be primarily due to the larger contribution of the increase in area. As there are grave doubts about the Index Number Series of Area (which incidentally is used as a deflator for calculating the Index of Productivity) it would be advisable to avoid going into the question of relative contribution of Area and Productivity to the growth in production.

For industrial growth, we have the Revised Series of Index of Industrial Production with the Base: 1956=100. After shifting the base to 1951, we get a linear rate of growth of 9.7 per cent per year. That the growth-rate in the industrial sector should be higher than that in the agricultural sector, is to be expected in a developing economy. What is somewhat unexpected is the wide divergence between the two.

The national income data provide another source from which the sectoral growth-rates may be derived. The net national output in 1948-49 prices originating from the agricultural sector increased from 43.8 abja rupees (annual average of 1949-52) to 57.6 abja rupees (average of 1959-62) resulting in an increase of 31.5 per cent during these years (Table). For the corresponding period, the increase in the net national output in the rest of the economy (termed the non-agricultural sector) was from 45.6 abja to 68.3 abja, resulting in an increase of 49.8 per cent. If these figures are viewed from another angle, 37.8 per cent of the total increase in national output during the period was contributed by the agricultural sector and the remaining 62.2 per cent by the non-agricultural sector. It is apparent that the rate of growth was relatively small for the agricultural sector as compared with that for the non-agricultural sector. This would make the income-parity ratio between the two sectors less favourable to the agricultural sector over the decade; other factors such as labour-force movement and terms of trade remaining the same. This picture is slightly altered when the national output is measured in current prices. Under this method of calculation, the output in the agricultural sector shows an increase of 39 per cent as against an increase of 54.4 per cent in the non-agricultural sector. In other words; 42.1 per cent of the increase in the national output during this period was contributed by agriculture as against 57.9 per cent by the non-agricultural sector. The contribution of the agricultural sector to the total increase in national output was relatively larger (42.1 per cent) when measured in terms of current prices instead of constant prices (37.8 per cent). This difference can be attributed to the change in the terms of trade in favour of agriculture (Price-parity ratio 102.72).*

Growth in National Output

	1949-52	1959-62	Increase	Increase percentage	Share in total increase
	Constant prices (1948-49)				
Agriculture@	43.8	57.6	13.8	31.5	37.8
Non-agriculture@ @	45.6	68.3	22.7	49.8	62.2
Total	89.4	125.9	36.5	40.8	100.00
	In current prices				
Agriculture	48.0	66.7	18.7	39.0	42.1
Non-agriculture	47.2	72.9	25.7	54.4	57.9
Total	95.2	139.6	44.4	46.6	100.0

* Three-year average centred round 1950-51.
** Three-year average centred round 1960-61.
@ Includes animal husbandry, forest and fisheries.
@ @ The rest of the economy.

Labour force: The changes in the composition of labour-force between 1951 and 1961 as revealed by the population census, are presented in the following Table. There were, however, some drastic changes in the concepts and definition used in the two censuses, and extreme caution is needed in drawing conclusions based on these figures. Particular mention may be made of the marked increase in the labour-participation rates from 39 per cent in 1951 to 42.98 per cent in 1961. On the whole, it can be said that the increase in the labour-force between 1951 and 1961 revealed by the table exaggerates the situation due to an underestimation by the 1951 census and overestimation by the 1961 census. Anyway, the most significant factor which emerges from the table is that the proportion of the labour-force employed in agriculture remains almost the same (72.13 in 1951 and 71.79 in 1961) over the decade. This would imply that the change in the relative position of the two sectors due to differential growth-rates would not be affected by this factor inasmuch as there was no change in the disposition of the labour-force.

Terms of trade: The third factor which would affect the relative position of the two sectors would be the change in their terms of trade. Various methods have been used to determine the terms of trade: (a) of the agricultural sector vis-a-vis non-agricultural sector; and (b) of the farmers in terms of the ratio of prices received to prices paid. The usual method used for the former is to study the relative movements in the prices of agricultural and non-agricultural commodities and the ratio between the two. This should not be strictly termed as terms of trade inasmuch as the weights used in the construction of the wholesale prices would be very different from the weights of the commodities entering into the trade between the two sectors. In any case, information regarding the movement in the prices of these two groups of commodities would be of some interest and is given in the following Table.

Price Indexes

	1949-52	1959-62			
Agricultural	100	107.45	107.45 / 104.60	=	102-72
Non-Agricultural	100	104.60	107.45 / 105.84	=	101.52
Total	100	105.84	104.60 / 105.84	=	98.82

Population and Labour-Force by Sectors

(Figures in million)

Year	Population	Working force	Agricultural workers*	Non-agricultural workers	% of agricultural workers to total workers
1951	356.88	139.52	100.63	38.89	72.13
1961	438.31	188.42	135.26	53.16	71.79
Change 1961-51	81.43	48.90	34.63	14.27	(-) 00 34

*(1) The term " agricultural workers " includes: (a) `cultivators', or the industrial category I of the 1961 census; (b) `agricultural labourers', or the industrial category II of the 1961 census; and (c) workers engaged in `livestock, forestry, hunting and plantations, orchards and allied activities' but not those engaged in mining and quarrying, or, in other words, only a part of the industrial category III of the 1961 census.

(2) The 1961 data are taken from: Census of India, Paper No. 1 of 1962, 1961 Census: Final Population Totals.

Employment, Output, Income Per Worker, and Income Ratio in Agriculture and the Rest of the Economy

Year force	Total Work-agriculture	Workers in non-agri-culture	Workers in agriculture	Output in non-agri-culture	Output in per worker	Agri. output output per worker	Non-agri. Agri. Non-agri.	Income ratio 1
1	2	3	4	5	6	7	8	9
		In millions	In Rs		prices	Rupees		
1951	139.52	100.63	38.89	43.4	45.3	431	1165	0.37:1
1960-61	188.4	135.3	53.1	59.1	68.9	437	1297	0.34:1
1970-71	237.7	170.7	67.0	77.14	99.70	452	1488	0.30:1
1970-71	237.7	165.6	72.1	77.14	99.70	466	1383	0.34:1
1975-76	266.9	191.7	75.2	88.13	119.93	460	1595	0.29:1

Assumptions: (i) Population increases at the compound rate of 2- 35 per cent per year; (ii) Work-force increases in both sectors at the same rate as that of population; (iii) Proportion of workers in the agricultural and the non-agricultural sector remains the same as in 1961 (71.8 and 28.2); (iv) Output in the two sectors increases at the same rate as experienced during 1948-49 to 1960-61 (agri. 3.7 per cent per year compound, non-agri. 3.76 per cent, National Income Data); *(v) In row IV in the Table, figures are worked out on the assumption that the ratio of the agricultural and the non-agricultural income in 1971 remains the same as in 1961.

By and large, the movements in the prices of the two groups of commodities have been on parallel lines. In the year 1955, however, the index for the agricultural commodities declined by as many as 12 points from the base year but that for the non-agricultural commodities fell by only one point. From this year onwards, the rise in the price index of the agricultural commodities has been somewhat steeper than that of the non-agricultural commodity price-index. In the year 1961, the two indexes stood almost at the same level.

Index Numbers of Wholesale Prices of Agricultural to Non-Agricultural Commodities.

(Base: 1951-53 = 100)

Weights	Agricultural commodities (680)	Non-agricultural commodities (320)	All commodities (1000)
1950	113	99	109
1951	122	117	120
1952	102	104	102
1953	107	99	104
1954	99	100	100
1955	88	99	92
1956	102	105	103
1957	109	108	109
1958	112	109	111
1959	118	111	116
1960	124	121	123
1961	126	127	126

Source: Economic Survey, 1960-61, Directorate of Economics and Statistics, Ministry of Food and Agriculture, p. 56.

Information regarding the ratio of prices received to prices paid by the farmers is available only for a few regions. (see Table.) The Punjab Board of Economic Enquiry has been compiling this information for the last 25 years. Similar information is available for the last decade in some other states like Assam, Kerala, Orissa and West Bengal. Extreme caution should be exercised in making use of this information without a detailed scrutiny of the methods and techniques used in the construction of the index. The differences in the crop patterns of these regions are significant.

Orissa, Assam and West Bengal are predominantly rice-growing areas, while the major crops in the Punjab are wheat and gram. Kerala's 'agriculture' is dominated by coconut, tapioca and pepper. Weights given to different commodities in the construction of the indexes of prices received naturally vary, as they should. But the marked variations in the weights given to commodities entering into the indexes of prices paid, particularly in regard to family consumption.

Index numbers of parity between prices received and prices paid.

Year	Assam (1944-= 100)	Kerala (1952-53 = 100)	Punjab (1938-39 = 100)	Orissa (1939-= 100)	West Bengal (Previous year= 100)
1951-52	131.6*	- 91.7	-	-	
1952-53	103.9	- 98.5	110.02*	-	
1953-54	102.1	95.2	101.2	103.02	-
1954-55	99.6	85.2	89.9	113.81	101.1*
1955-56	96.4	82.4	99.1	126.24	98.9
1956-57	106.7	83.4	102.7	135.54	-
1957-58	118.6	81.9	96.9	123.92	-
1958-59	109.3	83.0	103.2	121.84	107.3
1959-60	99.1	92.8	94.8	-	98.2
1960-61	107.3	92.1	95.3	-	102.6
1961-62	115.5	88.8	87.8	-	98.7
1962-63	105.6	84.1	84.9	-	97.9

* Calendar years, e.g.. 1951 is identified as 1951-52 and so on, in column one.

Source: Directorate of Economics & Statistics, Ministry of Food & Agriculture, Government of India.

48 per cent for clothing in the Punjab and eight per cent in Bengal—are difficult to explain. Similarly, the basis for weights given to commodities purchased for farm production is quite arbitrary in some cases. Apart from the technicalities of the construction of the index numbers, the method of collection of the data and their dependability leave much to be desired. However, for the sake of completing the record of available information, the parity indexes for these states are given in Table.

The statistical evidence regarding the terms of trade, apart from its inadequacy and qualitative deficiencies, does not lead to any firm conclusions. The sectoral national-income estimates in constant and current prices, indicate a positive shift of the terms of trade in favour of agriculture. Perhaps there is something in the (national-income-estimation procedures, which has such a built-in bias. The question needs a more careful and critical examination. Conclusions based on the wholesale-price index, would depend upon the year from which the trend is measured. Of the 12 years for which the data are given in above Tables years, the price index was favourable for agriculture, and the positive difference in its favour was, on the whole, larger than the negative difference against it. The data on the parity of the prices received to prices paid for Kerala and the Punjab definitely indicate that the terms of trade have gone against the former; Orissa shows exactly the opposite trend, and West Bengal a mixed trend.

The experience of the progress in the agricultural and non-agricultural sectors during the period 1951-61 may be summed up as follows:

(1) The gross product derived from the agricultural sector increased at the compound rate of 2.7 per cent; the growth-rate in the non-agricultural sector was 3.76 (1948-49 to 1960-61 National Income Statistics).

(2) The proportion of workers engaged in the agricultural sector declined fractionally from 72.13 in 1951 to 71.82 in 1961. Consequently, there was an insignificant increase in the proportion of the work-force engaged in the non-agricultural sector, from 27.87 in 1951 to 28.18 in 1961.

(3) The incomes per worker in the two sectors in 1951 were 431 rupees and 1,165 rupees respectively. In 1961, they had crept up to 437 rupees and 1,297 rupees respectively. As a result, the income parity of the workers in the two sectors declined from 0.37:1 to 0.34:1. It should be mentioned that the paltry rise of only six rupees in the per-agricultural-worker income is, in some measure, due to the sharp increase in the agricultural work-force, a part of which may be purely definitional. If the 1961 participation-rate is applied to the 1951 population-data, the work-force in 1951 would be

larger and the per-worker income would be smaller (approximately Rs. 392). In that case the increase in the per-worker income in agriculture, during the decade, would amount to 45 rupees.

Ground Realities

We may now examine some facets of the situation as it will emerge after a ten-year period ending 1971 and a 15-year period ending 1976; under certain specific assumptions. The projection examines the impact on the per-worker-income ratio of the two sectors under following assumptions

(1) Population will grow at the compound rate of 2-35 per cent during this period;
(2) The growth-rates in the two sectors will be the same as observed during the decade 1951-61; and
(3) The proportion of workers engaged in the two sectors will remain the same as in 1961.

The result of the projection shows that after a ten-year period, i.e. in 1971, the per-worker-income ratio in the agricultural and the non-agricultural sector will decline from 0.33: 1 in 1961 to 0.30: 1 in 1971, and to 0.29: 1 in 1975.

Apart from the deterioration in the relative position of the worker in the agricultural sector, as revealed by the above projection, the implications of our assumptions, that the ratio of the work-force in the two sectors will remain constant, need to be examined. On this assumption, the work-force in agriculture would expand from 135.3 millions in 1961 to 170.7 millions in 1971- resulting in an increase of 35.4 millions; in 1975 it will reach 191.7 millions-resulting in an increase of 56.4 millions in 15 years. The current pressure of population on land is already excessive, and one of the objectives of planned economic development is to reduce it. As we saw in Section III, we have not succeeded in doing so during the last decade. The above mentioned calculations indicate the magnitude of the task the agricultural sector will have to face in the next decade in regard to the employment situation.

Faced with this situation, it will be convenient to argue that the transfer of workers from agriculture to industry should be accelerated. But the industrial sector faces an equally difficult task.

Under the assumption of no change (from 1961) in the proportion of workers in the two sectors, by 1971, the non-agricultural sector will have to find employment for 13.8 million people. If the income-parity ratio is not to deteriorate for the agricultural sector, it will have to take in additional five million persons. If the workers' proportion in agriculture is to come down to 65 (instead of 71.8 in 1961), the total absorption by the non-agricultural sector will have to be of the magnitude of 28 million workers in 1971. We have not worked out the capital requirements of employing such a large number in industries. It will depend on the pattern of industrialization, a discussion on which will lead us into the controversy of employment-oriented v. surplus-generating industrialization.

The situation as is developing presents an awkward dilemma for the planner. If industrialization is not speeded up, the employment and the income situation in the agricultural sector will become explosive. With the acceleration in the rate of population-growth in the current decade, if the growth-rate and the rate of labour-transfer remain the same as in 1951-61, there will be an increase in the per-worker income in the agricultural sector of only six rupees in 10 years (1971). The situation will improve only if the growth-rate is significantly stepped up or there is a massive transfer of workers from the agricultural to the non-agricultural sector or both. The experience of the first three years of this decade has demonstrated how difficult it is to step up the growth-rate in agriculture. I am not suggesting that this experience of the first three years would be typical for the entire 1961-71 decade. Far from it; but neither would any facile optimism be in order. It is also necessary to point out that there are limits to the expansion of agricultural commodities from the demand side as well. Though in the context of the present shortage this aspect of the problem may not be immediately relevant, its relevance for long-term planning should not escape attention. Agricultural surpluses can be quite embarrassing, not only in the developed countries, but also in the developing ones. Not only are the export prospects of primary commodities somewhat dim, but the income-elasticity of domestic demand also will, sooner or later, begin to exercise a curb on expansion. As and when this happens, the gains of improved production may be lost through adverse terms of trade. Transfer of workers from agriculture to other sectors of the economy-which themselves are not free from the growing problem of unemployment and under-employment-is also not easy. Apart from the social and the psychological problems involved in it, the magnitude of capital requirements for employment in large industries, and organizational effort that would be needed if employment is to be found in decentralized and small-scale enterprises, would be stupendous. The situation demands a highly competent and wise economic statesmanship.

Thirteen

Local Self-governance

Emergence of Leadership

It is not only the urban-induced power of the private moneylender and the private trader that affects the success of co-operatives when it manifests itself either inside or outside the society. Affinity is not confined to these two; it extends to the leadership in the village whether this is based on property or derived from connection with the administration. The bigger landlord has ways which conform with those of the moneylender, and indeed, as we have said, he is often the moneylender or trader himself. The village headman is also drawn from the same class, and it is usual for these to have connections which link them not only to the sources of finance but to the seats of administrative power. Subordinate officials, revenue and other-including those of the relatively low-paid co-operative department-have often no alternative but to stay with these village leaders and be dependent on them for ordinary amenities when they visit the village or camp in it for a few days. In this and other ways is initiated a process of association with those who wield power and influence in the village and who for that reason have their own uses as the local instruments of an administration which resides in towns and cities and which in varying degrees is inaccessible to the ordinary villager. This close conformity of association and interests between the subordinate officials of Government and the more powerful elements in the village is a matter to be borne in mind as of great significance in explaining the failure of implementation of the policies and directives, co-operative or other, emanating from the higher levels of the administration. Sometimes, temporarily overawed by superior official authority or enthused by missionary-minded officers, an important measure of co-operative policy, for example, may in fact be translated into practice in the village; but it is not often that the effect is lasting; frequently the directions merely remain on paper, especially where they involve some disadvantage to the more powerful in the village. Acting in concert with these, the subordinate official, whose functions take him to the village, creates for the benefit of the superior officers what might be called the illusion of implementation woven round the reality of non-compliance.

Several factors in the village help to create this effect, not least among them the powerful influence of caste. If the leader is of a particular caste, it is unusual for others of the same caste in the village to report to superior authority that things are otherwise than us reported by the leader and the subordinate official. This marked tendency towards the promotion of an impression of change around changelessness of active obedience to behest around stolid resistance to instructions, which only the most persistent and detailed supervision from above can check, has always to be taken into account in assessing the worth of reports that the policies of Government have been put into operation in the village. The consideration is one which must qualify both satisfaction and belief when it is found stated, for example, of a particular area, that tenancy laws have been enforced, or that moneylenders are not operating without due authorization, or that co-operative societies are actively functioning from year to year. The status quo and the non-compliance are often achieved conjointly and at great effort by the leading elements in the village and the subordinate agencies of Government. The balance attained may be the result of some completely new alignment of forces, of some new distribution of perquisites or of some new passing of 'consideration'. The persons who suffer in this process are the weaker and disadvantaged elements of the village for whose benefit the directives and policies are conceived. Among the combinations of factors which thus operate against the interests of the bulk of those who reside in the village is the rigidity of caste feeling in conjunction with the power derived from money, land, leadership, and above all, the affiliation with the superior forces of urban economy. The rigidity of caste loyalty remains, while the original division of caste functions no longer does. The result is that the landlord who may also be moneylender, the moneylender who may also be trader and the educated person who may also be subordinate official, all these through their association with the outside urban world of finance and power wield an influence in the village which at many points is diverted from the good of the village to the benefit of the caste or even of a close circle of relatives.

Good Administration

Besides Planning, an important aspect of the larger context with which we are concerned, by reason of the bearing which it has on our recommendations, is Administration. We have elsewhere made various suggestions which come under this head: organisation of training, strengthening of co-operative departments, formation of new cadres, etc. From the standpoint of a programme such as is here envisaged, the reorganisation required in respect of the co-operative departments alone will be considerable. But the administrative problem in the larger context, in so far as it has relevance to co-ordinated programmes of national development of which this may be regarded as a part, is much wider than re-organisation of cooperative departments or the training of the personnel of those and other departments and institutions. The particular items to which we propose to confine our brief remarks in this chapter are: (1) the selection and training of the personnel concerned with such programmes; (2) the effectiveness of implementation as ensured by supervision; and (3) the wider question of reorganization at different levels in the context of development.

As we have already emphasised, not only the training but also the recruitment of the personnel will have to be looked at from the point of view of the new functions. Thus, a capacity for sympathy, understanding and responsiveness, in the sense in which we have used those terms in relation to the rural environment and to the needs of different rural classes, should be among the qualities to which importance should be attached in recruiting new candidates. For, unless that capacity is initially present and is fostered and encouraged at all stages, the warning would be relevant that "to exchange the landlord for the tax-gatherer, the merchant for the agent of State monopolies and the moneylender for the State Bank official, may prove to be not progress but enslavement."

To the extent that official attitudes are rigid, unresponsive and unimaginative, they will stultify the progress in every one of the directions envisaged. In particular, they will be fatal to the objective of evolving State-partnered co-operative institutions, especially at the rural level, into fully co-operative institutions at the earliest possible stage. Moreover, it is here that the administrator and the official will be called upon to discharge the extremely difficult task of helping others to help themselves; in other words, while doing important work as an officer of government, yet so to perform it as to make himself dispensable within the shortest possible time.

Efficient and Honest

Besides sympathy and informed responsiveness, two important requirements are obviously honesty and efficiency. On the latter it is needless to dwell. There is evident in India today a sad lack of honesty in different degrees and at different levels of administration and governance. In a programme for the positive economic benefit of the weaker, in conditions in which certain sections of the rich and the powerful will ever be interested in the failure of the programme-both broadly and in the detail of its effect on themselves in so far as it is their position of advantage and their power of competition that will be sought to be weakened-it is more than ordinarily necessary that the strictest honesty should be enforced and dishonesty punished. The fact has to be faced that the sociological soil of India today is more favourable to corruption and oppression than to cooperation and planning. Corruption has its roots not only in men's characters but also, and from the point of view of social remedy more relevantly and more deeply, in men's institutions. In India at present, the largest single factor institutionally responsible for corruption may be said to be the lack of egalitarianism where this lack is most basically present, viz., in the Indian village. For, corruption is the exchange of some form of favour against the public interest for some form of satisfaction of private interest. The latter is offered by the man who wants the favour. But favour against the public interest implies that someone else is disadvantaged, viz., the man who cannot offer the satisfaction. This is the weak man. The greater the degree and extent of inequality between strong and weak, rich and poor, the greater the reason and the larger the occasion to seek favours. Perfect egalitarianism, if that were possible, might almost be said to be a perfect safeguard against corruption. These considerations make it all the more important to demand the highest standards of honesty not only of those concerned with the implementation of programmes of development, but also of those in public life, administrative and political, generally.

On the need for ensuring by efficient supervision that there has been actual implementation, we would observe that there are two big illusions in India which too often take away people's thoughts, often involuntarily, from the realities of action and effect. These are the legislative and administrative illusions. Legislation says, 'This shall be done,' and after such interval as may be dictated by propriety, expediency or sometimes sheer inefficiency, Administration answers back, 'That has been done.' While Legislation and Administration thus proceed from one exchange to another, the old realities often continue their former sway. In the context of development the failure to translate into administrative reality what has been laid down as governmental policy would vitiate all programmes except on paper. The utmost importance should therefore be attached and the strictest standards of efficiency enforced in the execution of policy, and in the supervision of execution, at all levels.

Reforms in Administration

Many schemes and many suggestions for the reorganisation of the administrative set-up in order that the needs of independent India may be more effectively served are before the Government of the day. As in the reform of co-operative administration, so in that of general administration, especially in relation to the function of development, the main focus should be the village. It is necessary to emphasise this because, despite the welcome tendency to design certain important new measures of administration-such as National Extension-with the village in mind and round the village as centre, this requirement, which is basic to India's further development at this stage, is often lost sight of in the more comprehensive schemes of reorganisation. One sometimes comes across individual 'co-operators' who appear to think that co-operative re-organisation and development are best fostered by ensuring for its premier non-official bodies a continuity of political contacts at Delhi and a variety of international contacts at Geneva. But much greater than its need to go to the capitals of the world for guidance is the need of Indian co-operation to make, at long last, an effort to go to the Indian village for study and reflection and for genuine attempts to develop and reorganise. So too, for Indian administration as a whole, a vast field of research and action remains to be covered in the villages of the country. On lessons derived from rural India, rather than on those learnt from the unrelated experience of foreign, industrially more advanced and in the socio-economic and political aspects-radically different countries, will have to be based both the assessment of administrative needs and the modification of structure to meet those needs. In the administrative structure itself are present two interrelated but not always coordinated aspects: the new and growing aspect of development and the old and 'basic' aspect of normal administration. The main task before the country being the bringing about of economic development in terms of simultaneous progress towards social egalitarianism, the prior function of the administrative structure as a whole-including the basic-may be said to be the promotion of conditions in which such development and progress will be possible. The indigenous situation, then, by which must be dictated all plans of administrative reorganisation, is wholly dissimilar to that, for example, of countries whose administration is geared to the free play of political and economic forces.

Considering the problem of administrative reform in the extended light of the analysis and proposals the most important needs may be said to be these. There is first of all the need for Government to make its administrative role in the village more and more that of a beneficent authority and less and less that of the tax-gatherer which, for the most part, it has been till recently. Secondly, again in the village, there is the need for Government to assume the function of real partnership in economic development-especially of the middle and lower groups and not merely that of administration on the one hand or of advice and 'extension' on the other. Thirdly, there is the need not only to simplify development administration at the village end, as in National Extension Service, but also to achieve effective co-ordination between (i) the different administrative agencies of development, including that of Local Self-Government and (ii) those agencies and the machinery of basic administration. A large field remains to be explored in connection with the more effective association of the local bodies of administration—panchayats, local boards, etc.-with local projects of planned development, e. g., those relating to minor irrigation, no less than roads, public health or primary education.

Measures for Governence

Here we present at a brief review, in a very broad outline, of the changes that have been taking place in the rural life of India under the impact of the various measures of the Indian Union Government.

The choice of the subject has been prompted by the following considerations:

Transition of Society

Indian society has been experiencing one of its greatest transitions in history since the advent of the British rule. Its technological foundation, its economic structure, its social institutional framework based on the caste-system and the joint family, its political organization, its ideological orientation and cultural value systems have been undergoing a qualitative transformation. As the British rulers generated changes in Indian society basically to serve their own interests, these changes were not uniform or symmetrical and, therefore, created specific types of contradictions and antagonisms within Indian society.

After the withdrawal of the British from India the Indian people have entered a new phase of existence; independence has released their initiative and creative energies. The Government as well as other agencies have been evolving and operating various schemes to bring about changes in the social, economic, political and cultural life of the people. The study of these changes is fascinating and instructive as it gives glimpses of the social change affecting one-fifth of mankind.

Among the various agencies attempting to alter the social life in India at present the state has acquired signal significance as a factor ushering change. It has been effecting social changes by creating, to use Talcott Parsons' phraseology, "situations in which people must act" as well as by operating on `subjective' elements-their sentiments, goals, attitudes and definitions of situations.

The Constitution of the Indian Union has already formulated the goal towards which Indian society is to develop.

Historical Factors

Before we survey the measures adopted by the government of the Indian Union to realize this goal, it is necessary to visualize concretely the type of rural social structure which it inherited from the British rulers and which became the basis on which it operated.

(a) The British rulers, as is now well-known, had dealt an almost fatal blow to the rural organization which existed for centuries on the foundation of an almost independent and autarchic village community, collectivist in spirit, based on the village possession of land and unity of agriculture and industry, producing for local needs and functioning through three main institutions, viz., the Joint Family, the Caste and the Village Panchayat, and paying tribute to the state or the intermediary collectively and in kind out of the actual produce.

(b) They introduced situations "which were external to the social system as a whole" and "independent of the internal institutional structure, or the immediate situations in which large masses of people acted," by almost destroying the collectivist through hierarchic foundations of the social order and by introducing the individualist, competitive gestalt within it. They introduced private property in land through Zamindari and Ryotwari land tenures. They substituted in place of payment of revenue in kind by the village community on the basis of a definite share from the produce, one in cash from the individual, with the inevitable result that the motif of the entire agrarian economy shifted from production for use to production for market, first to secure cash for the payment of revenue and secondly to adjust to the new setting introduced by the British. Thus the agrarian economy was enmeshed into the web of the Indian and world market. By ruining village artisan industries through pushing their own machine-made goods, they destroyed the self-sufficiency of village life. They undermined the authority of the caste and the village panchayat by bringing the village under the rule of laws made by the centralized state and depriving the old institutions of their penal powers.

(c) While Britain thus destroyed the old economic and social equilibrium by introducing capitalist economic forms in India, no new equilibrium emerged, since she thwarted free economic development in general, and industrial development in particular, which would have militated against imperialist economic interests. The Indian rural scene as a result of this underwent a transformation based on increased impoverishment of the mass of the rural population, an increasingly deteriorating agrarian economy, sharp changes in rural class structure and fossilization of rural, social and cultural institutions.

(d) This resulted in the lop-sided and unbalanced position of agriculture in the national economy, mass ruination of artisans, over-pressure on land, increasing diminution in the size of the holdings, growth of subdivision and fragmentation of land leading to the alarming increase of uneconomic holdings, low yields, rise of massive indebtedness of the peasant population, extending grip of moneylenders, traders, landlords and substantial farmers over poor peasantry, steady passing of land from cultivators to creditors and resultant growth of absentee landlordism and rise in the number of landless labourers. In the zamindari areas, the letting and sub-letting of land resulted in the extensive growth of functionless non-cultivating rent-receivers creating a chain of intermediaries (tenants, sub-tenants and sub-sub-tenants) whose cumulative burden had to be borne by the actual tiller of the soil.

(e) In the social sphere, the operation of the laws which transformed land into a commodity capable of being bought, sold, mortgaged, leased and partitioned, in the economic context described above, engendered centrifugal tendencies in the joint family and led to its increasing disintegration. According to the Report of All India Agricultural Labour Enquiry Committee, the average size of the rural family has dwindled to 5.01 persons. The consequences of the shrinking of family in terms of human relations, emotional and attitudinal imbalance deserve to be stressed.

(f) The caste system experienced a peculiar jolt under the impact of the British rule. Caste ranking and economic status have been closely co-related. "Caste rank is particularly manifest through ritual symbols; a group which was economically well off could acquire ritual hallmark to raise its relative position in the hierarchy."

The impact of the British rule and the developments that took place under it were different on different castes. Some of the upper castes of the old social order acquired control over land and became land owners. Some of these took to trading, money-lending and such other business. A number of the intermediate castes, as a result of the operation of the laws of market economy, acquired lands and developed into substantial farmers or rich tenants. Many other castes and sub-castes, having lost their occupational security and having no alternative means of employment, took to agriculture, becoming small farmers or agricultural labourers, or vegetated in their traditional occupation. The scheduled castes, depressed classes and aboriginal tribes were more and more transformed into agricultural labourers, agrestic serfs or bond-tillers.

Thus, in the rural area, as a result of the dynamic but increasingly deteriorating economy, a profound socio-economic transformation took place during the British rule. Certain castes acquired a monopoly of economic power and resources. Certain other castes belonging either to upper or intermediate categories struggled to wrest control from the successful caste groups. Other castes suffered a further decline in their economic status. The agrarian area became a vast cauldron of fiercely competing units where the old hierarchy of caste system based on birth, status and ritual hallmarks, was being transformed into a new hierarchy based on the increasing monopoly of wealth, power and culture. However, it should be noted that this competition predominantly, operated within the matrix of the caste structure. Castes were competing with castes. There were shifts of power from some of the upper castes either to other upper castes or to some of the intermediate castes. The economically weak lower castes, though they became still weaker in this conflict, also initiated and developed struggles for the removal of their disabilities and the betterment of their conditions. It was unfortunate that this historical process of occupational changes of castes and their new correlations was not properly observed and its significance evaluated till very recently.

The Countryside

A brief picture of conditions in the rural area will assist us to understand the nature of the legacy inherited from the British period by the government of the free Indian Union.

Land concentration, predominance of uneconomic holdings, a third of the agricultural population reduced to the level of agricultural labourers, a large portion of the non-agricultural rural population also living in a precarious condition, dependent on the prosperity of agriculture, and, further, a substantial section of even the agricultural owners and agricultural tenants on medium or small-sized farms desperately struggling for survival on meagre agricultural production-such has been the picture of rural social life in India.

Provision for employment for millions of peasants who are unemployed but whose unemployment is disguised, as also for the ruined and unemployed non-agricultural section of the rural people; adequate wage for the agricultural labourers; proprietary rights and economic units of cultivation for the tenants; and economic holdings for the lower and middle strata of peasantry, along with proper credit facilities, marketing opportunities, suitable conditions for growing crops in a manner which would enable them to compete favourably with the prosperous and rich farmers-these are some of the fundamental requirements of a vast section of the rural people. In addition to these, they need to be provided with better seeds, fertilizers, adequate supply of water and better transport and marketing facilities. In short, the fundamental task confronting new government was to provide proper opportunities to all agricultural producers to compete on equal terms in the market.

As Chester Bowles very aptly sums up "Land inequality is a bottleneck clogging the creative energy of the people; a bottleneck that must be broken" and further "Land reform is not a solution of course; it is the first essential step to agricultural improvement, to consolidation of fragmented holdings and to the development of village co-operatives."

Official Steps

The government of the Indian Union has adopted a number of measures to reconstruct rural social life. They can broadly fall into the following categories:

Measures Affecting Political Life, their Impact. The granting of universal franchise to the people by the state has been one of the most significant events. Millions of individuals, irrespective of caste, rank, sex or any other differentiation, have secured the right to vote. Thus the entire rural population has been brought into the political whirlpool. Of the two-hundred million voters, the overwhelming majority belongs to the rural areas. The picture and some of the results of the first election are now available. Implications of such elections in generating various currents have now become more distinct. The very organization brought into being conducting elections in 1951 had great impact on the rural people. Ninety-thousand polling stations were established; 224,000 polling booths built. A systematic campaign was launched to explain the mechanics of voting to the people. Balloting was spread over one hundred days. Voting by party symbols printed on voting papers of different colours was evolved to suit the illiterate masses. Symbols having caste or religious significance were not permitted. About 1,800 candidates contested the 497 seats in the House of People, and over 15,000 candidates for the 3,283 seats in twenty-two assemblies. Numerous parties organized their propaganda campaigns. The four largest parties had secular politico-economic programmes. Numerous minor parties on provincial level sprang up. A total of 106 million people voted in the elections.

This single measure of the government generated powerful social and political ferment in rural India, the implications of which are too profound to be fully comprehended. It exposed the rural populations to the battery of ideas formulated in their programmes by various political parties and groups. It created a new type of social and cultural climate and process. Political discussions, meetings, processions and demonstrations were unprecedented events, new phenomena in the life of the countryside. The election processes agitated extensively for the first time the almost inert life of the rural people and created a new mobility, physical, mental and emotional, among them. It created conditions for the rise of numerous institutions of political, economic and cultural significance, some of them progressive, others reactionary (caste, communal, semi-feudal, social and economic and others). During the elections, economic issues came to the forefront and divergent class interests were revealed. Even propaganda carried on to work up caste sentiments had to resort to distinct economic appeals. Even voting on the basis of caste loyalties disclosed that specific castes usually aligned with specific political and economic parties. It is unfortunate that sociological and anthropological literature which is mounting up in India has not paid proper attention to this aspect of the contemporary rural life almost electrified by the elections and resultant mass political awakening of the rural people.

The effects of this development on different age groups, different sexes, different castes and provincial groups, as well as on different classes have to be assessed. It has created a situation, a climate, in which various ideologies and outlooks, passions and emotions, will ally, clash, modify one another or even result into various amalgams. In centuries of its existence, the rural community never lived such rich turbulent life, never experienced such unique events. The entry of the rural millions in the orbit of active politics as a result of the grant of universal suffrage and elections is a veritable new point of departure in the history of rural society pregnant with incalculable possibilities.

***Measures Affecting Economic Life*:** The government of the Indian Union has taken various measures to reconstruct the economy of India on the basis of what it describes as the principle of Mixed Economy. To reconstruct rural economy it has adopted measures which can be broadly classified into the following categories:

(a) Measures to extend and improve the extant agriculture.

(i) Reclamation of certain lands for cultivation.

(ii) Construction of major and minor irrigation projects, some of them of multi-purpose nature.

(iii) Production of improved seeds, fertilizers, and tools as well as insecticides.

(b) Measures to reform land relations

(i) Vesting of the estates of the intermediaries (Zamindars, Taluqdars and others) barring certain properties such as home farm lands, homesteads and others in the state on the basis of payments of compensation to the inter-mediaries.

(ii) Placing of limitations on future acquisitions of lands by different classes of people.

(iii) Tenancy reforms designed to reduce rents, give security against eviction, and give tenants an opportunity to acquire permanent rights over the land by payment of fixed compensation subject to landlord's right to resume cultivation of a certain area for his personal cultivation.

(iv) Restrictions on sale and mortgage, letting and subletting of lands.

(c) Measures to protect farmers from the oppression of Creditors:

(i) Numerous measures to regulate private money-lending.

(ii) Measures to scale down debts, etc.

(d) Measures to bring about an all-round development of rural areas, resulting in the strengthening of the national economy as a whole:

(i) Establishment of Community Development Blocks and National Extension Services.

(e) Measures creating new organizations to assist the process of the betterment of the life of the rural people:

(i) Establishment of co-operative societies, Vikas Mandals, Gaon or Gram (Village) Panchayats as well as Nyaya Panchayats.

(f) Measures to assist some of the small-scale and cottage industries in rural India.

We shall briefly indicate the effects of these measures on rural life of the people as well as their impact on different classes of rural society.

No measures have been evolved which would provide employment on a sufficient scale to solve even to a reasonable extent this major problem of the rural society, or which would give better conditions of living or land to the agricultural workers comprising about one-third of the agrarian population. As David G. Mandelbaum has rightly pointed out " The lowest castes, those who are mainly landless labourers, often gain nothing at all from the irrigation projects and the redistribution of land. They have nothing to begin with, nothing which can be improved, no means of getting an economic start and so they remain economically as well as socially disadvantaged. The gap between them and other villagers frequently widens rather than diminishes on account of development projects."

As irrigation facilities, seed, fertilizers and improved tools, are not given but are to be paid for the advantages of these facilities are taken predominantly by those who have financial resources to purchase them. As the Community Project Evaluation Report points out the advantage is taken mainly by substantial farmers.

The measures to abolish intermediaries suffer from two basic defects. The compensation to be paid to the intermediaries runs to 550 crores. It is a huge burden on the community. These measures also permit large tracts of land to remain in the hands of Zamindars and others as personal property. Further, as the compensation to be paid by tenants is very heavy, only substantial tenants can purchase proprietary titles of the lands taken from the intermediaries.

With regard to tenancy legislation it may be observed that "about 50 per cent of tenants on small plots, where fleecing by landlords can be as serious as on large, were not covered" and further, "tenancy regulations are unworkable because the landlord is still left in a powerful position," and still further "ever since tenancy legislation has been first talked about, the alert landowners had been carrying out widespread eviction in order to remove many of the occupancy claims."

Measures adopted to check the ravages of the moneylenders have hardly borne fruit. The report of the Rural Credit Survey very convincingly brings this out. These measures have been effectively circumvented and the moneylender is still supreme as he alone holds the key to finance necessary for meeting both the consumption and the production needs of the lower strata of the rural society.

Institutions established by the government like Co-operatives, Vikas Mandals, Gram Panchayats and Nyaya Panchayats are also assisting in practice only the richer sections of the rural population and are further controlled by them. The Community Project Evaluation Report very significantly discloses this in the following words: " When one considers the pattern of membership in village organizations, be they co-operative societies, Vikas Mandals, Gram Panchayats or Nyaya Panchayats, one clearly finds that the membership is confined to the larger cultivators and that the smaller cultivators as well as agricultural labourers have practically no stake in the organization of the village."

With regard to the Community Development Projects and their impact on rural life, the Evaluation Report has brought to light the following facts:-

(a) The advantages of improvements are taken predominantly by substantial farmers. (b) The contributions to be made by the village people are felt as very burdensome by the lower sections of the people. (c) The organizations emerging in these areas for bringing about rural change are dominated by upper sections of the rural population, the poorer ones having" no stake in them". (d) The initial enthusiasm born of great hopes in the projects is slowly declining among the lower strata of the population.

Other Factors

To sum up, as a result of the government measures to reconstruct economic life of the rural people, great changes have taken place in the socio-economic structure of the rural society. Some of the old classes (feudal and semi-feudal) have been largely crippled; some (substantial farmers) have been strengthened. Middle and lower sections have not benefited. The process of economic disintegration of these sections is advancing. (i) The measures have resulted in transforming many zamindari type of landlords into a class of substantial farmers and capitalist agriculturists. (ii) By numerous tenancy and other laws referred to above, the government is helping to create a class of prosperous peasants out of substantial tenants or a section of the medium-sized cultivators.

This class of prosperous peasants only can take advantage of the numerous facilities, such as improved seeds, better fertilizers, irrigation, efficient tools, better roads and also improved marketing facilities, thereby improving their production and sale of the product.

On the other hand, the vast mass of unemployed persons, large sections of the owners of uneconomic holdings, the mass of poor peasants and agricultural labourers, either remain unaffected by these measures or adversely affected.

A sharp conflict of interests and a resultant social cleavage are developing in the rural areas as a result of the measures of the government, Central and State. On one side there are prosperous peasants, landlords, village moneylenders and traders and the richer sections of the rural people. On the other, the middle and small cultivators, the mass of land labourers and ruined non-agrarian population.

As observed earlier, social castes and economic classes are closely correlated. As a result of this, the conflicts of these classes even take the form of conflicts of castes. Thus rural areas are seething with new caste tensions, sometimes visible in elections, sometimes in economic struggles, sometimes in the struggles in local organizations.

These new patterns of tensions are slowly emerging in the open. The tensions are becoming more widespread and are moving unfortunately in the direction of sharper conflicts.

The rural life of India is undergoing transformation under the impact of Government measures. The types of changes that are taking place have been narrated in their broadest outline. What will be the direction and tempo of these changes? Will the democratic political objective fit in with the newly-emerging class and social antagonisms in Rural India? Will rural social life experience another round of tensions and antagonisms? Can these contradictions be resolved without changing the very motif and mode of production? What institutional transformation will be required to establish both economic prosperity and social harmony in the rural life? These are some of the fundamental questions posed before all social scientists.

The rural change that is generated by the Government measures is tending to sharpen the contradictions among various classes in the rural society and in the context of caste and other institutional background is slowly unleashing tensions, antagonisms and collisions, the implications of which have to be properly comprehended if the direction of the development of one-fifth of mankind is to be assessed and influenced.

Various Institutions

An extremely important aspect of such an approach, in so far as the cultivator is concerned, is obviously the creation of an organization within the village which can be entrusted with the programme of production and other economic activities designed for the village as part of the bigger programme in the agricultural sector of the Plan. The search for such an organization may be said to be one of the main preoccupations of the Planning Commission. The position reached may be illustrated by the following extracts. These paragraphs appear in the Peoples Edition of the First Five-Year Plan (1953):

"It is greatly to be desired that in the agricultural part of the Plan, the village as a whole should be actively associated in fixing targets and working for their achievement. In recent years the State Governments have shown a welcome earnestness in establishing panchayats as civic bodies charged with general responsibility for the collective welfare of the village community. Many activities, such as framing programmes for production, obtaining and managing governmental grants for building roads, tanks, etc., introducing improvements in agricultural methods, organizing voluntary labour for community works and assisting in the implementation of legislation for economic and social reform, will fall within the purview of the panchayat.

"On the other hand, for the working of individual programmes of development, where the specific responsibility and liability of a member have to be ensured, a more binding form of association is necessary. Specific and practical tasks of reclaiming land, providing resources for better cultivation and for marketing the village produce are best performed through co-operatives. It is, however, very necessary that co-operative agencies in the village should have the closest possible relationship with the panchayat. Though in the discharge of their functions the two bodies have specific fields in which to operate, by having mutual representation and by common *ad hoc* committees for certain matters, it will be possible to build up a structure of democratic management through both the organisations."

'Village production councils' were the device thought of at an earlier stage as mentioned in the following quotation from the Report of the Grow Afore Food Enquiry Committee, 1952:

"There are also village institutions that can be set up where they do not exist. Panchayats can be established under laws in force in States. And for every village or group of villages, according to conditions, there should be a multipurpose co-operative society for providing credit and supplies and giving other assistance needed by farmers including marketing. Close working relations should also be established with schools which can become useful centres of social education. On the question whether village panchayats or management boards or multi-purpose societies should be recognised as agents for implementation of development plans, opinion is divided. Some States favour the former and some the latter. There is also the Planning Commission's suggestion for village production councils. Each area should decide this on its own special needs and conditions. But it is worth emphasising again that no solution can be found to the problem of rural betterment unless local co-operation is secured to the maximum possible extent and the support of the best leadership is enlisted."

The Progress of the Plan (January 1954) contains the following passages which seem to indicate hat village panchayats where possible, and *ad hoc* committees otherwise, are now favoured as instruments of development within the village.

"In the planning and implementation of the programme in the Community Projects and National Extension Areas the maximum use is being made of local popular organisations like Panchayats and Union Boards. Wherever Panchayats or Union Boards, organised along traditional lines, are effective, they are always utilised. In some areas, success has been achieved by entrusting developmental activities to *ad hoc* non-statutory bodies. These organisations have various names. In Madhya Pradesh they are called Gram Vikas Mandals; in Orissa, Gram Mandal Samities; in Madras, Gram Seva Sanghams, and in West Bengal, Palli Unnayan Samities. Participation of the people in developmental activities organised by these bodies is helping in the development of village leadership."

"Village panchayats have, thus, a vital role to play in the sphere of land reform and it is urgently necessary to establish a network of panchayats all over the country-side."

The problem itself was originally thus stated in the First Five-Year Plan (larger edition) in a passage in which the co-operative form of association, as a target if not an actuality, was considered to be the most desirable:

"According to their needs and experience, village communities will discover the arrangements which serve them best. There has to be a great deal of trial and experiment before patterns of organisation which will best promote the interests of the rural population can be evolved. Nevertheless, it is important to work towards a concept of co-operative village management, so that the village may become a vital, progressive and largely self-governing base of the structure of national planning and the existing social and economic disparities resulting from property, caste and status may be obliterated."

We have reproduced these extracts to illustrate the ineffectiveness of the search hitherto conducted for a body within the village which can assume responsibility for the execution of that part of the village plan which is concerned with agricultural production and development. If the analysis presented in this Report has some validity, the opinion may be hazarded that in most villages neither the panchayat nor an *ad hoc* committee would be an appropriate organization for being entrusted with this part of the task. Both these are likely to represent precisely those elements in the village which, by and large, operate against the interests of the middle and small cultivator. Here again, the more realistic approach seems to us to be to promote in the first instance those conditions which are necessary before such an organization can function successfully in the village in the context of better farm production and better farm business. For fulfilling this prior requirement, the effort on the part of the State, in the circumstances we have set out in detail, has to be a deliberate, concerted and nation-wide economic endeavour in combination, on a co-operative basis, with the weaker elements in the agricultural population itself. By and large, it is only State participation of this magnitude and direction that would constitute the needed approach. Into such an approach would then be fitted State activities such as National Extension and Community Development Project which, however important, cannot by themselves create conditions within the village which can be relied upon to retain their momentum after aid and supervision are withdrawn or reduced. The main task as recognized by the Plan is the generation within the village itself of forces which through their organic relation with village life and economy will continue to operate for the development and prosperity of the village. The creation of such forces by means which are not too costly in personnel and finance, which, in other words, can be adopted on a country-wide scale within a reasonable period, may be said to be the main problem of planning in relation to the important rural sector of the Plan.

Enthusiasm Required

To the socio-economic problem which today confronts the country, the approach has necessarily to be constructive and constitutional; and if only for this reason—there are others such as, for example, are pertinent to the Indian tradition—the approach of violence and class conflict and of 'revolution' in terms of these two, is of course a priori excluded from consideration, but the gigantic constructive effort which this imposes on the State as well as the people and their institutions is the reverse of inaction, *laissez-faire* and lack of concerted purpose. All the more is it necessary, in such a context, to devise positive institutional modes of approach which, among other goals, lead to the resolution of conflict and mitigation of caste and class disparity, and the promotion of new factors of unity across the older divisions.

In the village itself, nothing is so important in this context as to build up a new loyalty of production—of common economic effort in the widest sense—across the loyalties of caste and the disparities of riches, influence and economic privilege. If the cultivators of the village, medium and small included, owned, if need be along with the State, the rice mill to which the harvested paddy was taken, if they converted their sugarcane into sugar in a factory which was co-operatively organized for them, if they were effectively served with both credit and marketing services by a rural co-operative society working in co-ordination with a co-operative marketing society at the erstwhile mandi and if in gradual process they combined to consolidate their holdings, or to organize a co-operative farm which reduced their expenses and increased their yield-in all these ways would be brought about a new sense of participation in common effort for the common benefit together with a new feeling of fellowship for those who shared the economic function, but not necessarily the caste, in common with themselves. In this new context, the association of the producer would not merely be with other producers, big or large, medium or small, but also with the State through their local representatives, i.e., the officials serving in the department or deputed to the society with whose guidance and alliance, together with the assistance of the finances made available by Government, the conditions and disparities of the older order could be made gradually to disappear. Only out of such association, socially and economically beneficent, with one another and with the State, would be born that enthusiasm for development which is recognized to be absent today in most villages in India despite large-scale efforts on the part of the Administration to improve the lot of the villager. This lack of enthusiasm may be illustrated from recent official experience. In fact, say the Grow More Food Enquiry Committee, with reference to that campaign," the movement did not arouse nation-wide enthusiasm and did not become a mass movement for raising the level of village life." "Measures of reform," records the Progress of the Plan "have so far been enforced mainly through the revenue agency, but as the reforms take on a more radical character, it becomes more and more important that the people should be associated as fully as possible in their implementation. A new social and economic order cannot be built up without popular enthusiasm and the assistance of local leadership and initiative." The recognition of the planning authorities that, for the next phase of the Plan, the design of development should be `from the village upwards' is itself evidence of the need to enlist the active interest of the villager in those measures for his economic benefit which today have failed to rouse him to whole-hearted participation. This want of enthusiasm is a measure not of the smallness of governmental effort but of the vastness of the socio-economic disparity which the villager senses to be the main fact which conditions his life and which the policies and programmes of Government are seen by him to have left entirely unaffected. If, as may be assumed, in the larger context of the other disadvantaged groups in town and village, the next Five-Year Plan includes various programmes of economic amelioration, the same want of enthusiasm may be foreseen from these groups, if the same lack of effect is perceived by them to be inherent in the well-meaning and even costly efforts of the State conceived for the benefit of those very group.

Problems to Cope With

The programme of development outlined in this Report—the development of co-operative credit, of co-operative marketing, processing and other economic activity, and of rural banking in order to facilitate the other two types of development—is concerned with the two main classes of rural producer: with the cultivator mainly, and with the handicraftsman incidentally. In the context of future planning, it may be assumed that, for the first, there will be an even bigger programme of agricultural production; and for the second, a large-scale programme for the development of cottage industries. For both, it may be further assumed that the next phase of the programme will be governed by the announced concept of planning upwards from the village. It is of the essence of such a concept that the new Plan will be no mere projection into the next five years of the many unfinished projects or continuing activities of the present Plan, but something else besides; for, such a projection of the present Plan, followed by its cutting up into local sections, would not constitute each such section a 'plan upwards' from the particular locality, whether that locality be a village or a district. Mention has been made of the search for a suitable body inside the village which can take up and pursue a programme of agricultural development in which all the cultivators of the village can participate. This search for an appropriate village organization is symbolical of the wider effort to convert the present more or less super-imposed programme of economic improvement into something more in the nature of an organic development from within the village itself. From what point or nucleus shall this body of villagers be built up: from non-existent co-operative society, national production council, factious panchayat or, ignoring all these, from just an *ad hoc* committee in the village?

The problem has not been solved because it is largely insoluble in present conditions. The search, as already indicated, is for something which can only emerge if the conditions requisite for it are first created by a State-partnered programme which, among other things, includes important aspects of agricultural economic activity besides credit-facilities for that activity; it will not materialize as the result of any mere programme for extension, supervision and administration. In the sphere of rural industry, the new Plan will come up, not only against a combination of all these obstacles, but in addition the fundamental difficulty of promoting and sustaining small units of production, which, in respect of most of the types of goods they produce, will be confronted with the competition of the much larger units of urban industry which are both better organized and, in their technical aspects, more advanced and progressive. It may be assumed that this effort will nevertheless be made and the needed lines of development formulated in the programme for the Second Five-Year period. About the supreme importance of such an effort there can be no doubt, for it will be directed towards the fulfilment of a vital requirement of both the unemployed and the underemployed in the rural area; whether cultivator, handicraftsman or labourer. Indeed, the accord of priority to rural industry over most forms of urban industry is already implicit in both Plan and Constitution. From the basic economic objective of increase of wealth, in conjunction with the basic egalitarian objective of reduction of disparity, it follows that, as between different forms of production of new wealth, those should in particular be encouraged and established which, in the very process or situation or production, tend to promote the distribution of the added wealth in the more needed directions, as distinguished from its further concentration at the relatively more saturated points. Such an approach, already implicit in the concepts and precepts of planning, if not in its practical expression, may be expected to be made explicit in the Second Five-Year Plan and substantially embodied in the new programmes it will lay down for the industrial, including agro-industrial, sector of rural production. We have throughout kept this important and inevitable, though still largely potential, development in view in designing the State-partnered credit structure, co-operative as well as commercial, of our recommendations. We have also, it may be recalled, as comple-mentary to such a structure in the short-term sphere of credit, suggested the co-ordination of policies in respect of bodies such as the All-India Handloom Board, the All-India Khadi and Village Industries Board, the State Financial Corporations, etc., for the provision of the facilities needed in the context of the block and working capital requirements of State-sponsored, and possibly State-partnered, rural industries.

Fourteen

Panchayati Raj

Systematic sociological study of the structure and process of Panchayati Raj has not been conducted so far. The studies have emphasised only partial factors either exogenous or endogenous that influence the working and growth of the panchayat system: mostly administrative, legal, economic and isolated institutional (leadership, factions, caste etc.) factors have been emphasised particularly in the context of their implication to the working of the panchayats. Inadequacy in such studies lies not in the wrong choice of variables for analysis but in the narrow theoretical frame of reference and conceptual categories, in terms of which facts are interpreted. Diagnostic and didactic orientation has predominated over the scientific and analytical. The first attitude emanates from an exaggerated claim for social sciences through *ad hoc* studies and surveys to suggest cut and dried formulae for the solution of problems of social planning and reconstruction and the second emerges from an essentially historical fact which profoundly affects the Indian elites 'image' about panchayats. The historical fact lies in the significance attached to panchayat system and village society by Mahatma Gandhi. The institution has thus come to symbolise not only a structural innovation but also a moral commitment and an ideology.

Sociological evaluation of working of panchayat system would not rule out the analysis of this institution from the standpoint of values or ideologies but they would constitute the subject matter of enquiry rather than be the tools or concepts employed for analysis. Such a study would attempt the establishment of relationship of the structure and value system implicit in this system with other systems at various levels of their structural and functional differentiation and growth. Panchayats would be treated as a sub-system of relationship and socio-political norms working within the structural framework of the large scale society, right from the village to the region, to the state and the nation. Reciprocity of relationship and the emerging consequences, both intended and unintended, of the mutual interaction of the various structural and normative 'types' would indicate the overall process and problem of change.

Such comparison would not only bring to the surface the implications of panchayats on the village social structure in specific setting but would also point out the integral and differential aspects of the net balance of the forces of change that influence other major national institutions and processes such as democracy and planning. Questions to be asked would be: What is the structural and normative character of the indigenous system, where panchayats are introduced? What is the degree of the correspondence or lag between the indigenous and introduced systems? What bearing these structural and cultural innovations have upon the national society? How is the process of change at various structural levels throwing up alternative and equivalent norms and roles? And which factors promote or thwart their growth and institutionalisation? If we intend to assess the system of village panchayats in terms of above queries, a more systematic theoretical frame of analysis would be required. Bailey has recently made an attempt towards comparative structural analysis of political systems and values at the level of village, constituency and the state (F. G. Bailey, 1963) but fails to evolve a systematic method of enquiry for all the levels. Among the methods employed by him, he finds resemblance with anthropological method at his village level study, political science method at the constituency level study and historical method at the state level of analysis. This methodological eclecticism has thus led to a piece of work which has limitations of all the three types of studies without their advantages. For a better study this methodological multiplex is to be substituted by structural functional analysis as mentioned above. It will offer an integral view of all levels of social realities as well as all levels of structural complexities.

The application of the structural functional method in rural analysis has so far been confined to the study of the processes of change in caste stratification. This has led to the unfortunate neglect of the class structure and its consciousness in the rural society. The reason for the caste-centredness of the rural sociology in our country lies in its direct kinship with the works of British and Indian social anthropologists who have, through the study of caste, emphasised the cultural factors in social change rather than the role of economic and political factors and the interest-groups. Thus, the casteism', 'dominant castes', `factions', etc. are some of the concepts which have been used as camouflage to divert the attention of sociologists from the strategic area of the class structure. Moreover, because of this neglect, structural functional studies tend to be more static and fail to interpret the relationship between economic status and political power. Study of rural social processes through class relations and its structure would introduce in structural functional analysis that methodological richness which would also bring about the much coveted synthesis between the dialectical and functional approaches to the understanding of the dynamics of social structure.

Concept and Perspective

A micro-cosmic study from the structural point of view was conducted in six villages of Eastern Uttar Pradesh where panchayats were simultaneously established in 1949 on the basis of adult suffrage rather than nomination of functionaries by Tehsildar as existed prior to it. Not only in the six villages but in the whole of the Eastern U.P., these elections projected very vigorously the latent class consciousness which was seething against the landlords who till then enjoyed supreme power in the villages. The nature of this class conflict was accentuated by the peasant movements against rackrenting, sharecropping, elections, etc. common in this area and which were led by congress leaderships since 1939 or even earlier. The first election in 1949 thus, marked a state of initial euphoria among the peasants and landless labourers to dispossess the traditional ruling elites from power. It was a confrontation of a self-confidence populistic force with a dominant class whose future was uncertain since the Zamindari Abolition Act was getting through the assembly. Zamindari was subsequently abolished in 1950. Yet the func-tionaries of the "Zamindar Association" gave a bitter fight to the peasant candi-dates in all the six villages. Zamindars, however, could only win in two villages out of the six. In other four villages the office of President went to peasants, one of them was an educated school teacher and the other three, semi-literate peasants. The offices of the adalti panchas, however, went in every village to landlords or the village banias due to literacy being a qualifying pre-condition for this office.

From 1949 to 1953 there followed a long period of inter-nescine intrigues, faction-fights, in the four villages where the feudal group had lost. It was now that a conflict ensued between legal rights and social structural realities. The average land-holding of ex-landlords in all the six villages compared six to twelve times that of the peasant holdings. Most of the peasants and agricultural labourers had to depend for the land for sharecropping, sub-tenancy, farm employment and money-lending etc. upon the feudal families. With these patronages the latter began to introduce internal dissension in the class solidarity of the village In two villages they kept the village presidents engaged in one or the other litigation for the whole term of the panchayat; in the other two they systematically victimised the supporters of peasants village presidents. The landlords were educated, had acquaintance with the officers, were familiar with the pulse and rhythms of bureaucracy; the peasants-presidents except the one (teacher) were unfamiliar with this milieu. Yet they kept the solidarity intact and did not break.

The pressure made upon the power aspirations of the peasant class, however, in the elections of 1953 when the ex-landlords changed their strategy of election along with pressure group tactics. They would quote illustrations of the lack of feuds and tension and developmental work (petty in nature though) done in those villages where ex-landlords were made presidents; they used mainly pragmatic arguments of peace in the village and general prosperity. The result was, that in four villages out of six, ex-feudals became presidents defeating peasant candidates. The other two villages where peasant-presidents still kept the hold included the former educated teacher and a prosperous peasant, both again returned as presidents. The tension continued in these two villages. Even attempts were made to get the teacher dismissed from the higher secondary school of which the management was in the hands of the ex-landlords; but in these villages the traditionally dominant class was itself internally divided. In other four villages with the ex-landlords as presidents the conflict passed from inter class level to intra-class structure. In two villages even out of these four, the contestants were from among the ex-landlords themselves. In this situation, peasants began to benefit from the faction rivalries among the group in power.

The cycle in the dynamics of power was, however, complete in the third election of village panchayats in 1962 when in all the villages except one (where the teacher was president) ex-landlords were returned to the office of the village presidentship. In three of them the contest for presidentship was among ex-landlords themselves, in the other two they won against peasant candidates. Thus the process of regression in the power structure of the village had run a cycle.

This brief account of the political process in the six village communities may represent a unique situation which may not be identical to many others. However, the whole gamut of the change described above maybe summarised in three stages which might have some degree of validity for other regions as well, (1) the initial assertion of the ex-franchised peasantry for its power in rural community, (2) the long drawn period of group conflict between the power climbers and the traditional power elites. (3) the withdrawal of the peasant leadership from the arena of power. Now the question is, could this process be explained in terms of the social system as a whole? What will be the advantages of such a systematic approach over the eclectic ones employed so far?

Processes of Transition

Social processes can only analytically be isolated. In reality no single system of relationship or behaviour is free from the contingency of other relations and situations. Moreover, operation of any social system implies some pre-requisite processes and complementary roles. Whenever an old system or institution is replaced by a new one, the degree of its success, stability and growth would depend upon effective and quick development of these pre-requisites. Thus, the response of the existing social structure becomes a pre-condition for the success of an institutional innovation. In case of the above village panchayats we could classify following traditional structural institutions and forces into which the new system was introduced. (1) the pressure of a traditional ruling elite, (2) vast economic and cultural gap in status between these elites and the new climbers, (3) persistence of a diffused form of institutionalised approval with some section of peasantry in the villages in favour of the traditional group, (4) lack of counter-balancing pressure from outside to reinforce the aspirations of the climbers (No help from political leaders, peasant associations, caste panchayats could be effectively available to these villagers), (5) direct conflict between legal or constitutional prerogative (voting power) with established social and economic scale of stratifications e.g. class structure and caste (particularly former) and (6) absence of effective complementary changes in the social structure along with that in power system. The Zamindari abolition was no doubt a very radical complementary change but this too in practice meant increased legal prerogatives than real (in terms of goods and services). A survey that was conducted about the benefits accruing to various classes as a result of Zamindari abolition, revealed that ex-tenants and labourers did not feel benefited by the measure. The rule for the acquisition of Bhumidhar's right in land on a lump sum payment of 10 years rent by the peasants drained off the resources even of the medium sized tenants who could have been the potential climbers in the rural power structure.

On the other hand the panchayat system though acclaimed by many as an indigenous institution was introjected into the village power structure with many radical nuances of modernity such as; (1) voting on the basis of civil status, rather than ascriptive status which prevailed in traditional panchayats; (2) introduction of a certain degree of bureaucratic rationality in the working of panchayats in place of the former traditional communal sanctions; (3) greater interlinkage of this institution with institutions of higher scale at the level of block, district and the state; and finally (4) introduction of an overall value system of a rational democratic polity. None of these sociological norms were present in the same form in the traditional village panchayats and the introduction of the new had a far reaching significance for the value system and social structure of the rural society. The above attributes of the new panchayat system required that proper institutional supports should have been forthcoming to reinforce its expected norms in the body politic of the villages. In technical sociological language it was necessary to assess the presence or possibility of the growth of the structural-functional pre-requisites for the success of panchayat system.

The nature and pattern of these pre-requisites would differ firstly, as the social structure and culture of the indigenous systems would differ and secondly, as the form and content of the institutional innovation would itself vary. For this matter, the delineation of the structural-functional pre-requisites of the panchayat system would require a thorough understanding of the nature of the village communities, as well as, of the panchayat system, its legal, social and political and cultural implications. On the basis of the existing knowledge about these, a fairly reliable formulation of these pre-requisites may be possible and in its background it may be further possible to analyse the significance of the case history of the panchayats mentioned above.

For a proper success in the working of the panchayats in the villages, the structural-functional pre-requisites could be (1) reduction in the nature of disparity in real income and land ownership of various groups;. (2) greater occupational mobility in the villages; (3) rapid increase in the new types of economic activities (structural and infra-structural) to strengthen the base of rural economy and accelerate its social dynamics; (4) rational price policy to maintain a balance between rural-urban and agro-industrial sections and sectors respectively for control of the differential power and dependence relationship; (5) structural support to the specific and instrumental roles through reform in the indigenous sub-systems and support from large-scale social structures; (6) radical changes in the nature, and scope of communication system; (7) increased interaction among the various sub-structures of rural society (caste, kin-groups and lineages, etc.) through common participation at secular level of activities, cultural, economic and political, and finally (8) growth in equalitarian and secular symbolism (institutions, ceremonies, festivals, public gatherings, etc.) in the rural culture accompanied by its effective linkage with the culture of Indian nationalism.

These pre-requisites make it adequately clear as to how futile it would be to evaluate the success and failure of village panchayats in terms of its own organisation and working and to blame the institutions for many commissions and omissions for which it could not be held responsible. Moreover, it would also reveal the theoretical difficulties in the understanding of the processes and problems of village panchayat in terms of such sub-structures of this system as (1) problem of effective leadership; (2) lack of corporate (democratic) mechanism for decision-making; (3) existence of casteism and factions; (4) lack of effective administrative inter-linkage etc. etc. These are, in fact, consequences or functions of the interaction of the indigenous social structure and value system of the villages with the social structure and values of the village panchayats. These emanate from the total structural setting of the rural society and none of these alone could lend itself for correction and reconstruction for the desired working of the system as such. Why there has not arisen secular utilitarian and rational leadership in villages? Why there is factionalism and groupism in the decision making processes of the panchayats? Why new climbers to power cannot succeed? Answer to these and scores of such questions lies not in the symptoms but in the texture of the body-social of the rural society. Hence the need for analysis not in terms of isolated institutions but the total rural social system.

In case of the six villages to which reference has been made also in case of many others in the Eastern U.P., the effective existence of the structural-functional pre-requisites mentioned above has not been there. The average per household land-holding for ex-landlords in these villages is 28.5 acres and that of the ex-tenants only 1.6 acres. The average monthly income of the two compares as rupees 270 per month for the ex-landlords and rupees 60 per month for ex-tenants. The only economic innovation in the villages since 1947 has been cooperative brick-kilns which give seasonal employment to some agricultural labourers; most of the agricultural holdings including those of the ex-landlords are subsistence enterprises with little farm surplus which is consumed by industrial consumers' goods due to unfavourable price policy. No new roads except few shram-dana pavements have been constructed during the last thirteen years; no new primary schools have been opened since 1949 except a junior high school in one village; the adult education through night schools has never worked effectively; two new branch post-offices have certainly been opened due to large number of migrants in collieries, cloth mills, and for those gone for manual labour in Bihar, West Bengal and Bombay; in all these villages there are about 40 students reading in high school and intermediate colleges, about 15 are studying in degree colleges, there are 10 graduates and three post-graduates. Eighty per cent of these students who are studying in colleges and those who are graduates belong to ex-landlord families. There is no equalitarian interaction between ex-landlord families and ex-tenant families, complete hierarchical distance is maintained; even the very poor ex-landlord family, in fact poorer than average ex-tenant, maintains strict social distance from other classes, these ex-landlord groups have serious internal feuds and factions, but work as a consolidated front when the power or prestige of the whole class is threatened; at such occasions even traditional factions melt away contrary to the findings of Oscar Lewis.

In regard to the structural reinforcement from macro-social structure (at the level of block, constituency, state and finally national level) there has been no significant development. There is no interaction with political workers of the villages except during the periods of general elections; there is general unconcern with the block developmental meetings, police and revenue officers' visit to the village creates more stir in the villages than block development officers, involvement with national currents of events or even problems at state level is very little; not a single daily newspaper is subscribed by any member in any of the six villages; village panchayats have radio sets in four villages which are used only by the family members of the village presidents. The two macro-structures which influence village life are judicial and administrative bureaucracy, the influence of the latter is more effective and pervasive. Influence is unidirectional rather than reciprocal; between the administrative bureaucracy and the villagers the mode of relationship being more of compliance rather than consensus. The sociological value of this contact is not only limited but very often negative. It would be interesting to investigate how as the scale of bureaucracy moves from police administration to revenue to developmental the negative reaction of villages slowly, diminishes though it is never absent. Just as villagers relationship to bureaucratic macro-structure is of indifferent compliance, the same to political macro-structure is that of skeptical-indifference.

Relationship at Equal Level

There also exists an intimate relationship between the villagers cold and critical image about the political parties including the Congress and the sequential expropriation from them of the power in the village panchayats by the ex-landlords. As in course of the years following the abolition of landlordism the sting of oppression and control of the feudal group has waved from their memory and has been replaced by feline tactics of indirect control through manipulation of their emotions and interests. The average villagers' awareness about economic and material handicaps, has progressively increased and has created a kind of collective frustration which is evident in their reaction towards public policies and institutions. Feeling among them has gained strength that ultimately the C.D.P., the Panchayats and the assemblies etc. are for the privileged few. This feeling has further gained conviction due to consolidation of land holdings in the region (1956-57) which according to villagers has benefitted the big land owners (ex-landlords) only.

Now, this picture of the general condition of the villages deviates significantly from the various structural-functional pre-requisites and also from the norms implied by the new Panchayat system mentioned above. Obviously, looked at from this scale of evaluation, structure and process of Panchayat system has not made the expected impact on the rural society. Should we then consider Panchayat system a failure? Far from it, the question should rather be asked, was there a better alternative? Generally speaking, the answer to this question would be in the negative. Barring a few specific strategies about the implementation of the system and legal lacunae etc. the system as a whole had no alternative form of implementation. Within the structural framework of the rural society and its stratification system the process of gradual expropriation of the agricultural labourers and small peasants (ex-tenants) from power is a normal process and could only have been controverted by a very radical and harsher form of land reform which was perhaps repulsive to the collective conscience of the political leadership in power. A leftist version may perhaps be that this leadership itself is reactionary. The hypothesis is rather controversial, at best a truism from a sociological point of view. Leadership is itself a response thrown up by the society in the wake of the forces enshrined in new demands and innovations. At each level of socio-cultural adjustment the extent of deviation in the traditional and emergent form of leadership would invariably have its structural limit, assuming a normal or even accelerated process of social change.

However, in course of this discussion, we have now introduced in our analytical framework sufficient number of variables to sum up the implications of the facts presented in relation to the institution of village Panchayats, its structure and process of change. Some of the broad inferences that could be drawn are as following:-

(1) The Village Panchayat system, like various similar social innovations in India has been introduced more as a radical cultural institution rather than structural. Its structural characteristics suffer from serious handicaps due to lack of complementary social changes. It has, so far, been instrumental in activising a process of

social change only through alteration in the civic responsibilities and expectations of the villagers rather than changes in their class status and economic positions. Consequently, whenever, the inconsistency between the two becomes manifest through the interplay of politics-cultural processes of the Panchayats, it leads to either violent group conflicts or regression in power. In the cases quoted above, it has led to transition of power from the climbers to the traditional elites.

(2) Accompanying the former process, the intriguing problem of concentration of economic and socio-cultural benefits accruing from various institutional measures, e.g. C.D.P., cooperatives etc., to the substantially richer class of the villages is not surprising but is the normal consequence of the existing social conditions. It is unrealistic to isolate the aspects of economic and cultural power from the political, in order to justify the halfway measure of social change symbolised by the Panchayats or the Panchayati Raj. Panchayats have only succeeded in conferring upon the villagers certain legal rights which could not be put into effect for the absence of means to enforce them.

(3) Yet from one point of view the system can be justified viz. the integration of social structure. The case history of the power dynamics of the villages quoted here passes into three phases: (a) initial disequilibrium in power when power passes from traditional elites to the climbers; (b) period of acute group tension and conflict equivalent to the process of "strain towards consistency" and finally (c) the restoration of the equilibrium when the traditional elites come back to power. Thus, in the latest phase, social structure has gained a new level of social integration on a substantially different principle of cultural norms, adherence to which is more disguised than real. Hence from a strictly sociological viewpoint the change may even be desirable yet from an ideological point of view

(grass root democracy, socialistic pattern, distribution of power etc.) it is not. Ideologically the requirement is not merely of integration but a certain level and form of integration which Panchayats have certainly not been able to achieve as yet.

(4) Both from cultural and structural point of view the Panchayats introduced radical and far-reaching measures of innovation. In view of it, not even the successes but also the failures of the system would have radical consequences for the whole rural society. This, however, is visible to even a casual observer of rural life, and the magnitude of this measure is bound to grow with administrative and economic diversification of rural life. Mainly, the process is linked up with economic growth and increased social communication. But suitable checks on the class structure of the rural society would be imperative for the ideological success of the Panchayati Raj.

(5) Panchayats have been conceived not as isolated institutions but integral to the whole politico-ideological set-up of the Indian society. It was, therefore, expected that the administrative and ideological inter-linkages with institutions at the higher scale of operation and organisation in the country would reinforce this system. Due to unavoidable structural impediments this has not happened so far. For the same reason this process cannot even be expedited beyond a certain limit and should only grow steadily with overall process of social growth.

(6) Methodologically the analysis of the working of Panchayats offers better insight into the success and failure of the system if analysed from a dynamic class-structural point of view rather than through stereotypes of analytical categories like caste, leadership and faction. Analysed in this frame better insight is gained not only in the functioning of the system as such but also its inter-linkage with other social structures and the social system as a whole.

System at Work

As we observed earlier, the Village Panchayat as a statutory institution, emerged for the first time under the British rule. The traditional village councils experienced a decay as a result of the Village administration by the agencies of the Central Government, extension of the jurisdiction of Civil & Criminal Courts to the rural areas, growth of modern education, communication, introduction of the novel land revenue system, police organization and such other factors during the British period. The British Government with a view to preserve and stabilize its political control over rural areas gradually adopted various measures for reorganizing the village panchayats. It appointed a special Commission on democratic decentralization in 1909. This Commission stressed the need for revitalizing village panchayats for handling local affairs. Subsequently, various legislative Acts were passed in different provinces for the creation of local self-governing bodies in villages. Illustrative of this, are the Bengal Village Self-Government Act of 1919; Madras, Bombay and United Province Village Panchayat Acts of 1920; Bihar and Orissa Village Administration Act; Assam Rural Self-Government Act of 1926; Punjab Village Panchayat Act of 1935 and others. These new Panchayats were entrusted with such assignments as looking after village sanitation, lighting and were also empowered to try minor cases like theft, simple hurt, offence of cattle, trespass, etc. Various kinds of grants-in-aid, taxes, cesses, rates, tolls, fees, income from property, fines, donations and a portion of land cess were the general sources of income of Village Panchayats. There was no uniform practice for the establishment of Village Panchayats. Some provinces like Bengal, Madras, the United Provinces and the Punjab, declared specific areas as Panchayat areas. In Bombay, the Village Panchayats Act of 1939 made it compulsory to establish a Panchayat in a village with a population of 2000 or more. Thus it can be seen from the above perusal that the village Panchayat, as a formal statutory body, with officially sanctioned functions and powers and with specific financial allocation, emerged for the first time during the British period.

History

After independence, the development of village panchayats has received a fresh impetus. As per the Directive Principles of the Constitution (Article 40), the State is expected to take steps to organize Village Panchayats and attribute to them such powers and authority as may be necessary to enable them to function as units of self-government. Besides this Directive, the phenomenal increase in planned developmental activities after independence also brought home the need for the village panchayat as an integral part of decentralised administration. As a consequence, practically all the provinces took steps to improve the legislations with a view to promote rapid development of panchayats as well as entrusting them with greater responsibilities. Accordingly, almost all the provinces have enacted different legislations for providing requisite legal framework for the establishment of a village panchayat.

According to Nanavati and Anjaria, "The number of Village Panchayats increased from 83,093 in 1950-51 to 1,23,670 at the end of March 1956, and again increased to 1,64,358 at the end of March 1958. The number of villages covered was about four lakhs out of a total of about five lakhs of villages in the whole country. There has been good progress in the establishment of Village Panchayats in Uttar Pradesh, Punjab, Rajasthan, Kerala, Himachal Pradesh, and the erstwhile States of Madhya Bharat and Saurashtra, where almost all villages are served by panchayats. The pace has been somewhat slow in Assam, West Bengal, Orissa, Mysore and Andhra; while in other States, progress has been steady. As regards the working of Village Panchayats, possibly not more than 10 per cent of the total number of Panchayats are functioning effectively, roughly half are average and the remaining 40 per cent are working unsatisfactorily." In the year 1965 there were 2,19,694 Village Panchayats functioning in the country covering approximately 99 per cent of the entire rural population.

"The Village Panchayat Committee of the Congress Party, after a careful investigation of the working of Panchayats in 1954 made the following recommendations. The Panchayats provide a sound basis for the establishment of healthy, democratic traditions in the country. The Village Panchayats should not only serve as units of local self-Government but also as effective institutions for securing social justice and fostering corporate life, leading to conditions of fuller employment laid down in the Constitution. The State should therefore provide scope for the Village Panchayats to perform in the village society, functions such as credit, marketing, supplies, etc. The function of the Panchayats should include municipal, social, economic and judicial activities etc."

Similarly, the First Five Year Plan recommended that legislation should confer on the Panchayats specific functions relating to village production programmes and the development of village lands. The Second Plan further amplified this proposal, by classifying the functions as administrative and judicial. The functions in administrative sphere are defined as (1) civic, (2) development, (3) land management and (4) land reforms.

Secondly, with regard to finance it was suggested that "allocation to the Village Panchayats by the states may be in two parts, a basic proportion of 15 to 20 per cent of the land revenue and an additional grant extending upto 15 per cent of the land revenue on condition that the Panchayat raises an equal additional amount by taxation or voluntary contribution."

The Second Plan also emphasised the need for creating a well organized democratic organization at the district level and suggested that the Village Panchayats should be organically linked with popular organizations at a higher level. Now we shall briefly refer to the recommendations of the Study Team on Community Projects and National Extension Service.

Suggestions for Betterment

Panchayati Raj in India owes its origin to the findings and recommendations of the Study Team on the working of Community Projects and National Extension Service under the auspices of the Committee on Plan Project, which is popularly known as Balwantrai Mehta Committee. From the point of view of the Mehta Committee the major shortcomings of the Community Projects and National Extension Service lies in its failure in generating the necessary enthusiasm among rural people for the programme and its implementation. According to the Committee, each development block has an Advisory Committee composed of the official and non-official representatives but they have no roots amongst the people and have no powers and responsibilities. All planning and execution is done by the block-staff, who are responsible for the proper and timely utilization of the block funds. In the opinion of the Committee the block administration functions more bureaucratically and has not imbibed the spirit behind the programme. For generating people's enthusiasm for the programme the Committee recommended that all development programmes in the block areas should be entrusted to representative institutions that can evoke local interest and initiative and the block staff and other officials should be placed at the disposal of those institutions. The Study Team also recommended for the provision of sufficient funds and sources of revenue for these local institutions to enable them to discharge their new duties. With this view in mind, the Committee suggested the formation of the three-tier system of local Government i.e. at village, block and district level. The three-tier system consisted of directly elected Panchayats at village level, Panchayat Samiti at block and Zila Parishad at district level. The Panchayat Samiti should have a life of five years, and should possess the power to scrutinize and approve the budgets of village Panchayats. Its functions should include the development of agriculture, improvement of cattle, promotion of local industries, welfare work, public health, and administration of primary schools etc. As almost the entire rural development work would come within the purview of the Panchayat Samiti, the Study Team suggested the following resources should be assigned to them.

"(i) a percentage of land revenue collected within the block, which should not be less than 40 per cent of the State's net land revenue, (ii) cess on land revenue, etc. (iii) tax on professions, (iv) surcharge of duty on transfer of immovable property, (v) rent and profit accruing from property, (vi) net proceeds of tools and leases, (vii) pilgrim tax, tax on entertainment, primary education cess, proceeds from fairs and markets, (viii) share of motor vehicles tax, (ix) voluntary public contributions and (x) Government grants."

Further: "to ensure the necessary co-ordination between the Panchayat Samitis, a Zila Parishad should be established consisting of the Presidents of Panchayat Samitis, members of the State Legislature and of the Parliament, representing the area and the district level officers. The chairman of this parishad would be the Collector. The Parishad would have the power to examine and approve the budgets of the Panchayat Samitis. It would also generally supervise the activities of the Panchayat Samiti but it would not be invested with any executive functions."

The Central Government while accepting the proposals of the report recommended its implementation to all the States but the States were left free to make their own variations on the general pattern. All States that endorsed the proposal of the Centre adopted at their Zila and village level, the general pattern. At intermediate level, although most of the States took the block as unit, some States like Mysore and Gujarat opted for the taluk. At village level, all States favoured direct elections for the Village Panchayats, but again at intermediate level, most of the States preferred indirect elections, few having opted for direct. At district level, all elections are indirect.

It has been observed that, real power in the three-tier system is at the middle tier, with the Samiti President, and he is the key figure in the whole set-up. He has no interfering collector and he is not only president, but the chairman of all the Standing Committees. The senior official in the Block, the B.D.O. is his executive officer, and a word in the ear of ministerial friends can always secure the BDO's transfer if he is not alienable to the president's wishes."

Aims and Objectives

The main objectives of Panchayati Raj as laid down in third Five Year Plan are as follows:

(1) Increasing agricultural production,

(2) Development of rural industries,

(3) Fostering co-operative institutions,

(4) Full utilization of local manpower and other resources,

(5) Assisting the weaker sections of the community,

(6) Progressive dispersal of authority and initiative with emphasis on the role of voluntary organization, and

(7) Fostering cohesion and encouraging the spirit of self-help within the community.

The village production plans should include the following two programmes:

(a) Programmes such as supply of credit, fertilizers and improved seeds, plant protection, minor irrigation etc., for which major assistance has to come from outside;

(b) Programmes such as digging field channels for utilizing irrigation from large projects, maintenance of bunds and field channels, digging and maintenance of village tanks, development and utilization of local manurial resources, etc. which call for effort on the part of the village community or the beneficiaries.

Now we shall briefly summarise the main functions of the three-tier system, at village, block and district levels respectively. This being the general pattern minor variation in the programme of activities do exist in different States.

At village level the main functions of the Panchayat are (a) provision of a water supply, (b) maintenance of minor irrigation, (c) school buildings etc., (d) family planning, (e) development and co-operation, (f) construction of wells, latrines etc.

Major Functions

They cover agricultural improvement, development, co-operation, sanitation, primary education, social education, cottage industries, emergency relief. It works through Standing Committees for (a) production programmes, (b) social service and finance, (c) taxation and administration. Block Development Officers are regarded as on deputation to the Panchayat Samiti and are liable to be transferred in consultation with the pradhan. The Samiti pradhan exercises administrative control over the 'Vikas adhikari' (meaning development officer) and the staff within the block.

District Boards

The functions of Zila Parishads include coordination and consolidation of the plans of the Panchayat Samiti, supervision of the activities, distribution among the Panchayat Samitis of the *adhoc* grants allotted to the district by the State Government etc. Pramukh of Zila Parishad can visit, guide and advise the Panchayat Samitis. Coordination between the work of the various departments is secured through the District Development Officer, who is normally the Collector and he is responsible to see that the amounts placed at the disposal of the Panchayat Samitis are being properly utilized and that the 'Vikas adhikaris' of this team are discharging their functions adequately as extension staff.

Available Funds

It can be seen from the perusal of the functions of the three-tier system that most of the functions of these three layers of the Panchayati Raj institutions are of a supervisory nature." The district Panchayat acts as the agency of the State, the taluka Panchayat acts as the agency of the district Panchayat and the village Panchayat as that of the taluka Panchayat, for fulfilling certain previously laid down targets. Of course, the agency functions do not exhaust the list of all the responsibilities of various local institutions. There does remain the scope to initiate a limited programme of development on their own. As for the financing of the agency functions, it can be presumed that the principal agency will provide finance to carry out the functions which have been delegated to the lower agencies. It is mainly for the functions undertaken at the initiative of the village, taluka and district Panchayats that the problem of resources arises."

Further: "A review of the resources proposed to be made available to various local bodies in the Panchayat Raj Legislation shows that the main reliance is placed on land revenue. The total collection of the land revenue in a district will be distributed among various bodies in varying proportions. These bodies are also empowered to levy cess on land revenue at various rates. Besides land revenue, they also have a nominal share in forest revenue and a portion of royalty from sand and morveum etc. They can also levy a cess on water rates. But their main independent source of income viz. land revenue is a highly inelastic one."

The above observations succinctly sum up the position with regard to resources of the Panchayati Raj at various levels.

Fifteen

Government's Role

The State Government has reserved the right to cancel or reject any resolution or order passed by a Panchayat Samiti or in case of emergency the Collector can also suspend a resolution of the Panchayat Samiti and report the case for orders to the State Government. The State Government also retains the right to supersede or dissolve a Panchayat Samiti or Zila Parishad if it has failed to exercise, abuse or exceeded its power.

Smooth Pattern

On January 12, 1958, the National Development Council endorsed the recommendations of the Balwantrai Mehta Committee. Since then Panchayati Raj is under implementation in Andhra Pradesh, Assam, Bihar, Gujarat, Madras, Maharashtra, Mysore, Orissa, Punjab, Rajasthan, Uttar Pradesh and West Bengal. The other States have either enacted or are in the process of enacting legislations to introduce a similar system. The Bihar Government has established the block as the primary unit of administration for all Government Departments and have assigned enlarged functions to the Block Advisory Committee. With regard to Gujarat, V. S. Vyas, remarks ;

"In Gujarat, as in several though not in all States, the linchpin in the Panchayati Raj set-up is the district level institutions. All that has been done in the Panchayati Raj legislation is to give more powers to the district administration and to democratise the set-up at district level. There is hardly any significant change whether in the powers and responsibilities or in the composition of village Panchayats which have been in existence from 1958. At the taluka level, though a new democratic body has come into existence, it does not have any independent responsibilities at least none which cannot be borne by either the district or the village Panchayats."

In Madras, the local administration of the village vests in the Panchayats. Then there are Panchayat Samitis at Block level and Advisory Coordinating Committee at the district level. Most of the functions of the district local boards are taken over by the Block Panchayat Union. In Andhra Pradesh, Panchayat Samitis are established at Block level, and the developments are transferred to these Samitis. The relation of the Block Samiti with the village Panchayats are presumed to be of a coordinating and advisory nature. The District Committee is also assigned work of supervising and guiding the activities of the Samitis at the Block level. In Uttar Pradesh, the District Councils have gradually replaced the District Boards. This council is expected to handle all the departmental development activities of the Government. In Maharashtra Village Panchayat Mandals set up for every district are the main executing bodies of Government developmental programme. In Mysore, Taluka Boards function as advisory bodies for the Community Development Blocks in their areas. The District Development Council generally supervises the working of the Taluka Boards and provide guidance and assistance in co-ordinating their work. In other States also the three-tier system of the Panchayati Raj is based more or less on the above pattern.

We now propose to examine the functioning of the Panchayati Raj in action. We shall begin with Rajasthan where the Panchayati Raj was first initiated.

One of the important criteria for assessing the success of Panchayati Raj is the extent to which it has succeeded in fulfilling the objectives of village production plans and thereby increased village production.

P. K. Chaudhari makes very pertinent observations with regard to the functioning of the Panchayati Raj in Rajasthan. With regard to village production plans he points out "that the so-called village production plans that we have now are nothing but paper plans prepared by the village level workers in consultation with a few village elders and the Sarpanch of the Panchayat. No serious attempt has been made to prepare genuine village plans incorporating targets for each crop and for every family in the village."

Further: "Panchayat Samitis and Village Panchayats are prompt to take up and execute programmes for which the Government provides loans, grants or subsidies so as to avail themselves of this assistance. But programmes which have to be carried out with local resources and initiative lag behind."

With regard to the functioning of the Zila Parishad, the same author points out: " In its present form the Zila Parishad as an institution appears to have become redundant. In spite of its status, it has played no effective role. The Zila Parishads to the Panchayat Samitis are all of an advisory nature having no sanction behind them. If the advice is not palatable, the Samitis usually ignore it."

Further while narrating evils of indirect elections he remarks:

"In Rajasthan there are 7,394 village Panchayats and 232 Panchayat Samitis. In 1960-61, 25% of the elections of panches and Sarpanches were unanimous; of sarpanches, 38.80% were elected unanimously. But unanimous election of Panchayat Samiti pradhan were rare. In most cases, there were keen contests for the office of pradhans. The Congress contested the elections as a party. During these contests, cases of forcible confinement and kidnapping of sarpanches occurred on an alarming scale. The kidnapped persons were released at the place of elections, just in time to cast their votes. In a few cases the sarpanches were sent on pilgrimage to Hardwar, etc., for sight-seeing to Kashmir at the expense of the prospective candidate for the office of pradhan so as to prevent them from coming under the influence of rival candidates."

Further: "These elections witnessed the worst features of indirect elections when the electoral college is small and the office is one of power and patronage. The assumption that direct election is more expensive than indirect was disproved. None of the contestants for the office of pradhan spent less than what an average Assembly Candidate spends (actual expenditure, not that submitted to the returning officer). Another unhappy feature of indirect elections also manifested itself—political and other pressures as well as money played a deciding role in them."

Standing Committees

It is the Standing Committee which is a real functioning body in the Panchayat Samiti. The Samiti has delegated its vital powers and functions to this body. With regard to the performance of these bodies the above author remarks: "Members of Panchayat Samitis are generally more interested in transfers, postings, and appointments of Samiti staff than in developmental activities. This is what the State Evaluation Organization has to say about the duration of meetings of the various Standing Committees. On an average the meetings of the Standing Committees on Administration and finances were the longest while those of the Standing Committees on production were the shortest. It is interesting to note that a fairly large number of meetings of the Standing Committee lasted for only 15 minutes. Hardly any business could have been transacted in such meetings and they were just called to complete the formality of doing so.

Officials' Responsibilities

Implementation of 'Panchayati Raj' has caused deep apprehensions in the minds of the officials. According to Chaudhari, "there is evidence of growing deterioration in the relations between officials and non-officials in the Panchayat Samitis. Instances of friction between the pradhan and the Vikas Adhikari are on an increase".

"Whenever the Pradhan happens to be educated and assertive conflicts with the Vikas Adhikari are frequent. A clear demarcation of the sphere of action and powers and functions of the two is urgently called for."

With regard to the impact of the Panchayati Raj on weaker section of the rural population, the same author remarks: "Panchayat Raj has not brought relief to the weaker section of the community. There has been no perceptible increase in the flow of benefits of development to the economically and socially weaker section of village community. According to the 1961 Census, the State has a population of 21 millions, of which Scheduled Castes constitute about 3 millions and Scheduled Tribes about 2.1 millions. Yet there is not a single Scheduled Caste Pradhan in the whole of the State. Out of a total of 7,394 Sarpanches, the number of Scheduled Caste Sarpanches could be counted on one's fingers. And only in predominantly tribal areas do we find a few sarpanches and pradhans belonging to the Scheduled Tribes. Rural leadership is still in the hands of the relatively well-to-do classes in the village which control all vantage positions in panchayati Raj."

Findings on the functioning of the Panchayati Raj in Mysore also broadly corroborate the above observations. Manu in this connection remarks that "under the Mysore Panchayati and Local Boards Act, Panchayati Raj institutions have been turned into bureaucratic cells. There is no organic link between different tiers of Panchayati Raj nor do the sources of revenue allocated to each bear any relation to the functions it has been charged with."

Further: "The Mysore Village Panchayats and Local Boards Act, 1959 the working of the Act has revealed glaring imperfections which affect the basic tenets of the Panchayati Raj like decentralization of decision making power, organic relationship between different tiers and democratisation of administration. The objective of increasing people's involvement in the development efforts of the State has not been attained because of the unrepresentative character of the District Development Council."

Now we shall examine the impact of democratic decentralization in Rajasthan and Andhra Pradesh as revealed by the survey conducted by the Central Institute of Study and Research in Community Development. The study of Panchayati Raj in Rajasthan and Andhra was done by Harold Hoffommer and D. C. Dubey.

With regard to Andhra Pradesh, the Report of the survey observes that "the fact that 35 per cent of the people are still not aware of the programme of Panchayati Raj, is indicative of the ground still to be covered in acquainting all the villages with even a minimum awareness of the programme."

Further: "Although 45 per cent of the respondents are indicated by this analysis to know about the objective of the programme, typical comments indicate that this understanding is only at a first level, for example, most of these respondents regard the main objective of the programme as that of providing amenities for the village. They fail to see in Panchayati Raj the opportunities for developing agriculture and the other constructive phases relating to village life and welfare."

With regard to the areas of the functional leadership of the Panchayats in respect of various aspects of village life the study provides some interesting information. This can be seen from the table reproduced from the study as below.

Areas of Functional Leadership: Rajasthan.

(1)	Settling Disputes (with neighbours 76; within caste 32)	108	responses
(2)	Loan for Irrigation	91	"
(3)	Disease in standing crops	18	"
(4)	Sickness among cattle	15	"
(5)	Sickness of family	14	"
(6)	Loan for daughter's marriage	8	"
(7)	Planning of next years' crop	6	"
(8)	Selling crop	2	"

Areas of Functional Leadership: Andhra.

(1)	Settling disputes (with neighbours 71; within caste 42)	113	responses.
(2)	Loans for irrigation wells (Panchayat direct 18; Panchayat through village level worker 13)	31	
(3)	Disease in standing crop	13	"
(4)	Sickness among cattle	9	"
(5)	Loan for daughter's marriage	6	"
(6)	Family sickness	3	"
(7)	Planning for next year's crop	3	"
(8)	Selling crop	1	"

Focus of leadership problem situation encompassed.

(1)	Family	Family discord, Planning next year's selling crop farm.
(2)	Panchayat	Dispute with neighbours, Loan from Govt. (Irrigation, Wells)
(3)	Extension Agency & Specialists	Disease in standing crop, Sickness in cattle, Sickness in family.
(4)	Caste Group	Caste disputes.
(5)	Money lenders	Loan for marriage of daughter, Selling crop.

(Source: 'A Sociological Study of Panchayati Raj in Rajasthan and Andhra Pradesh', Harold Hoffsomer and D. C. Dubey, pp. 76 and 89.)

It can be seen from the above table that in Rajasthan as well as in Andhra Pradesh, the functional leadership provided by the Panchayats in such vital matters as planning of crop production is very inadequate. Only 6 respondents in Rajasthan and 3 respondents in Andhra Pradesh consulted the village panchayats in their planning for next year's crop. The reason underlying such poor response can be of a serious nature. The respondents in all probability might have a feeling that the panchayats have hardly any effective solution to offer them in this vital problem. The planning for crops involves the problem of existing structure of land holdings. The structure of land holdings in turn, depends on prevailing pattern of land-relations and ultimately upon prevailing system of property relations. The resolution of this problem is beyond the jurisdiction of Panchayats.

Similarly, the failure on the part of the large number of cultivators to consult Panchayats for crop sale also indicate the control of the moneylender over the peasants' crop. The cultivators because of their economic dependence on money-lenders have very little choice in selecting agencies for selling their crops.

With regard to the administrative framework of Panchayati Raj Vyas remarks: " What is being attempted in Gujarat, as in the other States, is the decentralization rather than devolution of power. The distinction is fundamental. Decentralization involves control by local branches of a Central department; while genuine devolution of power would mean transfer of control to lower levels of Government. Panchayati Raj Legislation aims at the decentralization of power of different Central departments. A simple test to distinguish between decentralization and devolution is to find out the agency which is the reservoir of power, though it might delegate some of its power to the talukas, district or State. As it is, the main source of power is the State which merely delegates its power to the lower limits." Further, "The limits of this system of decentralization are better understood when it is realised that our economic planning is highly centralised."

In connection with Gujarat the author observes: "The absence of any provision for setting up Gramsabha is a real lacunae in Gujarat Panchayati Raj Act. Without effective control by the village people there is every danger of gram panchayats degenerating, literally in the rule of five persons."

The implementation of the 'Panchayati Raj' has led to the emergence of the novel forms of political tensions and conflicts in rural areas. The findings of the Report of Panchayati Raj Research Project conducted by the Department of Economic & Public Administration of the Rajasthan University has amply demonstrated this fact. The survey was conducted under the direction of Prof. M. V. Mathur (ex-member of the Santhanam Committee) on Panchayati Raj finances. Some of the findings of the Report are reproduced below.

Leadership at the Local Level

Firstly, the introduction of Panchayati Raj has given a fillip to the emergence of a local leadership which though not independent from the State leadership is in a strong bargaining position vis-a-vis the political bosses at State level.

Secondly, the pradhan of the panchayat Samiti is an elected rival for the sphere of influence as far as the legislator is concerned. The former wields much more real power than the MLA and thus grows into a potential contender for the legislator's position.

Thirdly, the failure of public leaders in politicalizing Panchayati Raj affairs and their incapacity in generating loyalties based on platform of action and programme has revived and strengthened the traditional loyalties.

Fourthly, inadequate preparation of the large mass of really backward and downtrodden people in securing their due share in powers vested in these institutions has given an opportunity to the local vested interest to perpetuate itself with the aid of new resources provided by the State.

Fifthly, the wide gap between hopes raised by the slogan of Panchayati Raj and the actual sphere of work of these institutions has led to impatience and frustration on the one hand and in-built dynamism on the other.

Sixthly, the widespread tension between the administrative machinery and elected representatives and the usual tendency of the State Governments to protect the administrative wing has given rise to a deep-seated sense of hostility amongst the new and emergent leadership against the present new political monarchy.

Observations made by Hugh Gray, (fellow in South Asian Studies at the Oriental & African Studies, London,) who spent a year studying Panchayati Raj in Andhra Pradesh also corroborate the findings of the Report referred to above. According to him, " Panchayati Raj has provided a new framework for political and caste struggles between rival landlords (by this I don't mean feudal landlords but substantial land-owners), jealous of their prestige and determined to maintain and if possible strengthen their district power network. Needs have never been the ultimate criteria for help, except in the very broadest sense and in the individual instance there has always been patronage. Today, the Samiti president disposes not only of the Samiti jeep but of important sources of patronage, such as for instance, the postings of primary school teachers. Through his political majority the president decides who shall receive individual well subsidies and taccavi loans, these are rarely if ever given to political opponents. The prestige of the individual Samiti members depends on what they obtain for their village in concrete physical benefits."

Further: "The aim of decentralizing political power has to a great extent been achieved. But the main aim of arousing popular enthusiasm for community development has been less successful. One sees this by the amounts of money which lapse, particularly for roads and schools, when it is a question of the public's contribution amounting to 50% instead of 25%."

According to Gray: " Villagers do not yet feel that the Raj is theirs, they still think of it as the landlords. Panchayati Raj has established a new forum in which the members of the dominant landowing castes, fight each other for prestige and power. Before, they remained as lords of their villages or went to the Legislative Assembly, in between was a vaccum. In Andhra Pradesh, where the Congress party is dominant, the Samiti Presidency is fought for on a caste basis and a Reddi, Kamma or Velma almost invariably emerges as Victor, except when a Brahmin successfully manipulates the caste factor in his favour. In districts where the

Congress party is in a minority the caste factor is muted and the party cuts across caste, but the caste variable is always present and manipulated even by the communist party.

"Whatever politicians may still be doing inside their houses, outside they will dine and accept alcohol from anybody. Political parties are ritual levellers, and the higher no longer dare to appear polluted by the lower who have votes to give them. This does not mean that the boundary maintaining forces of caste are dead but that they are utilizing more secular forms and the dominant agricultural castes battle each other for control of the State Government and the new bodies set up by Panchayati Raj."

In his concluding remark the above author makes a very pertinent and revealing observation. According to him." I would argue that there can only be common interests in egalitarian communities, which Indian villages are not: It seems to me that the shifting of the conflict of interests and opinions, serves not the emergence of synthesis from thesis and antithesis, but the interests of powerful individuals and groups. The consensus which emerges is always the view of the rulers and not the ruled."

The bureaucratic nature of the new power elite that has emerged as a result of the implementation of the Panchayati Raj is very ably depicted by 'Seminarists'.

The author observes that: "in Rajasthan, where the BDO is in many cases a junior I.A.S. Officer the president of the Panchayat Samiti writes his annual report. How impartial these reports are can easily be judged by the dilemma of the BDO. He is expected to carry the people with him but, more often than not, this simply means an ability to be tactful, without antagonising the unscrupulous. There is not a politician of consequence who is not either a building contractor or a road builder, an office bearer of the local cooperative. The BDO has to humour him or else he is easily transferred as tactless, inefficient bureaucrat lacking in the spirit of extension."

With regard to the impact of the Panchayati Raj on the weaker sections of the rural society the above author's findings deserve consideration.

He remarks: "The impoverished small cultivator who is sought to be put on his legs by Panchayati Raj is gullible enough to accept his old bare level of subsistence. No eggs for him, no fish for him, not even a reasonable quality of the paddy or wheat which he produces."

Further: "Firstly, Panchayati Raj is used more as an empty slogan to catch the fancy of the voter who has already exploded the myth of the common good ....Secondly, democratic decentralization is not possible within the limits of perpetuating a regime. Not when Panchayati constituencies are delimited suitably to preserve group strength; elections are staged without adequate rules, administrators are either appointed or removed to suit the interests of political representatives, presidents of Zila Parishads are nominated and not elected; accounts are audited inordinately late, the collection of arrears of land revenue and loans is willfully postponed and schools and buildings and roads and wells are constructed in chosen constituencies. What earthly chance can the illiterate and backward, the gullible and innocent villagers have against the organised conspiracy? Whether it is Bihar or Orissa, the Punjab or U.P. the story is the same."

The implementation of the Panchayati Raj has led to the strengthening of caste system. Number of scholars have pointed out this fact. Prof M. N. Srinivasa in his essay on 'Caste in Modern India', observes that the power and activity of caste has increased in proportion as political power passed increasingly to the people from the rulers and the establishment of the Panchayati Raj in Rajasthan and Andhra has given a new fillip to caste.

Leadership in the Making

Dr. Pradipto Roy, in a paper throws significant light on the new elite that has emerged in rural areas in recent years. According to him the main characteristics of the rural leadership today are as follows:

"In short, the characteristics that distinguish the emergent leaders who are participating in the new organizations from non-participants were-first, higher socio-economic level in a rational sense i.e. higher income, more material possessions and more education. The new participants as would be expected, had a higher level of contact with the extension agency and more secular orientation to life." Further in summing up the overall characteristics of the new leadership in rural areas the author observes:

"The picture that emerges of the leader is a person of high economic status, some education, good contacts with extension agencies, a large family and a somewhat rational orientation to life."

Similar trends are also noticed by B. Ganguly in his paper entitled: 'The Emerging Leadership pattern under planning in Rural Bihar', submitted to the conference we referred above. He remarks: " Moreover casteism has raised its head in a virulent form in recent years and sometimes second rate political leaders have been fanning caste tensions for getting support of voters. Zamindars, who were in most cases the natural leaders of the villages have lost their leadership and in their place have cropped up a class of semi literate leaders. In many cases the contractors, school managers, muharris, kutibs, karparardars, cooperative secretaries, and Banias are the village leaders. Mukhias, Up-mukhias, Sarpanches and Dalpatis very often crop up from the class of leaders who really belong to the Kamkanchana group, now clamouring for kirti. People of the 'Karma' and 'Dharma' groups are in the background. When MLAs and M.P.s take part in village politics, there is a better leadership no doubt, but party politics pollutes even the rural society. Even some Sarvodaya workers are hesitating to take up village leadership lest they might be corrupted by power and lest their participation in gram panchayats means lending whole hearted support to the Congress policy with which they are not in complete agreement."

The same author further observes that there were bitter quarrels and fights over Panchayat elections, often under the patronage of political parties. Mukhias, Pramukhs and others were found to be more concerned with making contracts etc., than in promoting village welfare.

The studies conducted by the Planning Commission recently, further reveal that most of the Sarpanches in the villages surveyed by the Commission were recruited from upper caste.

We are reproducing below some more findings on the impact of the Panchayati Raj in rural areas. Recently a sample survey conducted by Prof. Y. M. Sirsikar, revealed that 'rural politics in Maharashtra tends to become more competitive than constructive' and traditional factors like caste, social status and wealth play an important role in Panchayat elections.

The survey has pointed out, 'the rural elite', consisting of the well-to-do peasantry, lawyers with an agricultural background and a few businessmen, display an increasing power consciousness. Politics threatens to become more competitive than constructive. 'Ideology would seem to count less than power consideration.

"The political structure in rural Maharashtra exhibits a mixed character, modern and traditional. The leaders are elected on party tickets by secret ballot and defined procedures. At the same time, traditional factors such as kinship and caste are in evidence and the party structure itself is threatened with infiltration by these traditional elements."

Further the survey also shows that as many as 71.2 per cent of the office bearers of Zila Parishads are drawn from the Maratha Caste. This means that the Marathas are 'heavily over-represented', since they constitute only 40 per cent of the total population of the State. Brahmins hold less than four per cent of the seats in the Panchayat institutions. This poor showing on their part is attributed to the shift of the Brahmin population from the rural to urban centres in recent years.

Referring to the age-group of leadership the survey reveals that 63.4 per cent of the Panchayat officials belong to the age-group of 31-45, the younger ones (between 25 and 30 years) constituting only 9.8 per cent. The percentage of office-bearers of up to 25 years is 3.6. Only 4.2 per cent of the officials are above the age of 60.

Thus the leadership in rural Maharashtra at present appears to be concentrated in the hands of the 31-45 age group.

The survey also points out that most of the leaders of Zila Parishads entered public life and political parties very recently—some not even more than a year prior to their election. Referring to the education and social values of the new rural elites, the study reveals that there were no illiterates among the new rural leaders, though more than 30 per cent had no English education. Only 25 per cent had passed the matriculation examination. There were a good number of graduates.

Another interesting revelation of the survey is the significant change in social values. For instance, against only 31.7 per cent of the Panchayat officials being connected with temple or such other religious activities in their respective areas, 66.7 per cent were found to be intimately connected with educational institutions. This indicates that education has become a matter of immediate concern for the rural leadership.

Another intensive inquiry into various Panchayat Samitis in the Punjab conducted by the Gram Swaraj Sangha concluded that these institutions have failed due to factionalism: " So long as there is a clash of interests—and it is idle to pretend that there is no such clash in the villages—such divisions cannot be wished away."

The Times of India in its editorial points out that the accumulating evidence shows that incompetence, moreover, is compounded by factionalism and that the Panchayati institutions (like all too many of the co-operative societies in the rural areas) are becoming instruments in the hands of the privileged sections in the countryside for their own advancement.

"Some months ago the Department of Economics and Public Administration of Rajasthan University completed a study of Panchayati Raj in the State; and its report is a sobering document. In the agricultural sector, the introduction of Panchayati Raj has had little impact on productivity; rather, it is `bogged down' in the complexities of distributing taccavi and other loans, and the recovery of these loans is disappointingly low. Democratic decentralization, it seems has generated development consciousness; but this has not led to the growth of social solidarity. In the sphere of social reform, it has had little direct impact, and its indirect impact has been negative. Clan and caste loyalties are finding renewed expression through Panchayati Raj institutions. If similar candid studies were conducted elsewhere, we might find that the situation in the other States is equally bad, if not worse. After all, Rajasthan continues to be hailed as a pioneer in democratic decentralization, one which has given a bold lead to the other States."

It can be seen from the above observations that the new leadership that has emerged in agrarian areas as a result of various Government developmental measures is essentially recruited from new landowning class. It has been also indicated that this leadership coming from higher income groups equipped with better education and with superior material resources at its command has acquired a more rational outlook on life. This new leadership is also bureaucratic and corrupt in character. The study conducted by the Planning Commission has also pointed out that most of the village sarpanches are recruited from upper castes. This leadership also exploits caste sentiments for promotion of its interests. Thus, the replacement of traditional leadership of Zamindars by a new land-owning class is a new phenomenon that has emerged in rural India after Independence. The above observations also reveal that the new land-owning class is emerging not only as an economic, but also as a political and social leader in agrarian areas. The above studies also indicate how this new leadership is slowly developing its grip over administrative authorities like Block Development Officer and other officials. Thus the new land-owning class is emerging as a most powerful and potent force in agrarian India in recent years. The positive significance of the Panchayati Raj as per the strategy of the ruling class in India lie in accelerating this process in rural areas.

It may be noted here that the Panchayati Raj as implemented by the Government of India is quite different from the one as visualised by Gandhiji and Vinobaji and other Sarvodaya leaders. The Panchayati Raj or 'Gram-Swarajya' as envisaged by latter centred round the idea of reviving the self-sufficient village community with the spinning wheel as the base of the village economy. The social and economic life of the village community according to the concept of Gandhiji should be guided by the laws of morality. One of the most important ingredients of these moral laws is that every owner of property should consider himself to be a trustee on behalf of the people. The concept of gramdan, as evolved and propagated by Vinobaji represents the ideal image of such self-sufficient village community.

The Panchayati Raj as implemented now is the very opposite of this. Far from reviving the self-sufficient village community as cherished by Sarvodaya, it subjects every aspect of village life, agricultural production, animal husbandry and fisheries, education and public health, etc., to the direction and guidance emanating from the centre, as well as the State Head Quarters.

The establishment of socio-economic systems within the matrix of mixed economy as envisaged by the Indian Planning Commission makes it inevitable that the administration should have a large degree of centralization as it is impossible to build up a modern industrialized economy without having a centralized administration.

On the basis of the evaluations made by above official enquiries and the findings of the experts, the impact made by the Panchayati Raj on rural India can broadly be summed up as below:

(1) The implementation of the Panchayati Raj has given a new fillip to caste systems in Andhra and Rajasthan.

(2) The Panchayati Raj has further intensified the factional struggles and group rivalries among the contesting groups for power.

(3) It has given birth to a new variety of non-official bureaucrats in rural areas.

(4) It has further intensified the tensions and conflicts among the administrative personnel and taluk leaders.

(5) It has brought politics of manipulation' right up to the village level.

(6) It has successfully directed the mind of the rural people from resolving their basic economic and social problem to intrigues for power from village to taluka level.

(7) It has given rise to intensified form of nepotism and corruption through patronizing selected group of individuals.

(8) The ruling party has successfully created through Panchayati Raj an organised group of its supporters who form its social base today in rural areas.

(9) It has further generated power hunger and consequently power tensions in rural areas.

(10) The production plans which panchayats are expected to implement at the village level have largely remained only paper plans. Thus, the Panchayati Raj like Community Development has proved a total failure in effectively enforcing production plans at village level and thereby contributing in increasing agricultural production.

(11) The Panchayati Raj has failed in benefitting weaker sections of the rural society.

(12) The new rural elite emerging from the higher income and more educated section of the rural society is dominating the Panchayati Raj today.

(13) The Scheduled Castes and the Scheduled Tribes members have no effective choice in Panchayat Samitis which is a real governing body. To the best of our knowledge no scheduled caste member has been selected as the Pramukh of the panchayat Samiti in any state. The Scheduled Tribes Pramukhs are found only in tribal areas. Thus, the weaker sections of Indian rural society are left almost completely unrepresented in the Panchayati Raj institutions.

(14) Panchayati Raj has also failed in generating local enthusiasm for Government projects. This is evident from the fact that it has failed in enlisting the cooperation of the village people for the voluntary projects which demanded more contribution from the people in kind or cash. It has succeeded in undertaking only those projects which are mainly financed by the Government.

What are the implications of the above findings for rural India? Can Panchayati Raj successfully resolve our agrarian problem within the matrix of the present social structure of rural society? Can it successfully implement any production plan in the existing pattern of land relations? Can it generate any sense of unity and cooperation and enthusiasm in class, caste and faction ridden rural society in India? Is any 'democratic decentralization' possible in the hierarchically graded society? Will it be too much to assume that in the absence of the basic prerequisites for effective application of 'democratic decentralization' the present programme of the Panchayati Raj only serves the function of expanding the social base of the ruling party and the Government by recruiting larger number of their supporters at different levels in rural society?

Issues at Stake

The inspiration for Panchayati Raj is derived from the tradition of Panch Parameshwar, where God speaks through the Five, and official publications speak of 'Village Republics" as established historical facts, but do not list any sources for this well-established myth. By January 1957, every State had a Panchayat Act, and by September of that year 73 per cent of India's villages were covered by statutory panchayats with powers to enforce sanitation laws, to maintain the roads and protect the water supply. These were not autonomous bodies, and their activities were checked by State officials.

In India, most indigenous local consultative bodies seem to have had a caste origin. Within most castes, there were panchayats meeting to hear cases and arbitrate between fellow caste members involved in disputes, and punish offenders against caste rules and customs. Inter caste panchayats were also formed to hear disputes between members of different castes. There were also regional caste courts in some places hearing cases in which the people involved were from different villages. Disputes were also referred to Doras, Deshmukhs and Jagirdars for arbitration, and this was often paid for, an additional source of income to landlords. Before the introduction of British courts, justice was administered by the masters, or one's caste fellows.

The Indian Constitution deals with government at the Centre and State levels, and does not foreshadow Panchayati Raj as a form of political organization, except that States are directed in the Directive Principles to 'take steps to organise village panchayats... to enable them to function as units of self-government.' The declared aim, then, was the decentralising of democracy. There was also a more practical, immediate reason.

Important Factors

The main consideration which prompted their introduction seems to have been the need for provoking public co-operation and participation in national construction and development, in view of the slow momentum of economic growth compared with such countries as Israel, Yugoslavia and China.

The adoption by the Planning Commission of Panchayati Raj as the pattern of future political organization followed the report of the Balwantrai Mehta study team, and experiments carried out in Andhra Pradesh and Rajasthan. Since 1959, 'democratic decentralization' has been gradually extended throughout India. The Balwantrai Mehta report recommended the formation of a three-tier system of local government within districts, the three tiers to be indirectly elected and 'originally' linked. They were to be at village, block and district levels.

The report was enthusiastically received by the ruling party and its implementation recommended to all States, but States were left free to make their own variations on the general pattern. All States took as their top and bottom tiers the district and the village; at intermediate level, although most took the Block as unit, others (e.g. Mysore) took the taluk. At village level, all States decided on direct elections to the village panchayat, but again at the intermediate level, although most opted for indirect elections, some had direct. At district level, all elections are indirect.

In the State (Andhra Pradesh) where it was studying Panchayati Raj the Block is taken as the middle unit and direct elections are only at village level. The village panchayat is elected by secret ballot, the number of members proportional to the population. In Andhra, elections at village level are inevitably fought out on a caste basis in Congress dominated villages; the caste factor is intensified in these elections by the division of the villages into territorial wards.

In villages dominated by individual Congress landlords, or the Communist Party, there are no contested elections and the choice of the village panchayat is 'unanimous'. In the State of Madras, this expression of 'concensus' receives a monetary award-so much for the ideal that democracy should extend rather than curtail the range of choices open to the individual. After the village panchayat is constituted, its members elect a Sarpanch, and he becomes a member of the Panchayat Samiti.

The middle tier, the Panchayat Samiti, is composed (in Andhra Pradesh) of the thirty to forty directly elected Sarpanchas of the village panchayats, plus some co-opted members and members of the Legislative Assembly in whose constituency the Block is situated. Co-opted members are generally local politicians who are not interested in becoming Sarpanchas of their own villages, but wish to have a share in the power, patronage and perquisites deriving from Samiti membership.

At district level, the Zila Parishad consists of the presidents of all the samities, who are all ex-officio members, plus some co-opted members, M.L.A.'s, M.P.'s and such members of the Legislative Council and the All-India Council of State as have been directed by the State government to sit on the particular Zila Parishad. This provision was included to enable the Congress Party to assure themselves of a majority on any Zila Parishad which seemed likely to fall prey to another party.

The power wielded by a Zila Parishad chairman within a district depends on his personality, local standing, his skill in manipulating variables, and the interplay of his personality with that of the Collector. (In Andhra Pradesh, the Collector is chairman of the Zila Parishad standing committees, but the chairman of the Zila Parishad itself is a politician.) A strong Zila Parishad chairman, who belongs to a political faction within Congress opposed to that of the Chief Minister, is more likely to find himself with a strong Collector, than with one of his supporters. On the other hand, if the Zila Parishad chairman has powerful friends at State level, he can always get the Collector transferred elsewhere.

Under Panchayati Raj, the Collector's role is changing. Loud were the cries of nostalgia for the days of the British Raj when the Collector was a monarch in his own district, not a *primus inter pares* among district officers, heard at a recent seminar in Hyderabad, at which Collectors discussed their problems. But district officers are not the executive officers of Zila Parishads, and the Zila Parishad chairman's position is weak as compared with that of the Samiti's presidents.

Centre of Power

Real power in the three-tier system is at the middle tier, with the Samiti president, and he is the key figure in the whole set-up. He has no interfering Collector, and he is not only president, but chairman of all the standing committees. The senior official in the

Block, the Block Development Officer, is his executive officer, and a word in the ear of ministerial friends can always secure the BDO's transfer, if he is not amenable to the president's wishes.

If the membership of samitis is analysed, one finds they consist almost entirely of members of the dominant landowning castes, whatever the political affiliations of the members concerned. More caste, more land, more money, more education are still the requisites for political success.

Panchayati Raj has provided a new framework for political and caste struggles between rival landlords (by this we don't mean feudal landlords but substantial landowners), jealous of their prestige and determined to maintain and, if possible, strengthen their district power networks. Needs have never been the ultimate criteria for help, except in the very broadest sense and in the individual instance there has always been patronage. Today, the Samiti president disposes not only of the Samiti jeep but of important sources of patronage, such as, for instance, the postings of primary school teachers. Through his political majority, the president decides who shall receive individual well subsidies and taccavi loans; these are rarely, if ever, given to political opponents. The prestige of the individual Samiti members depends on what they obtain for their villages in concrete physical benefits.

Like Panchayati Raj, Community Development benefits which have reached villagers through landlord representatives and officials who share the same socio-economic and educational background, have reinforced traditional authority. Officials do not consider it their role to nurture new sources of leadership, and subvert the class and caste structures, which in rural areas reinforce one another. Indeed, if they attempted any such thing they would find themselves quickly transferred. But with Panchayati Raj, certain changes have come about.

Panchayati Raj has brought politics down to village level, and made government more intelligible. 'You can talk to the Samiti President', as one villager said to me. Eventually, when the new ways of access to power are utilised by educated members of the lower castes, the traditional authority of the dominant landowning castes may be broken.

The aim of decentralising political power, has, to a great extent, been achieved. But the twin aim of arousing popular enthusiasm for Community development has been less successful. One sees this by the amounts of money which lapse, particularly for roads and schools, when it is a question of the public's contribution amounting to 50 per cent instead of 25 per cent. (This is also partly a cause, partly a symptom of the failure of community development: what the leaders want is not necessarily what the villagers want. 'Who wants roads?' said a villager to me. 'I'll tell you, officials; politicians, landlords, but not us. Where there is a road the landlord will not have to pay us for taking his paddy on our bullock carts down to the main road.')

Where a 25 per cent contribution is expected, much more gets done, even though the public contribution in the forms of labour and material is often avoided. If villagers are asked if they favour Panchayati Raj, they tend to say' YES,' because, it has brought more money to the village. Villagers do not yet feel that the Raj is theirs, they still think of it as the landlords, Landlords are better than officials, because they are people you can talk to easily, but the government is still of 'them' not 'us'.

People's Platform

Panchayati Raj has established a new forum in which the members of the dominant landowning castes fight each other for prestige and power. Before, they remained as lords of their villages or went to the Legislative Assembly; in between was a vacuum. In Andhra Pradesh, where the Congress Party is dominant, the Samiti presidency is fought for on a caste basis and a Reddi, Kamma or Velma almost invariably emerges as victor, except when a Brahmin successfully manipulates the caste factor in his favour. In districts where the Congress Party is in a minority, the caste factor is muted and the party cuts across caste, but the caste variable is always present, and manipulated, even by the Communist Party.

On the positive side, villagers are becoming election minded and beginning to realise that the whole of life is not dharma and karma, and that social plumbing is an everyday possibility: that if the ballot is secret, they can sometimes resist the landlords' pressure. They are not yet consciously participating in decision making processes, but they do realise that they have a vote to use, and that it is something which has a value because it represents a choice.

Whatever politicians may still be doing inside their houses, outside they will dine and accept alcohol from anybody. Political parties are ritual levellers, and the higher no longer dare to appear polluted by the lower who have votes to give them. This does not mean that the boundary-maintaining forces of caste are dead but that they are utilising more secular forms, and the dominant agricultural castes battle each other for control of the State governments and the new bodies set up by Panchayati Raj.

It is presumably the virulence of caste in political parties which has led thinkers such as Gore and Jayaprakash Narayan to reject them in favour of 'partyless democracy'. Jayaprakash Narayan would like to see a hierarchical structure replaced by a system of ' ever widening never ascending circles', with the individual at the centre of each circle and the world as the final circumference. He wishes to base political organization on small communities expressing the general will by consensus rather than through voting. Gram Panchayats would be formed by 'general consensus of opinion in the Sabha.'

Thinkers like Jayaprakash Narayan seem to assume that there is some straightforward, simple entity easily identified as pertaining to the common good, which can always be stripped naked by discussion and acclaimed by all. I would argue that there can only be common interests in egalitarian communities, which Indian villages are not. It seems to me that the stifling of the conflict of interests and opinions, serves not the emergence of synthesis from thesis and antithesis, but the interests of powerful individuals and groups. The consensus which emerges is always the view of the rulers, not the ruled.

Search for New Sources

For Community Development and Panchayati Raj, the main problem is to foster new sources of leadership from the peasant and artisan castes, and to thus break the iron stranglehold which the landlords have on village life. Only in this way can popular participation be obtained, when the leaders come from the majority castes, not the minority dominant ones.

The more political parties cut across caste and provide an alternative focus of loyalty, the more likely is this to happen. Will the Congress Party continue to foster new men only when it is in danger of losing district control. What is needed at the moment is more activity—including adult education—by political parties in villages, not less. The cries one often hears of, 'let us keep politics out of the villages' always means 'let us maintain the authoritarian hierarchical status quo', and calling this a village republic does not change its nature. Where there is democracy and voice, there are political parties. Only in totalitarian villages do elections not take place.

There must be no backtracking. Panchayati Raj is a great step forward in Asia's only democratic country. Within this new system of local government, democracy must be increased, not lessened, with direct elections and candidates from opposed political parties at every level.

And the immediate problem is still how to increase popular participation in decision-making and community development schemes—the undoubted social revolution is a slow one, and the sweeping away of the dominant castes' power, a long process. But there is no going back unless it were going back on democracy itself.

Sixteen

Opportunities for Education

Important Factor

The significance of education in modern societies cannot be overestimated. A literate and educated people are a prerequisite both for maintaining and further developing these societies. The crucial need of education for the people in various spheres of modern social life (economic, political, social, ethical and others) has been unanimously recognized. We will see why this need arises.

Financial Restraints

In contrast to the multitude of self-sufficient village economies which mainly constituted the economic life of the pre-modern communities, the economy of a modern people has a national basis. Further even this national economy has been largely outmoded in recent decades and has become an integral part of the single world economy. The national economy, in fact, produces industrial, agrarian and other commodities, both for the national and international markets. Consequently, it is the world price movement of various commodities which finally determines the volume and the price of products in different production centres. An intelligent and correct understanding of the complex economic life of mankind as a whole therefore becomes necessary for all producers.

It was not so in pre-modern societies. In pre-British India, as observed earlier, the village farmer group produced just enough to meet the requirements of the village population and of the land revenue to be paid by the village collectively to the state. In post-British India the village farmer group has been producing for the local, national and even international market. If the village agriculturist is not to be a victim of the vicissitudes of the world market, he needs to be educated enough to follow the movement of national and world economies.

Lack of Awareness

Education is necessary for the modern rural aggregate also for political and administrative reasons. Formerly, the state exercised nominal sovereignty over the village. Its administrative machinery did not penetrate and function in the village. The village panchayat and caste committees regulated the life of the people. After the modern society evolved, the village has become an integral part of the political and administrative machinery of a highly centralized state. Since the modern state appreciably shapes the economic, social, and cultural life of the people, it is indispensable for the rural people to study its mechanism. The rural man needs to know a minimum of law, governing judicial and administrative processes as well as powers of various state organs. Further, in recent decades, various political parties have sprung up in the rural area. These parties struggle among themselves to win the support of the rural people with a view to gaining control over the state. It is, therefore, also necessary for the rural people to study the programmes and policies of these political parties. Both these reasons make it obligatory for them to have education.

Reasons for Backwardness

Education is essential for the rural people also for the broad social reason, viz., that all social relations between citizens are, in the modern society, governed by the principle of contract and not by status as in the former epoch. Contractual social relations are complex and multifold demanding from the citizen an understanding of the basic structure of the modern society and hence this need for education. The economic relations between citizens, the relations between the members of the family and other types of social relations, which in their totality form the complex variegated pattern of the modern society, are governed by laws based on the principle of contract. Only an educated citizen can have a comprehension of such a diversified system of contractual relations.

Restrictions by Ethics

There is another reason why the rural man must be an educated man. In the modern society the ethical life of the individual as well as of the sowety aggregate is increasingly being based on secular and humanist instead of on religious principles as in the medieval society. Equality of all men, individual liberty, development of human personality, reason as the determinant of human conduct-such are some of the principal conceptions which have been progressively determining the behaviour of the individual and the social aggregate. Modern education is absolutely necessary to comprehend these basic conceptions.

Cultural Card

Education is also the prerequisite for the study and assimilation of the rich culture which has developed in the contemporary age. Human knowledge of the natural world has registered a phenomenal advance in modern times, giving man a greater mastery over nature. Similarly knowledge in the sphere of social life too has immensely grown, thereby enabling man to mould his collective social life more consciously. Further, there has been a tremendous advance in the field of artistic culture also. A part of this rich modern culture has even acquired the character of a world culture. Education is indispensable for assimilating this mighty world culture so vital for enriching the intellectual and emotional life of the individual and thereby increasing his capacity to contribute to the advance of society. The best part of modern culture lays strong emphasis on individual liberty and social co-operation both of which are so essential for the development of the individual's personality and powers and for social progress. The citizen who imbibes such a culture will feel an inevitable urge to work for the creation of a society free from social antagonism and discord and based on social solidarity and individual freedom.

More Reasons

For the agriculturist, education is, in addition, necessary for understanding of the advantages of the use of such advanced agricultural techniques as tractors, fertilizers, harvesters and thrashers.

It must be also noted that the modern society throws up specific problems which only modern knowledge can successfully solve. For instance, the economic or political science embodied in Arthashastra by Chanakya cannot aid in solving the economic and political problems emerging from the soil of contemporary society. And modern education is the only means to acquire modern knowledge.

Just as old knowledge cannot assist in solving modern problems, educational methods of gaining old knowledge cannot help to assimilate modern knowledge. Modern science of pedagogy, modern methods of instruction and modern schools are required for imparting modern knowledge.

A shockingly large portion of the Indian rural population is submerged in gross ignorance and illiteracy. The problem of transforming tens of millions of those illiterate rural humans into educated and well-informed citizens is a problem of herculean proportion and still has to be resolved if the Indian society is to advance materially and culturally.

Background

We will first delineate the main features of education in the pre-British Indian rural society based on subsistence economy.

Education in the agricultural, industrial, and other occupational arts was imparted to the members of the growing young generation not in schools but in the process of their direct empirical participation in those occupations under the guidance of family elders.

Social education or education in the arts of social behaviour and adaptations was imparted to them by the family and the caste as the social life of the village people mainly moved within the family and the caste matrix.

The growing young generation received its moral and intellectual education largely from the priests, the Kathakars and saints, and also, to some extent, from the family.

The multitude of secular and religious functions, festivals and celebrations, which the family, the caste, and the village community organized and in which the youngsters of the village participated, served as the school for the aesthetic education of those youngsters.

The world outlook inculcated by that education was fundamentally religious. It propagated the concept of the divine origin of the world and of God's free will determining all phenomena and happenings. In addition to one supreme God it also taught the belief in a pantheon of gods and spirits behind all phenomena, significant and insignificant. Eclipses and earthquakes, floods and epidemics, were not scientifically explained but were declared to be the result of the wrathful actions of malevolent gods and goddesses. For instance, the eclipse signified the temporary suppression of the Sun-God by the two demons, Rahas and Ketu. The earthquake was the consequence of the movement of Shesh Nag who supports the earth on its colossal hood. The eruption of small-pox was the result of the ire of the deity Balia Kaka who, therefore, had to be propitiated by a proper ritual. Education, then, also encouraged belief in animism in tree gods, mountain gods and river goddesses.

Thus the rural people of the pre-modern society had a religious unscientific conception of the world.

The history of the past Indian society taught to the young generation was largely mythology. It dealt with the superhuman feats of god-kings. Even gods participated in the terrestrial battles between these god-kings. Such a history could not give a consistent continuous account of the development of the social, economic and political life of the people in the past and explain all historical transformations by means of secular causes.

The social education adapted the individual to the exigencies of joint family, caste and village communal life. Since the social structure was authoritarian, the social education was authoritarian too in spirit. It exhorted the individual to completely subordinate himself to the joint family, the caste or the village community. It disciplined him in the service of these institutions. Such a social education could hardly serve individual liberty or help the development of human personality.

All education including agricultural and craft education consisted of empirically acquired and hereditarily transmitted body of knowledge from the past. It was imparted to the young orally, mostly in the process of practice in arts, crafts and agriculture and participation in social life. There did not exist any technical institutes, musical and other art academies or schools of social sciences in the village. It was only in some distant urban centres that some educational and training institutions existed and functioned.

Impact with the west in general and Britain in particular and the resultant rise of modern society in India led to the spread of modern education among our people.

The new education was essentially secular and, on the whole liberal in spirit and content. This signified a shift from the religious and authoritarian to secular and liberal character of education. The spread of the modern education was, however, extremely slow and mainly restricted to middle and upper strata of the urban society. Very few villages had schools, and, even where they existed, the stark poverty of the rural people made it impossible for them to take advantage of the educational facility due to high cost. Further, since the modern education was introduced in India by the British mainly to meet the need of the personnel for their administrative machinery and economic enterprises, its liberal aims remained hazy or were even distorted. It did not set to itself the ideal of turning out citizens armed with modern knowledge who would use that knowledge for the untrammelled material and cultural advance of the nation to which they belonged. It was bereft of nationalist spirit and ideals. Nevertheless, it must be recognised that in spite of these serious flaws, the introduction of the new education brought the Indian people in contact with the liberal, democratic and rationalist ideologies of the modern west. Supersession of the pre-British education, authoritarian in spirit and largely superstitious in content, by the modern education, however defective, was an event of great significance in Indian history. Radhakrishnan's University Commission Report vividly depicts the achievements as well as the limitations of the system of modern education introduced during the British period.

The benefits of the modern education hardly extended to the rural India. The problem of education in the rural area was almost completely ignored by the British as is evidenced in the fact that, even after a hundred and fifty years of the British rule, 86 per cent of the total Indian population, including its advanced urban section, still remained illiterate.

A number of agencies worked for the spread of the modern education in India. The British Government, various foreign missionary bodies, Indian social reform organizations and subsequently political institutions like the Indian National Congress, were the chief among these agencies.

All these agencies, however, failed to achieve any appreciable result in the rural area.

The problem of rural education, it must be said, was not even thought out in all its complexity.

Post-independence Strides

With the advent of national independence, the problem of rural education has assumed urgent importance and new significance. The free Indian people have set to themselves the task of building up of a democratic, progressive, national life, which surely cannot be achieved when tens of millions of rural people are illiterate, ignorant and superstitious.

Campaign against the mass illiteracy among the rural people is the urgent task to-day. Further, treasures of rich modern knowledge have to be brought within their reach if they are to be effective participants in the creative work of national reconstruction.

For successfully evolving a comprehensive and scientific programme of rural education a number of problems germane to it have to be resolved.

We enumerate these problems below

1. Objective of Education.
2. Structure of the Machinery of Education.
3. Technical and other Means for its Spread.
4. Finance and Personnel.

Mottos and Aims

It is now recognized by eminent educationists that the present system of urban education lays unduly greater emphasis on the training of intellect than on the development of the physical, emotional, and moral aspects of the pupil's personality. Such education results in the one-sided and therefore defective development of the young generation. It fails to evolve an integral human being with an all-sided development of his personality.

The present system of urban education is further criticized on the ground that, during the long period of schooling which extends from childhood to almost adulthood, the role of general knowledge is over-emphasised. It is not related to concrete problems of real life. Consequently the educated youth, when he enters the arena of life after completing education, finds it difficult to grapple with the concrete problems of real life.

Various views have been advanced in the field of controversy over the question of education.

There are some who emphasise that education must have the liberal and humanist ideal before it. Others lay greater stress on the technical and practical aspects of education.

There are some who declare that the basic aim of education should be the development of the individual's personality. There are others who give greater importance to the cultivation of the virtues and qualities of an ideal citizen in the pupil.

There are some who desire secular education to be reinforced by religious training. There are others who sharply disagree with this view and uncompromisingly stand for purely secular education.

There is a group of educationists who are the exponents of a synthetic type of education which would help the development of all sides of the pupil's nature, intellectual, emotional, moral, and social, and help him to evolve into a synthetic man.

The view is gaining ground among a large number of social thinkers that the present education, which at the lower level, concentrates on the three R's, thereby concerns itself only with the development of the intellectual side of the pupil. They recommend that, instead of this, education should focus on three

H's, i. e., education of hand, heart and head. This will guarantee, they observe, the all-sided development of the pupil. Such education will result into the emergence of citizens, physically healthy and strong, emotionally rich, intellectually alert and capable of social co-operation. They will be valuable assets to the society.

The new Constitution of the Indian Union has stated in its Preamble that it aims at creating a democratic society based on "Justice, social, economic and political; liberty of thought, expression, belief, faith and worship; equality of status and opportunity." Further it aims at promoting among all citizens "Fraternity, assuring the dignity of the individual and unity of the Nation."

It implies the creation of a society free from all forms of inequalities and exploitation and based on individual liberty and social solidarity and cooperation.

For the realization of such an objective, it is necessary that the conception and the programme of education should be in harmony with and be derived out of it.

In his University Education Report, Dr. Radhakrishanan has given an elaborate picture of the social ideal depicted in the Constitution and has further described how it should be paraphrased and expressed in terms of the educational ideal of the nation.

Reconstruction of the Indian society as a whole in the spirit of the social ideal embodied in the Constitution would imply also the reconstruction of the Indian rural society in the spirit of the same ideal. Rural education should be therefore adapted to the needs of creation of the new and higher type of rural society envisaged in the future.

The study of a society reveals that the prevailing system of education serves the needs and ideals of that society. The educational system of a society based on self-sufficient economy serves the needs and ideals of that society. Similarly the present educational system sub-serves the requirements of the existing capitalist society based on a competitive and market economy and its social ideals.

A new educational system will have to be evolved if a new society based on co-operative socio-economic relations is to be created. It will have to instill virtues of social solidarity and social co-operation in the members of the young generation, uproot anti-social individualism, infuse social passions, and build up the ability for social co-operation among them.

The type of rural society which is programmed for construction should determine the educational system to be elaborated for the rural people.

The rural sociologist has to give the most earnest attention to this fact while making suggestions for a new system of education for the rural people.

Infrastructure

The success of an educational scheme like that of all schemes depends upon the machinery evolved for implementing that scheme. The scheme may be scientific and adapted realistically to social conditions and, further, the social ideal conceived by it may be noble, yet, if the appropriate machinery for its implementation is not forged, it will meet with failure.

The task of elaborating the organizational machinery for a scientific and comprehensive educational plan for millions of illiterate and ignorant villagers is a stupendous task. This is obvious when we consider that even the problem of creating a machinery for carrying out the minimum programme of the abolition of illiteracy among the rural people presents formidable obstacles.

The task raises a number of problems. What type of primary schools should be established for children? How will they be coordinated with such schools started for adult illiterates? In what manner will the primary schools be linked with secondary schools and the latter with higher educational institutions?

Further, should the schools in the rural area be open air or single room schools? Should they be specialized and differentiated or omnibus institutes? And, finally, how should the school time be adjusted to the exigencies of agricultural and artisan labour in which not only village adults but also youngsters participate?

The educational scheme will also raise such problems as those of the graded system of schools, suitable curricula to be evolved in the spirit of the social ideal in view, and the graded system of courses.

Based on Technology

During the last two hundred years, humanity has made amazing progress in the domain of technology. It has invented railways, steamships, aeroplanes, telephone and telegraph, radio, cinema and other marvellous technical devices. These devices constitute the valuable material means of integrating humanity into a single unit as well as of building up of a rich unified economic and cultural life on a national and even international scale.

Formerly the school was practically the only effective lever of education. After those astonishing inventions, the school can be reinforced by other means also.

These modern means, it must be noted, have not yet been sufficiently utilised for educational and cultural purposes in our country.

We will enumerate below some of the principal among these means which along with the school, are available for the rapid advance of education and cultural enlightenment of our people:

(a) School.
(b) Library.
(c) Museum.
(d) Movie.
(e) Radio.
(f) Mobile Van.
(g) Gymnasiums and Sport Centres.

A maximum and simultaneous utilization of these means will undoubtedly accelerate the process of extension of education and culture among the rural people.

We will refer very briefly to the specific role of these various means.

(a) *School*: The school should remain the principal lever of education. It can serve as the medium of formal education, patterned and planned.

(b) *Library*: The library adequately equipped with books scientifically dealing with varied subjects; with newspapers and magazines of local, national and even international significance; and with charts and maps; can be a rich reservoir of variegated knowledge, social, political, technical, economic and cultural. It can also enable the villager to follow decisive national and international happenings. The art section of the library can help him to develop a refined aesthetic sense and artistic taste. The library, when properly made use of, will help him to broaden his outlook, enlarge his vision extend the frontiers of his knowledge and to visualise local developments as an integral part of one single organic world development. He will thereby steadily build up a national and even international consciousness.

The library is particularly necessary in the village to-day, because, due to its absence, a large number of even those few, who have become literate through elementary village school education, cannot maintain their ability to read and hence lapse into illiteracy. As in the case of a bodily organ, a capacity atrophies when it is not continuously exercised.

The programme of providing the library to the rural area raises a number of problems. A veritable legion of them will be required for tens of thousands of villages in our country. Further, a good section of the village library should comprise literature adapted to the specific psychology, lower cultural level, and requirements of life of the village people. The production of such literature will itself present a task of stupendous proportion. The problem of fixing its content will bring headache even to expert educationists.

(c) *Museum*: The role of the museum as a source of knowledge is not often sufficiently realized even by the educated man. The various studies prepared by the League of Nations in the past vividly demonstrate the great significance of the museum in the educational programme for the rural people. Even a museum with a local scope has a great value for the enlightenment of the villager. It can bring him rich information about the geography, the geology and the topography of the local territory, its flora and fauna, racial stocks inhabiting it, its arts and crafts as well as its past embodied in historical- records and relics. This would enable the villager to get a vivid composite picture of the life and culture of the local people of whom he is a part, in various stages of their development. It would thus help him to develop a historical sense and thereby recognize the causal connection between the past and the present. It would further deepen and vivify his imagination, enhance his sense of appreciation and strengthen his habit of observation. It would also deepen his interest in the social and natural worlds in which he lives. This would engender in him the urge to transform those worlds.

The museum will prove a valuable reinforcement to the school and library in the complex of means of disseminating education and culture among the rural people. It will not only improve the quality and quantity of education but will also, further, serve as a priceless additional source of material and factual data for preparing an authentic, multi-sided history of the people.

(d) *Movie*: It is very difficult to realize the hidden potentialities of the cinema, one of the most outstanding inventions of modern times, for creative social use. It can be a most powerful means of disseminating the modern protean culture among the people on a mass scale. It can be a classic weapon of mass education. It is one of the most effective means precisely because it enables hundreds of persons simultaneously to imbibe education and culture visually. In minimum of time the cinema can transmit maximum of instruction and cultural information. Further, since it operates through a succession of visual images interpreted through words, it accentuates interest in the educational and cultural content of those images. It is, in addition, the most economical method of spreading knowledge because it does not involve the necessity of engaging a large personnel of instructors.

This marvellous instrument has not still been utilized for mass education in India. It should be adopted as rapidly as possible as a means for educating the rural population in the briefest possible time and also for making accessible to them the immense wealth of contemporary artistic and intellectual culture.

(e) *Radio*: Radio is another remarkable invention which, too, can reinforce the school as an auxiliary means of the education of the rural people. Ideally, each village should be equipped with a radio in the central place. Songs of great artists relayed by the radio will not only have recreational and emotionally nourishing value for the villager but will also develop his aesthetic faculty. Radio will further keep him acquainted with day-to-day events, both national and international. Further, talks given on radio do various themes by eminent experts and specialists will bring valuable knowledge to the village people.

(f) *Mobile Van*: Mobile vans, equipped with loudspeakers, radio, films, libraries and cultural objects, will greatly accelerate the spread of knowledge among the rural population. They can travel from village to village and bring enlightenment at the very door of the rural people. This would draw even its inert section, which lacks sufficient enthusiasm to visit schools or libraries into the orbit of modern culture.

(g) *Gymnasiums and Sport Centres*: The role of gymnasiums and sport centres as valuable means of physical culture and recreation should not be underestimated. They help to build up a physically sturdy and vivacious rural people. Further, by drawing the people in the sphere of vital and pleasant collective activities, they develop such qualities as social solidarity, co-operative habits, and social discipline among them. This is recognized by educationists and sociologists all over the world. The technique both of physical culture and sport has appreciably grown in quantity and quality in modern times due to the great advance of general technique. The modern gymnasiums are equipped with more complex and varied instruments than those of the previous societies. In the world of sport too, new games like cricket, lawn and table tennis, badminton, hockey and others have been added to the old ones.

Further, in former times, gymnastics and sports were isolated local activities only. In contrast to this, in modern times they have acquired a national and even international scope as is proved by national and international contests which are organized to-day. Not only are modern games and sports more specialized, differentiated and consciously planned but they have also become a permanent feature of the life of the society. This is unlike in former times when games and sports were only episodic phenomena mainly associated as subsidiaries with important social and religious functions.

It must, however, be noted that modern games, which have been practically transplanted from the West, have not still penetrated the rural area. This is primarily due to their expensive character.

Indigenous games and gymnastics bequeathed from pre-modern India still exist in the rural area.

One of the tasks confronting the rural educationist is to evolve a synthetic physical and sport culture which would be a creative amalgam of the best elements of pre-modern and modern physical and sport cultures.

The establishment of gymnasiums and sport centres, conceived in the spirit of such a scheme of synthetic physical and sport culture, in villages should be a part of the educational programme for the rural people.

This in brief is a survey of the role of various means, available in the modern age, for carrying out a comprehensive scheme of education and culture for the rural people. The problem is complex and the task colossal. However, the solution of this problem is vitally necessary for evolving a generation of sturdy people equipped with modern knowledge who alone can be the architect of a rural society based upon democratic and cooperative socio-economic relations and pulsating with rich cultural life.

For accomplishing this signal task it is necessary to abandon not only the old conception of rural education but also of the machinery to spread it. It is not only necessary to create schools and libraries in the rural area but also to establish museums, cinemas exhibiting educational films, radio sets relaying topical news and gymnasiums and sport centres, and, further, to organize a numerous fleet of mobile vans equipped with libraries, films and loudspeakers constantly engaged in their peripatetic educational and cultural campaign.

Man and Money

The principal prerequisites for a successful fulfilment of the programme of rural education and culture outlined before are first, the mobilization of the necessary finances and secondly, the creation of the personnel to man the gigantic venture.

The financial resources at the disposal of a nation for implementing progressive plans in various spheres of life, in final analysis, depend on the productive power of the social economy which, in its turn, is determined by the natural resources of the country, the technique of production in industry and agriculture, and above all, by the character of the social economy within which the production process is carried on. The extant social economy may help or hinder the free and rapid development of the productive forces of a society. The rural sociologist has, therefore, to be interested in the economic system prevailing in a country, study it, and decide whether it requires to be modified or even overhauled in the interests of the economic advance of the people and the resultant expansion of their material wealth. Only then the community can set apart finance requisite for the realization of comprehensive reform or reconstruction programmes including that of the rural education. Material prosperity and social and cultural advance of a people are indissolubly bound up. Culture is the spiritual perfume of the social economy.

The problem of teaching and directing personnel is another baffling problem. An enormous number of cadres of instructors, who have imbibed modern culture and who are, further, fired with social passion, will be needed for fulfilling the comprehensive educational plan.

A Great Task

Only when all the above mentioned factors-a comprehensive scientific educational and cultural plan, a properly elaborated organizational machinery, various modern technical devices, a large personnel trained in modern knowledge and, finally, adequate financial resources-are created, it is possible to liquidate illiteracy among the rural people and also to bring treasures of modern knowledge and culture to them.

The problem of the rural education-its scope, methods, means, agencies, finances and personnel-is one of the most vital problems confronting the student of rural society in India.

Seventeen

Religious Factors

Religion in Countryside

A thorough study of rural religion and its significant role in determining the life processes of the rural society should form an essential part of the study of that society. The following are the principal reasons for this

First, it has been observed by sociologists all over the world that rural people have a greater predisposition to religion than what the urban people have. The dependence of agriculture—the basic form of production in the countryside—on the hitherto unmastered forces of nature like rains and the near absence of scientific culture, which provides a correct understanding of the natural and social worlds, among the rural people are two main reasons for the greater degree of religiosity among them. Traditional religion composed of the crudest conceptions of the world holds their mind in its grip. Animism, magic polytheism, ghost beliefs and other forms of primitive religion, are rampant among the rural people to a far greater extent than among the urban people.

Secondly, the religious outlook of the rural people overwhelmingly dominates their intellectual, emotional and practical life. It is difficult to locate any aspect of their life which is not permeated with and coloured by religion. Their family life, caste life, general social life, economic and even recreational life, are more or less governed by a religious approach and religious norms. Religious conceptions also largely dominate their ethical standards; the form and content of their arts like painting, sculpture, architecture, folk-songs and others; as also their social and economic festivals.

This is specially true of societies based on subsistence economies of the pre-capitalist epoch when religion was almost completely fused with social life and when even the then existing secular scientific knowledge of man—physiology, medicine, astronomy, mathematics, agronomy, mechanics, sociology, ethics, etc. — was clothed in religious garb and was the monopoly of the priestly caste.

Thirdly, in societies based on subsistence economies, the leadership of the village life in all domains was provided by the priestly group. Hence the life of the village aggregate in all spheres was moulded in the spirit of religious ideas and dogmas and was controlled by religious institutions and leaders.

Fourthly, a new development took place in modern times in India after the advent of the British rule. The social, economic and political life of the village, as stated elsewhere, experienced a progressive transformation. The development and spread of capitalist economic forms led to the disintegration of the subsistence economy of the autarchic village. Further, a new and secular centralized state took over the administration of the village from the village panchayat and caste councils whose outlook was essentially religious and who were generally guided by religious conceptions and criteria even in secular matters.

In the new economic and political environs, new norms, basically non-religious and secular are derived out of a liberal democratic philosophy, emerged and began increasingly to supersede the authoritarian religious norms which for ages had governed even the secular life of the village population. The village people for the first time in history felt the impact of secular, and democratic and equalitarian ideas on their consciousness. A new ferment began to spread among them which has been steadily affecting their life and outlook hitherto coloured with religion. Also new secular institutions and associations, new secular leadership and social controls, began to emerge within the rural society.

This has resulted in a slow but steady decline in the hegemony and control of the leaders of religion over the life of the rural population.

It must be noted that, even then, religion still continues to exercise a powerful hold over the mind of the rural people and determines their behaviour in a number of secular fields. However, as a result of the operation of such material and ideological forces as modern means of transport like buses and railways and democratic secular ideas, as also due to the growth of secular economic and political movements of the rural masses, the historical tendency, though admittedly very slow, is towards a dereligionizing of increasing sectors of secular life of the rural people as also of their attitude towards purely secular matters.

The contemporary rural society in India has become a battle ground of struggle between the forces of religious orthodoxy and authoritarian social conceptions on the one hand and those of secular democratic advance on the other. It is essential for the student of Indian rural society to follow this conflict.

Comparison of Rural and Urban

Crude forms of religion comprising animism, magic, polytheism, mythology, ghost beliefs and others, which exercise sway over the mind of the rural population, should be distinguished from the refined and subtle types of religion and religious philosophy which are prevalent in cities among the urban intelligentsia. These refined and subtle religions and religious philosophies have been elaborated by great idealistic thinkers out of daring philosophical speculations on basic problems of life such as the problems of the nature of ultimate reality, the genesis of human knowledge and others, which markedly distinguish them from the naive religious beliefs generated in the rural atmosphere.

While rural religion tends to be crude and concrete in form, urbanized religion has tended to be abstract. While the rural population worships and falls prostrate before a multitude of gods and goddesses derived out of their animistic conception of the universe, the cultured educated section of the urban humanity subscribes to the idealistic view of the universe and discusses such categories as the nature of Brahman, Free Will and others.

Further, even critical rationalism and philosophical materialism are minority philosophical currents flourish in urban centres.

The rural sociologist needs to distinguish between the crude, almost static, rural religion and the refined and highly abstract urbanized religion which soars in the stratosphere of speculative thought and grapples with ontological, epistemological and other basic problems of philosophy. Further, he should also note that rationalist and materialist philosophical thought currents found in the urban society are almost absent in the rural area.

The roots of rural religion lie principally in the great, almost abysmal, ignorance and resultant fear of the forces of environment prevailing among the rural people. Refined urban religion, even if based on the erroneous idealistic interpretation of the world, is not born of mere fear. This distinction regarding the psychological roots of rural and urban religions is important.

Various Angles

The rural religion should be studied in its following three important aspects

1. Rural religion as providing a specific world outlook, a specific view of the universe;
2. Rural religion as prescribing a body of religious practices to the rural people; and
3. Rural religion as an institutional complex.

Each of these three vital aspects of the rural religion needs a few observations.

As a World Outlook. The world outlook provided by the rural religion includes such ingredients as (a) magical conceptions, (b) animism, (c) the conception of a bizarre world peopled by spirits, (d) the conception of a posthumous world of dead ancestors who have to be worshipped, and (e) mythology. The most striking feature of the rural religion is its dynamic conception of the universe, i.e., the conception of the universe as a theatre of the interplay of conscious freely acting elements. The rural religion unfolds such worlds as Pitrilok, Pretlok, Devlok, and Vaikunth

Dham, i.e., the worlds of dead ancestors, disembodied spirits, gods and goddesses, as also the celestial world. It also, in addition, conjures up worlds peopled by such deities as those of fertility, various epidemics, rivers and forests. In fact, the rural religion sees spirits practically behind all phenomena and creates a phantasmagoria of numerous uncanny worlds of spirits. Such a world outlook is fundamentally born of the profound ignorance of the forces of nature and of the nature of man. Ignorance breeds fear and these two are the interrelated twin sources of the world outlook fashioned by the crude rural religion. Since the world outlook, consciously or unconsciously, largely determines the social, ethical and other views of the individual and the social aggregate as well as their behaviour, its study forms an indispensable part of the study of the rural society.

As a Body of Practices. The body of religious practices prescribed by the rural religion is imposing. These practices may be divided into the following three groups:

Prayers: The individual is enjoined to offer prayer to various deities at home as well as outside the home. At home he is required to pray to the family god or goddess. The prayers are offered by the members of the family at the family alter. Every caste generally worships a special deity and maintains, if possible, caste temples where the deity is installed. All members of the caste are exhorted to regularly offer prayers to the deity, a god or a goddess. Further, every street or locality in the village has its own deity, generally Goddess Moholla Mata to whom the people residing in the locality have to offer prayers, specially during the Navaratra religious festival. There is also the village temple in which the village god is installed. Community prayers have to be offered to him. Further, prayers are offered also to the river goddess if the village is situated on a river, to the forest deity and to other deities of the locality. In addition, prayers have to be offered also to some or all gods and goddesses common to all Hindus. The prayer and worship aspect of the rural religion deserves a careful study because, in recent times, sections of the Hindus—the depressed classes—who were denied the right of temple entry, organized a number of struggles to secure that right. The issue of the right to enter public temples and worship and offer prayers to deities became even a political issue.

Sacrifices: The rural religion prescribes a variety of sacrificial acts to its adherents, which range from the sprinkling of some drops of water and scattering of leaves or grains in front of various deities to the offering of animal and, though rarely, even of human sacrifices to them. The rural religion is composed of various sub-religions and each sub-religion prescribes to its followers a particular set of sacrificial acts. Sacrifices are offered to a variety of gods and goddesses. There are the food god (Annadevata), the gods of different diseases (Baliakaka and others), the rain god, the river goddess, and a plethora of others. Sacrifices are offered to propitiate them and thereby disarm their wrath or win their favour. A sociological analysis of sacrifices is valuable for comprehending the conceptions of the rural people of the cause of diseases, floods and other devastating phenomena. It can also provide a clue to their social habits and styles of living. It will reveal their attitudes to the world and life. It may assist the rural sociologist to grasp how various castes practising different kinds of sacrificial acts, thereby, develop a hierarchic conception of the caste series. Such a study can further help him to explain certain psychological and cultural traits of different social groups. And finally it may aid him in tracing the past-history of Indian society, social, economic and cultural, of which the concept and practice of sacrifice were an organic outgrowth. Sacrifices to particular deities have a specific character and hence presupposed a specific concept of each deity. Those deities were born in the field of human consciousness at a certain stage in the socio-economic development of society. Mythology, in fact, is the history of society in terms of symbolism and since society changes, the pantheon of gods and goddesses too changes. The rural society has at present become the amphitheatre of the struggle between the conservative and the reformist religious tendencies and movements. The conservative social groups strive to preserve old religious practices while the reformist social groups are characterizing those practices as irrational and mentally deadening. They counsel a rational approach to problems of life. A study of sacrifices becomes essential if one were to properly understand this struggle, particularly because they play a very significant role in the life of the rural people. The culture of the rural people is predominantly religious and sacrifices also form the theme of the rural folklore which constitutes the major part of their culture.

Rituals: One of the significant features of the life of the rural people is its meticulous domination, even in details, by rituals. The conception of purity had been elaborated in the past Indian society to such an extent that it became a veritable principle. Rituals are the religious means by which the purity of the individual and the social life becomes guaranteed. The inherited rural religion prescribes a complex pattern of behaviour for the individual as well as for various social groups in all spheres of life, complex because rituals are associated with their numerous significant and even insignificant activities. Particular sets of rituals are dictated to a particular caste or sub-caste group so much so that distinct differences in the respective rituals which those social groups and sub-groups follow enable one to distinguish them from one another. Social condemnation and even the threat of ex-communication provide sanction for the strict enforcement of rituals among their members. Rituals are associated with most of the life activities of the rural people. A ritual is prescribed whenever the individual or the social group initiates an activity even though the activity may be, like food-taking, repeated in future. Before an individual Brahmin starts consuming the food in the dish, he is required to draw a magic circle round the dish and apportion some grains of cooked rice to the god or gods. There are rituals prescribed for a number of such ordinary mundane and secular activities. There are the bath ritual, the occupational ritual, the ritual to be performed when a person occupies a residential premises. There are separate rituals when the farmer begins sowing and harvesting. All landmarks in the process of agricultural production have been associated with specific rituals. Rituals have been prescribed for auspicious days and also for the start of a new season. When a child for the first time goes to the school, there is also ritual to be performed. In fact, the life of the rural human is a succession of rituals corresponding to a succession of activities he is engaged in from morning to night, from month to month and year to year, almost from birth to death.

Even the dead person is not to be left alone. Specific rituals have to be performed in the posthumous period for some days. In fact, we may remark that it is very difficult to locate in the Hindu society where religious observances end and secular practices begin.

As an Institutional Complex. The Hindu religion, which a preponderant section of the rural population subscribes to, is a conglomeration of numerous sub-religions and religious cults. A number of these sub-religions and religious cults have been institutionalized. Corresponding to these institutionalized sub-religions and religious cults there exists a number of religious organizations. Some of these religious organizations function on a national scale, some on the provincial and others on the local basis. They maintain Maths, Ashrams and Temples where their adherents flock to worship and to pray to various deities as also to listen to religious discourses. These religious bodies own property, often substantial. They maintain a permanent staff of priests and preachers who spread the doctrines of their respective sub-religions and religious cults among the people. Thus we have in the country such religious organizations as those headed by Shankaracharya, descendants of Ramanuj, Vallabha, Sahajanand and others, all differing again in subtle points of philosophy and rituals. Some of the sub-religions and religious cults have not been institutionalized. Their protagonists and preachers have not been integrated into regular organizations. The absence of state religions has been one striking characteristic of religion in India. This is in contrast to Christianity and Islam which became state religions in a number of countries of Europe and Asia. Religion in India was considered the concern of the community and not of the state. The religious organization was always distinct and separate from the state though a Hindu or a Muslim king might favour and support his respective religion.

Religious Authority

Europe, as history records, it was otherwise. There existed, in the Middle Ages, Catholic and subsequently Catholic and Protestant states. Till Kamal Pasha separated the state from religion, Turkey was a theocratic Muslim State. Hence we do not find in Indian history such struggles as that between the Pope, the head of the organized international Catholic religion, striving to maintain a system of Catholic states and Henry VIII who rebelled against Catholicism and transformed the English state into a Protestant one.

One significant feature of the life of Indian society in the past lay in the fact that great democratic mass movements took the form of religious movements led by outstanding religious leaders popularly known as Bhaktas (Sants). Since religion was a community and not a state matter in India these movements were not directed against the state (in contrast to Protestantism in Europe) but aimed at winning over the people to their programmes aid, through their initiative and action, bringing about the reform of society.

The popular democratic character of those Bhakti movements is evidenced by the fact that they generally stood for democratization of the Hindu society (liquidation of castes or caste inequalities) and for equal access to God and religious culture by all, including women, without the intermediary of the priestly Brahmin caste. Further the Bhaktas developed the vernaculars or the languages which the common people knew and spoke and themselves created a vast literature in those languages. Thus they also brought culture to the common people.

It must, however, be noted that a Hindu, a Buddhist or a Muslim king would often utilise his state power and state resources for the extensions of the particular religion he subscribed to. The state, however, had not a Hindu or a Muslim character. Religion was not a department of the state.

We will next refer to the group of men exclusively devoted to religion. This group can be divided into two categories, priests who have a fixed domicile and sanyasis who travel from place to place.

There are various kinds of priests. There are family priests who serve the religious needs of the family; the caste and sub-caste priests who cater to the needs of various castes and sub-castes; and the village priest who looks after the village temple and meets the religious requirements of the village community as a whole.

These priestly groups exercise a powerful influence over the life of the rural people, both religious and secular, since secular life processes are coloured by religion and before being undertaken, require to be hallowed by religion through rituals. Religion is even now largely interwoven in the texture of the secular life of the rural people.

The historical tendency, however, is towards a decline of the domination of the secular life of the rural people by the priestly group.

There are, in our country, in addition to priests, a large number of roving religious men (Sanyasis) who mostly tour in the rural area. Some of them are preachers of the religious cults to which they belong. Others are just holy men who hallow the village by their visit and design to taste the hospitality of the villagers for a while.

Sanctity of Temples

We will next evaluate the role of the village temple in the life of the rural people. This is because the temple has not only functioned as a place of worship and prayer but also has served as the main centre and initiator of village activities. It plays a significant part in the village life even to-day.

The temple has been associated with education in the village. For ages it maintained a school where the village youngsters of higher castes received religious and secular education. It organized for the village people religious discourses as well as Kathas narrating the past history of the Indian people.

The temple did philanthrophic and social welfare work in the village. It collected money and goods from the villagers with which it used to bring relief to the needy among them.

The temple organized collective social and religious functions. Under its auspices marriages were performed, social and religious festivals including village dinners were organized, and significant days like the New Year's Day were celebrated. In fact, a good proportion of the collective life of the village, religious and secular, moved round the temple.

The temple also embodied and was the guardian of all traditional culture, literary and artistic. Sometimes it even attached to itself and maintained singers, dancers and musicians. It must be borne in mind that the past culture was largely religious and even its secular part was clothed in the religious raiment. Hence, this inherited culture was associated with and guarded by the temple. Thus the village temple became the predominant centre of village culture; and the cultural life of the village, religious and secular, artistic and literary, moved round the temple.

The temple was the source of ethical values which regulated the life of the village people. The head of the village temple was the inexorable moral critic and controller of the actions of the villagers, though in recent times the control has been diminishing.

The temple played and also plays today an important role in the economic life of the village. All turning points in the process of agricultural production such as sowing, reaping, and others are signified by religious rituals. When an artisan starts his occupation, there is the inevitable ritual linked with the event. The temple through its priestly representative hallows the farmer's plough and the artisan's instruments, when they are first put to use, by means of appropriate religious rituals. Thus, the temple, the visible expression of the rural religion, plays an important role also in the economic life of the rural society.

The temple occasionally dispenses justice too. It adjudicates disputes between villagers with the authoritative voice of religion. It prescribes religious methods of expiation for even heinous secular offences.

Not only that. The temple further makes forecasts of future events through the priestly representative.

The temple serves as a social centre also. Even village gossip is largely carried on within the precincts or the periphery of the temple.

Public meetings are generally held near or in the temple since it is the most significant and spacious place in the village.

The temple provided largely in the past and provides to a less extent now, teachers, physicians, medicine men, ethical leaders, songster, experts in narrating past history before village audiences (Kuthakars), scribes, astrologers, astronomers, and soothsayers to the village.

There is a rich variety of temples in the village. There are caste and sub-caste temples as well as temples consecrated to deities worshipped by the village people in common with the entire Hindu community as a whole. There are also temples for the worship of deities of specific religious cults like the Shakti cult and others. There are, further, temples where local village deities are enshrined.

Some of the village temples are owned publicly; others are owned privately.

Case for Study

The study of contemporary rural religion is very essential for leaving a composite picture of the past cultural evolution of the Indian people. The history of Indian culture is still scrappy, is still in a fragmentary state. A controversy is still going on regarding the genesis of Indian culture and further phases of its subsequent development. Varied views have been advanced on the subject. Also problems such as, where the Indian culture originated and how it spread in different parts of India, also remain in the domain of debate.

Regional Angle

A study of various rural religions in various rural regions of India reveals certain common characteristics such as common patterns of gods and goddesses, common objects of worship, common rituals as well as almost common religious conceptions and myths. A number of these characteristics, however, exhibit regional variations.

Further, a regional rural religion also possesses features which are distinct and its own which it does not share with others.

This discloses two striking facts. First, the common characteristics of these rural religions indicate that they had their origin in a common Indian culture in the past and, in spite of regional variations, constitute a varied pattern of a single Indian rural culture even today. Secondly, in spite of common ancestry they are also distinct rural religions of various rural areas since they possess certain independent traits and elements.

A careful sociological analysis of this rich diversity of contemporary regional rural religions will assist to trace their evolution. It will, further, help to discover the genesis of these rural religions which spread along with great and frequent migrations of peasant communities from one part of India to others.

Even the varied geographical conditions of India have played a big role in determining Indian rural religion and its regional variations. Mighty rivers, mountainous territories, decisive trade routes, have influenced the character and content of these religions. The spread of modern railways, which have greatly neutralized the topographical and geographical factors in conditioning the cultural life of the people in modern times, makes it difficult for us to comprehend the significance of these factors in shaping the past Indian culture.

An inventory of the various religious beliefs, rituals and pantheons of gods and goddesses of various regional rural religions and a study of their common characteristics as well as their regional variations will help to evolve a scientific history of the Indian rural culture as it developed and spread for many centuries.

The study of the Hindu rural religion is particularly fascinating because of the rich variety of its content. Hinduism is a colossal diversified complex of religious beliefs and rituals. In its contemporary form it is an aggregate of religious dogmas and practices almost of all phases of development of human society.

Recording Scientific History

Further, a sociological investigation into Indian rural religion will disclose, though in a symbolic form, the past social, political, economic and ethnic history of India. It will unveil the history of economic and other clashes as well as of various social, political and cultural amalgamations of conflicting social groups in the past.

This is because the shadow world of religion reflects the real movement of society.

The studies of Egypt, Babylonia, Greece and other countries by eminent scholars like More, Maspero, Breasted, Frankfort,

Gordon Childe, Thomson and others have shown how a systematic study of the evolution of gods from tribal totems and fetishes to national pantheons unfolds the process of the transformation of tribal society into territorial political society. A study of the ideology and mythology of the rural religion in India may also unlock the secrets of changes in the Indian society in various stages of its evolution.

The rural sociologist in India has to study such problems as to why Shaivism spread in certain parts of India, how Vaishnavism spread in certain regions, why the Shakti cult took various forms in various zones. Migrations of gods and goddesses signify the migrations of peoples too. Fusion of gods and goddesses reveals the historical process of the fusion of peoples. The hierarchy of gods and goddesses and the branding of some deities as villainous and extolling of others as beneficient, unfold, though in mythological terms, struggles among ethnic groups and peoples and the subordination of some to others in real historical conflicts.

It must be noted that in addition to Hinduism which we have extensively discussed on account of its preponderance, other religions like Islam, Christianity and Zoroastrianism also have existed in the Indian rural society. It is, therefore, also necessary for a rural sociologist to make their study on similar lines for a thorough assessment of the role of religion in the life of the rural people.

Modern Influence

Further, the study of the rural religion is also very vital because, due to the impact of modern economic, social, political and rationalist forces, the rural society is experiencing a transformation, however, slow, in the present period. The transformation is taking place in all spheres of rural life including the sphere of rural religion. The ideology, the institutions, the rituals, the ethics, and the aesthetics of the rural religion are undergoing a change, though gradual, under the pressure of new material and cultural forces. It is the task of the rural sociologist to study this process to be able to predict the future of the rural religion which exercises a great sway over the mind of the rural people and the life processes of the rural society.

Eighteen

Caste System

A very peculiar type of social grouping which is found in India is the caste grouping. A student of the Indian society, who fails to closely and carefully study this variety of social grouping, will miss the very essence of that society. In India, caste largely determines the function, the status, the available opportunities as well as the handicaps for an individual. Caste differences even determine the differences in modes of domestic and social life, types of houses and cultural patterns of the people which are found in the rural area. Even land ownership exists frequently on caste lines. Due to a number of reasons, administrative functions have also been often divided according to castes, especially in the rural area. Caste has, further, determined the pattern of the complicated religious and secular culture of the people. It has fixed the psychology of the various social groups and has evolved such minutely graded levels of social distance and superior-inferior relationships that the social structure looks like a gigantic hierarchic pyramid with a mass of untouchables as its base and a small stratum of elite, the Brahmins, almost equally unapproachable, at its apex. The Hindu society is composed of hundreds of distinct self-contained caste worlds piled one over the other.

The increasing spread of the modern means of communication, the introduction of the British system of adminis-tration and laws, and the growth of modern capitalist competitive economy which shattered the subsistence economy of the self-sufficient village community, undermined more and more the functional basis of caste. However, the transformation of self-contained rigid castes into modern mobile classes has taken place in a peculiar manner. Certain castes have been monopolising the position of the privileged upper classes of modern society. Certain castes have been loosing previous status and functions and slowly submerging into the lowest class groups of modern society. This development has created a peculiar social structure in modern India with the result that, within the existing Indian society, class struggles have been often assuming the form of caste-struggles. The student of rural society is here confronted with one of the most complex types of social transformation in the socio-economic as well as in the ideological spheres. The caste system composed of caste groups in a state of increasing decay and undergoing a transformation into modern classes in a confused way and offering stubborn resistance to it, presents the epic spectacle of a social cyclones writhing in violent death agonies.

Caste Factor

One of the most urgent tasks before the student of rural society in India is to evolve an approach which will be able to appraise the social and cultural processes of that society within the matrix of caste structure.

Failure to develop such a perspective has, in spite of an immense accumulation of economic and other factual data, obstructed the elaboration of a living composite picture of rural society. The rural sociologist should concentrate on the following vital problems:

Economic Life

The economic life of rural society should be studied in context of caste, in its interrelation and interaction with caste.

Production: In the field of production the rural sociologist should study the extent to which functional and propertied groups correspond to castes. Such a study, for instance, as that of Bhuvel has revealed how far the new economic and political forces have undermined the homogeneous functional basis of old castes and also the distribution of property among them. It will thereby disclose the degree of disintegration and alteration of the status, privileges, and social and political significance of various castes. Secondly, it will enable us to comprehend the attitude of the Hindu as well as the Indian Mahomedans too, who are affected by the caste phenomena, towards the hierarchically graded caste structure of society as well as their reaction to the process of change which it is experiencing. Such a study, for instance, as that of Bhuvel has revealed how in some parts of the Central Gujarat, the Rajputs who owned land are declining in their social and economic status being increasingly supplanted by the Patidars.

Consumption: In the field of consumption the rural sociologist requires to study how castes greatly mould the pattern of consumption of respective caste groups. For instance, caste appreciably fixes the food and dress habits or the choice of utensils and other articles of its members. This caste-determined mode of consumption reacts on and influences production. The pure economic theory of consumption would be misleading and result into incorrect conclusions unless its modification due to the intervention of the caste institution is taken into account.

Indebtedness: The rural indebtedness, a striking feature of rural economic life, also requires to be studied in context of caste. Dr. R. K. Nehru has vividly pointed out in his exploratory study of a few villages what close relation exists between caste and indebtedness and credit in the rural area. Certain castes are predominantly composed of members who are almost hereditary debtors; some others of those who are mainly creditors. The rural sociologist should study the social and economic millieu and find out why it is so.

Habitat: Caste also largely determines the type of houses its members reside in their housing habits and the choice of village area where these houses are located. The village is generally divided into areas, each inhabited by the members of a particular caste. Further, even when some members of a caste cease to pursue the caste-determined vocation, they generally continue to reside in the same area and socially interact with other members of their caste.

Mobility: Another significant problem which requires to be studied is the co-relation between caste and economic mobility of the rural people. As a result of the operation of the forces of economic evolution of Indian society, a slow but steady and constant inter-change of functions among various castes has been taking place. Members of a caste gradually cease to perform the caste-determined function and take to occupations which other caste groups are engaged in. Further, for the same reason some castes slide down the economic ladder while some castes go up the ladder. Since these changes have an effect on the development of the rural economy and its nature, their specific study is necessary.

United Family

The study of the rural society should include the study of how caste and joint family—its two dominant social institutions-influence the social life of the rural individual and the rural aggregate. They are powerful forces determining their social activities and thereby play a big role in moulding their psychology and ideology. As observed elsewhere, a caste in the rural area is generally a cluster of joint families. Hence, the caste moulds the nature of the life of those families.

Deprived of Education

Caste also largely determines the attitude of the rural man towards education and even fixes the nature of the education which he intends to receive. A Brahmin child will, due to caste tradition generally receive education and that too predominantly religious in contrast to the Bania child who will be given secular education and the child of a depressed class who would forego all education. Further, it must be noted that education is not evaluated from the standpoint of individual development or social advance but from that of the caste tradition.

Religious Sanctions

How religious life is determined rigorously by caste, especially in the rural area, also deserves to be studied. While in cities religious practices are slowly shrinking, in villages they flourish luxuriantly even now. It is the caste that rigidly determines the place of its member in the religious life of the people.

Political Opportunities

Caste influences the political life to a greater extent in the rural area than in the urban centres. This is because caste consciousness is stronger among the rural people than among the urban people. Choice or rejection of candidates as well as the nature of propaganda in political elections are determined by caste considerations more in villages than in towns and cities. Caste ego is stronger among the rural people and hence exerts a powerful influence in shaping the political life of the rural aggregate. In contrast to this, extra-caste considerations considerably influence political prejudices and predilections of the urban population.

Norms and Values

Since caste largely determines the ideals and patterns of life of the rural social groups, it also considerably shapes the value systems prevailing in the rural society. The value patterns of the rural society bear a far greater impress of caste traditions than those of the urban society where extra-caste institutions and ideologies operate.

Emerging Leadership

Caste plays a big role in determining the nature and the personnel of the leadership of the rural society. Caste leaders are generally leaders also of the social, economic, political and ideological life of the rural society. As a consequence of this, caste struggles are often co-eval with social, political, economic and ideological struggles in the rural zone.

The study of the role of caste in the life of the Indian rural aggregate in all its spheres is thus vitally necessary for getting a correct picture of the Indian rural society and its life processes.

Common Attitudes

It is further necessary to study the actual functioning of the caste and the subjective reactions of its members to that functioning. A proper study of such subjective reactions of different caste groups to the almost all pervasive functioning of caste will enable the rural sociologist to comprehend that fundamental social phenomenon called social distance in the Indian rural society. It will explain the emergence and development of various grades of social superiority and inferiority complexes rampant among the rural people. It will also disclose how those subjective reactions of various groups crystallize as different group psychologies which express themselves in various cultural patterns.

Class Distance

The study will also enable him to comprehend what type of consciousness arises out of a social life mainly moving within the caste matrix. It will also aid the rural sociologist in his indispensable study of those socio-historic forces, which, across centuries, brought into existence the most complex and elaborate, the most systematised and logically worked out structure of organised and minutely graded group inequality, via., the caste system in India.

Constitutional Cover

The problem has acquired a special significance for the contemporary Indian people for a number of reasons. First, the Constitution of the Indian Union has assumed as its postulate the individual citizen and not caste as the unit of Indian society. Secondly, it has laid down equality of citizens and not hierarchically graded privileges based on the caste as the principle of State legislation. It has chosen as its objective a democratic social order free from inequality and special privileges. Finally, the existing socio-economic structure is also based on the principle of contract between free and equal individuals and not on caste privilege. Individual contract and not caste status is the basis of all rights and responsibilities today.

In Hinduism's Fold

This shift from the caste to the individual as the unit of society has brought about convulsive changes in Indian society transforming old social relations. It has been dealing shattering blows to the orthodoxy of Hinduism and the caste social order of the Hindus. The socio-psychological patterns, the religio-ethical norms and even the philosophical outlook of the Hindus determined by the old Hinduism are being increasingly undermined as the process of the transformation of the social relations advances. A democratic conception of social relations in all fields, social, legal, political, economic and cultural, is progressively replacing the former hierarchic conception of those relations. A study of the caste and of the process of its steady dissolution today will, further, inevitably make it necessary for the rural sociologist to study the historical genesis of caste and also of the Hindu religion and the Hindu culture which are closely bound up with it. It will also show whether Hinduism can survive as an ideology without the existence of caste, the social institutional expression and concretization of Hinduism.

A research in the subject of the origin of caste will also require a study of (i) past economic evolution of Indian society which at a certain stage made caste historically inevitable, (ii) its subsequent role as a formidable obstacle to further economic and cultural development of Indian society and (iii) contemporary forces which are steadily undermining caste and therefore also probably weakening Hinduism as an ideology and a culture.

Community Life

Joint family, caste and village community were the basic social institutions of the pre-British Indian rural society. It is the task of the rural sociologist to study the relations between them.

The process of dissolution of those institutions, however slow, commenced, as previously stated, with the impact of British contact after the conquest of India. It must be noted that the autarchic village had been the socio-economic unit of Indian society during the period of agrarian civilization based on a subsistence economy which intervened between the food gathering phase of social existence and the modern phase of competitive nation-scale capitalistic civil society founded on national economy and mobile classes. One unique feature of social evolution in India was that primitive food gathering tribal society was not historically succeeded by a society based on a slave mode of production as in Greece and Rome or by a society based on a feudal mode of production with serf labour which developed in the Western Europe during the Middle Ages. Slavery or serfdom was never the basis of social production in the long history of Indian society though the phenomenon of slavery might have crept in here and there. Due to complex ecological and socio-historical reasons, primitive collective tribal society seems to have been superseded in India by a unique type of society which persisted for a remarkably long period. It began to disintegrate only after the contact with the capitalist West in modern times.

Extensive historical research dealing with the most remote periods of past history of the Indian people together with the utmost exercise of the power of historical inference guided by a scientific theory of social development, are needed to trace the causes of the genesis of village communities in India. It is necessary to locate the peculiar ecological and socio-historical factors which brought about the emergence of a unique type of social structure based on those autarchic and collectively land-possessing village communities in India. Thereafter, it is necessary to probe into the problem whether caste arose as a socio-economic institution adapted to the exigencies of such a social formation.

Supremacy of the Learned

The next problem which, the rural sociologist should investigate is whether the doctrine of immutable casteism propagated by the Brahmins was the inevitable theoretical outgrowth of a society which remained unaltered and stationary for a remarkably long period as a result of unchanging technique and resultant unvarying division of labour. Was it because caste persisted for ages and subsequently became rigid and ossified, that an illusion was generated in the consciousness of the Hindu humanity that it was immutable?

It is also vital to comprehend why the Brahmin caste exercised ideological and social dictatorship over the Hindu people for centuries with rare episodic interruptions like the challenge of Buddhism and a few others. Was it because the Hindu people living in such a stationary society as mentioned above developed an organic predisposition to docilely accept and submit to authority and tradition? Was it, therefore, that they surrendered themselves to the social and ideological sway of the Brahmins who were not only the architect of authoritarian social and religious philosophies but were also the repository and monopolist of whatever scientific knowledge, astronomical, agronomical, medical and other, which existed in the past? Even regarding the uncanny forces of nature, they were the Brahmins who alone were supposed to have the religio-magical power of propitiating and mastering them through rites, incantations and other devices.

The Vital Factor

Numerous theories have been advanced to explain the origin, development, crystallization and ultimate petrifaction of the caste system. Most of them have been offered in the spirit of surmises only. The rest, though they have illuminated the problem, have given partial solution of it. A consciously planned out, systematic and still deeper study of the problem of caste, historically and in its complex interconnections with other social developments, has still to be made.

To unravel this problem it is necessary to study the ecological conditions of India in the past, which resulted in the peculiar economic development of Indian society and gave rise to the peculiar type of social formation as the village community. This may provide a valuable clue to the solution of the problem of the origin of caste. Then alone the significance of caste which has played such a powerful role in past Indian society and which is still playing considerable role in the life of the Indian people in general and the Indian rural people in particular can be fully grasped.